LEGENDARY LOCALS

OF

FILLMORE

CALIFORNIA

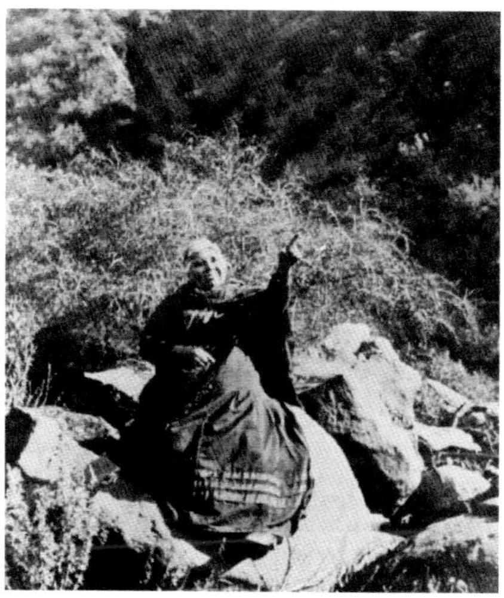

I0805807

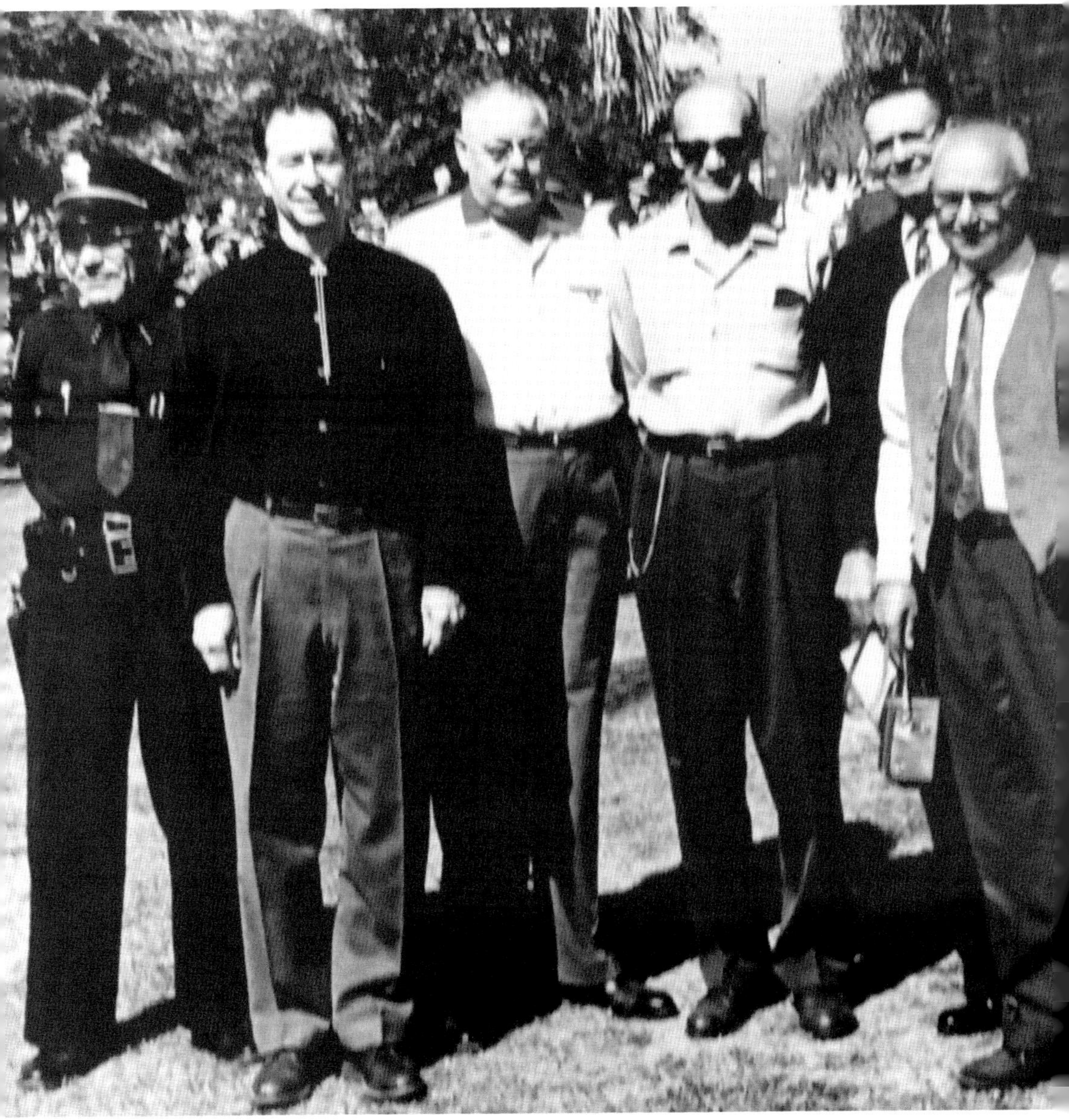

Fillmore Notables
Pictured from left to right are Chief Earl Hume, Councilman Loren Briggs, Councilman Bert Major, Councilman Fred Bryce, Councilman Ray Lindenfeld, and Mayor Robert Linville. Chief Hume was once the longest-serving police chief in the United States. (Courtesy of the Harold and Bernice Michel family collection.)

Page 1: Candelaria Valenzuela
Believed to have been the last of the Sespe Indians, Candelaria Valenzuela was born approximately 1838 in the Lord's Creek–Sespe Creek area in the Sespe backcountry, above Fillmore. Anthropologist John Peabody Harrington made wax recordings of Candelaria singing Chumash songs and reciting text. (Courtesy of Candelaria American Indian Council.)

LEGENDARY LOCALS

OF

FILLMORE

CALIFORNIA

EVIE YBARRA

LEGENDARY LOCALS

ISBN 978-1-4671-0192-9

Legendary Locals is an imprint of Arcadia Publishing
Charleston, South Carolina

Printed in the United States of America

Library of Congress Control Number: 2014947076

For all general information, please contact Arcadia Publishing:
Telephone 843-853-2070
Fax 843-853-0044
E-mail sales@arcadiapublishing.com
For customer service and orders:
Toll-Free 1-888-313-2665

Visit us on the Internet at www.arcadiapublishing.com

Dedication

To the people of the city of Fillmore, and the communities of Bardsdale and Piru, without whose tireless preservation efforts this book would not have been possible. To the families and individuals who shared their stories and precious time with me, and to my dear brother, Robert, who assisted with the photography and supported this project from the beginning. To Anna Bermudez for offering her encouragement from the onset. To my daughter, Elizabeth, and my son-in-law, Chris, for assisting me, and to my son, Robert, for all of his encouragement. In loving memory to my father, "Woody," and to my mother, Minnie, who always encouraged us to succeed. Thank you.

On the Front Cover: Clockwise from top left:
Dr. Richard Ramirez, professor and counselor (Author's collection; see page 90), Dr. Luis Sánchez, professor at California State University, Channel Islands (Author's collection; see page 90), William Shiells, 1900s businessman and civic leader (Courtesy of Shiells family collection; see pages 31–32), Marcelino "Woody" and Minnie Ybarra, leaders in the community (Courtesy of the Minnie Ybarra family collection; see page 109), supervisor Kathy Long, Fillmore representative (Courtesy of supervisor Kathy Long; see page 102),Marie Wren, businesswoman and civic leader (Courtesy of Marie Wren family collection; see page 99), Dr. Dorothy Leland, chancellor of the University of California, Merced (Courtesy of Dr. Leland; see page 106), Dr. Ofelia Romero-Motlagh, professor and counselor (Courtesy of Motlagh family collection; see page 113), Russell Hardison, businessman and civic leader (Courtesy of Hardison family collection; see page 40), Manuel and Anna Inadomi, co-owners of Inadomi Market and Department Store in the 1930s (Courtesy of George and Jeanette Inadomi family collection; see page 84).

On the Back Cover: From left to right:
Joe Gottardi searching for his family after St. Francis Dam disaster (Courtesy of Santa Clarita Valley Historical Society and Newhall Land and Farming; see page 71), Ernest "Ernie" and Becky Morales, civic leaders and former city mayor (Courtesy of Bob Cox personal collection; see page 68).

CONTENTS

ACKNOWLEDGMENTS

Thank you to everyone who assisted in this project. There are numerous families and helpful individuals who contributed to this project and who made time to discuss their family histories and share photographs. Michele McKinley, Bob and Diana Cox, Missy Pennington Cervantez, Kathy Corley Recicar, Diane Galvan, Melodie Smith Ramsey, Robert Ybarra, and Suzanne Lummis, thank you! Thanks also to Monty and Maio Winkler for their assistance and for sharing so freely, and a big thank-you to Bernice and Elizabeth Michel, Marie Wren, Myrna Taylor, Linda Starnes Faris, and to the many dedicated individuals who want to preserve family histories. I appreciate all the assistance from Lucy Rangel and Dr. Palazuelos and the Fillmore Unified School District. Thanks to Dr. Alan Pollack and the Santa Clarita Valley Historical Society for all of their assistance in helping to make this project possible. Thank you also to Martin Farrell, Publisher of the *Fillmore Gazette* and to Scott Duckett. A special thanks to Tom Hardison for his valuable insight and to Judith P. Triem for her assistance. Dr. Susan Falck of Ranch Camulos Museum was extremely helpful, as were the research docents of the Museum of Ventura County and Charles Johnson. Martha Gentry from the Fillmore Historical Museum shared many stories, and to Ernestine Lopez, director of the Candelaria American Indian Council, thank you.

Thank you to my family for the endless encouragement—especially my daughter, Elizabeth, and son, Robert; I could not have done this without all of your words of encouragement and positive critiques. Thank you to their father, Robert, for his support.

INTRODUCTION

The best way to tell a story is to show it with images that can take on a life of their own. The family stories that each person shared for this book are very personal, and now those stories have become part of the fabric of Fillmore-Bardsdale-Piru history. Many bared their souls and offered their photographs, knowing they would be shared with the general public and citizens of the community.

The city of Fillmore is unique, and many of the descendants of pioneer families still live in the area. There are also newcomers who have become integrated into the community. Piru has a special history, and its residents are close-knit; they share a special connection because the community is small and they know everyone. Bardsdale is distinct for having not changed very much. Many of the original families still have descendants living in the area. Everyone takes care of everyone else, and the sense of family is prevalent in Fillmore, Piru, and Bardsdale.

The More murder was all about the battle for land and water rights. Now, as it was then, there are concerns over worker rights and battles over wages, housing, and the basics for sustaining life in a costly economy. History demonstrates that our ancestors dealt with some of the same issues. By examining what they did differently, we may be able to learn from our past.

There are many more stories that need to be told and more photographs to be shared.

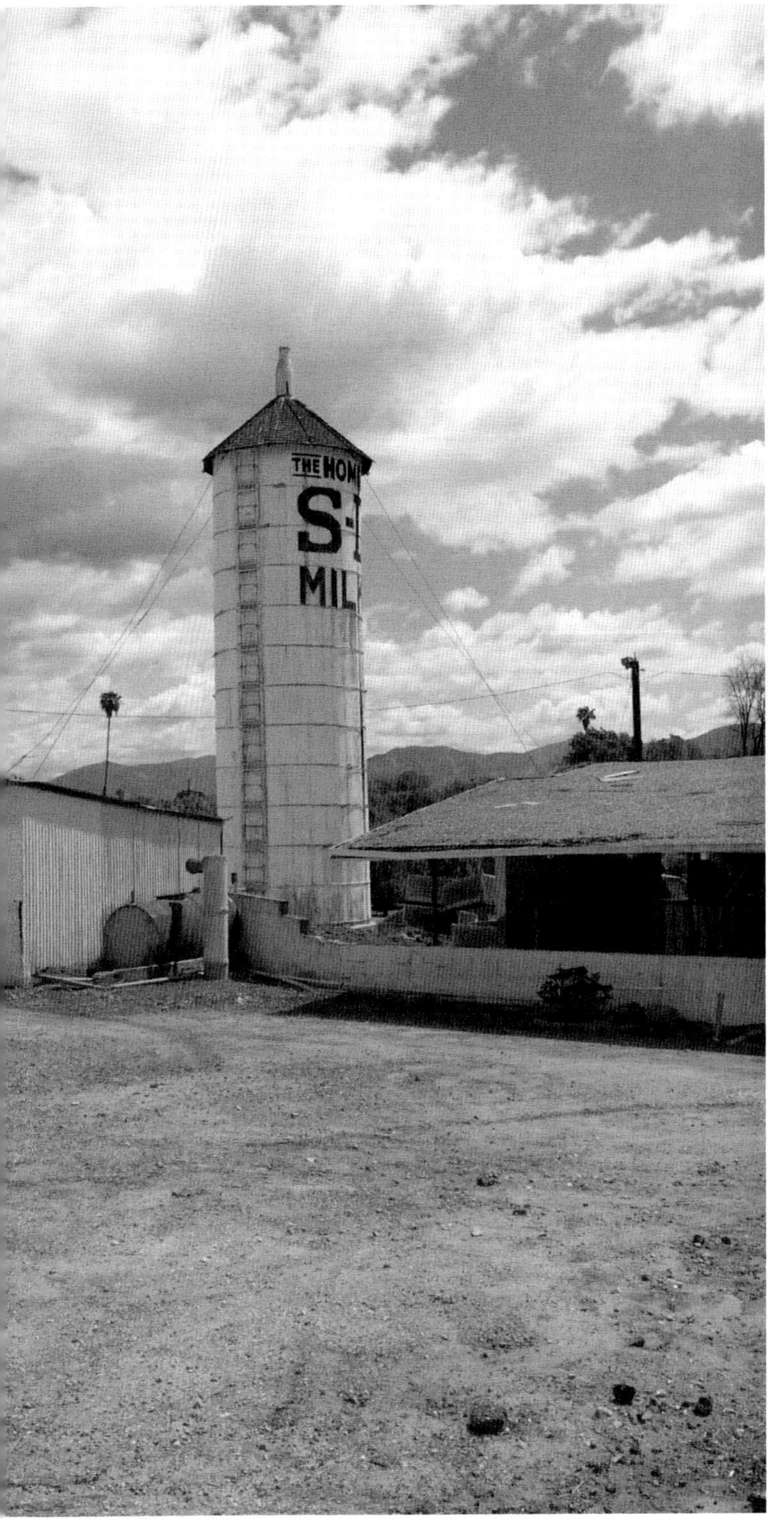

The Iconic Sanitary Dairy
The Sanitary Dairy could be seen from great distances as travelers ventured toward Fillmore, driving along Telegraph Road. It was also a place where one could purchase snacks, fresh orange juice, and, of course, milk. Clifford Hardison opened the dairy in 1916. (Photograph by Robert Ybarra.)

CHAPTER ONE

In the Beginning

The California ranchos took shape when the land grants were distributed to Mexican families by the various Mexican governors. The land was cultivated, and fruits, walnuts, olives, and vegetables were among the crops grown on the ranchos. The Californios developed a preference for self-government because they lacked representation in the governing body of faraway Mexico. In Los Angeles and outlying areas, they formed the Los Angeles Rangers, a group of men who upheld the law in what was becoming a lawless society. Ygnacio del Valle helped organize this group. Charles Lummis, cofounder of the Landmarks Club with Reginaldo del Valle, was influenced by what he observed at the missions in Ventura and Santa Barbara. He convinced the padres to preserve the missions. The Californios favored an aristocratic, feudal-style agricultural economy based on honor, trust, and trade without money—a form of bartering system. When the Yankees married their daughters, there was a sense of uneasiness because these men were not Catholic, and their capitalism and landgrabs threatened the rancho way of life. The feudal-style system of ranchos included village workers who lived outside of the adobe main house of the owner; the laborers—not slaves—were poor and could not own land, and were kept like serfs. The Mexican government in 1834 gave mission lands (800 million acres) to 600–800 Mexican people. Most of the missions had a minimum of 900,000 to 1,000,000 acres of land. The missions "claimed" most of the land along the California coast, but the land was lost and reduced in the final claims. The mission lands were secularized, they were broken up, and their property was sold or given away. Mission land had passed through the hands of 800 private families by 1846. The land claims were usually declared invalid. The California Land Law of 1851 was primarily designed to invalidate the Mexican land grants to pave the way for Yankees to take over the land. Anglo lawyers tricked Californios to sign leases to mortgages they could not afford and to pay the lawyers for the land they already owned. A combination of squatters, bankers, and lawyers took over the land once owned by the Californios, and many were reduced to poverty. Then, there were added taxes that landowners could not afford to pay, since they had never been levied in the past, so the transition to the new federal government was not an easy one. Rather, it marked an end to the era of ranchos and los Californios.

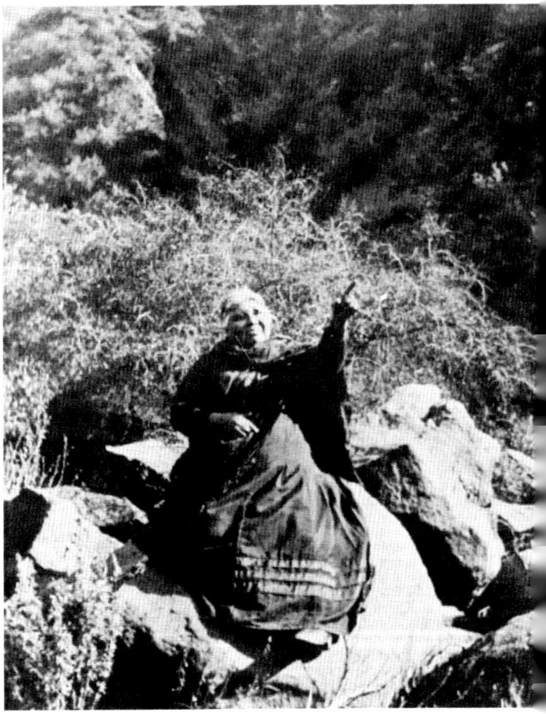

Candelaria

The last of the Chumash Sespe Indians, Candelaria Valenzuela had lived in the Chumash village known as Mahalal before the missions secularized the land. She was born in approximately 1838 on Lord's Creek in the Sespe area in the mountains above Fillmore. She was interviewed by both the anthropologist John Peabody Harrington and George Henley of the Smithsonian Institution in Washington DC, and she shared information about the traditions, language, and culture of her Chumash people. The Chumash are the only California Indian tribe who buried their dead in the ground, and they slept on true beds as they are known today—mats on raised platforms a few feet above the ground. Candelaria taught others how to weave baskets and how to dye the reeds for creative designs. For much of her life, she worked as a cook in Ventura County. She married and had four sons. (Courtesy Candelaria American Indian Council.)

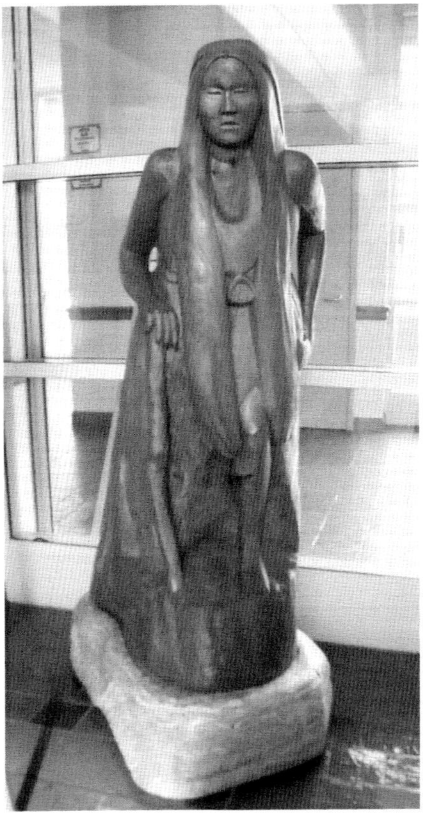

Statue of Candelaria

This statue, created by Apache sculptor Earl Dean Sistos in honor of Candelaria Valenzuela, is on permanent display in the Oxnard Public Library. Candelaria lived and worked with her husband, Jose Valenzuela, on Nick Peirano's ranch. On March 15, 1915, she was cooking in the grove on the field stove when she suffered severe burns. She died as a result of her injuries on March 17, 1915, at the age of 75. She shared the richness of her culture, traditions, and language with scholars, and her contributions are documented in the Smithsonian and in the archives of the Santa Barbara Museum of Natural History. (Courtesy Candelaria American Indian Council.)

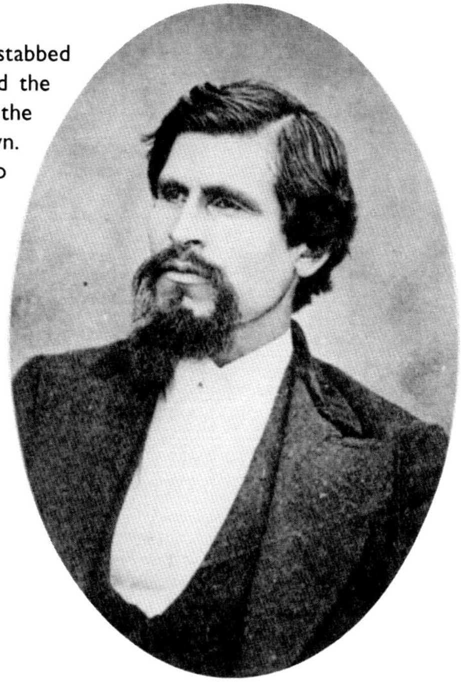

Tiburcio Vasquez

Tiburcio Vasquez was a born leader. He allegedly stabbed an American at a dance because his sister claimed the American had insulted her. Fearing the wrath of the Americans, he and a band of young followers left town. Soon after, a murder and robbery were attributed to him in 1852, it was said that he had joined the band of Joaquin Murrieta. Vasquez became a wanted man after he shot a deputy sheriff, but he continued to terrorize Southern California for 20 more years. (Courtesy Michele McKinley family collection.)

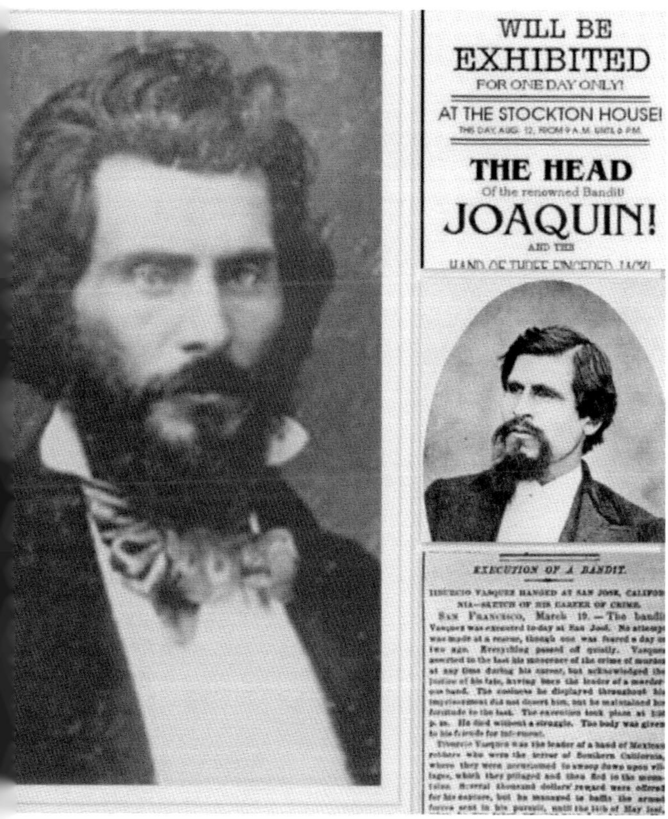

Joaquin Murrieta

Joaquin Murrieta would give riches to the poor and avenge those who were oppressed; in return, they would assist him in escaping from the law. Travel in the gold mine country was impossible for fear of Murrieta. California's governor hired a group of rangers to find him and kill him. Led by Captain Love, the rangers ambushed and killed Joaquin, his men, and his horse. They decapitated Joaquin for evidence, and the head was placed in an alcohol-filled jar and put on display at the Golden Nugget Saloon in San Francisco.

The notorious career of Murrieta lasted three and a half years as he made his way through Southern California. Tiburcio Vasquez and Joaquin Murrieta allegedly hid among the rocks of Devil's Gate in the Sespe backcountry. (Courtesy Michele McKinley family collection.)

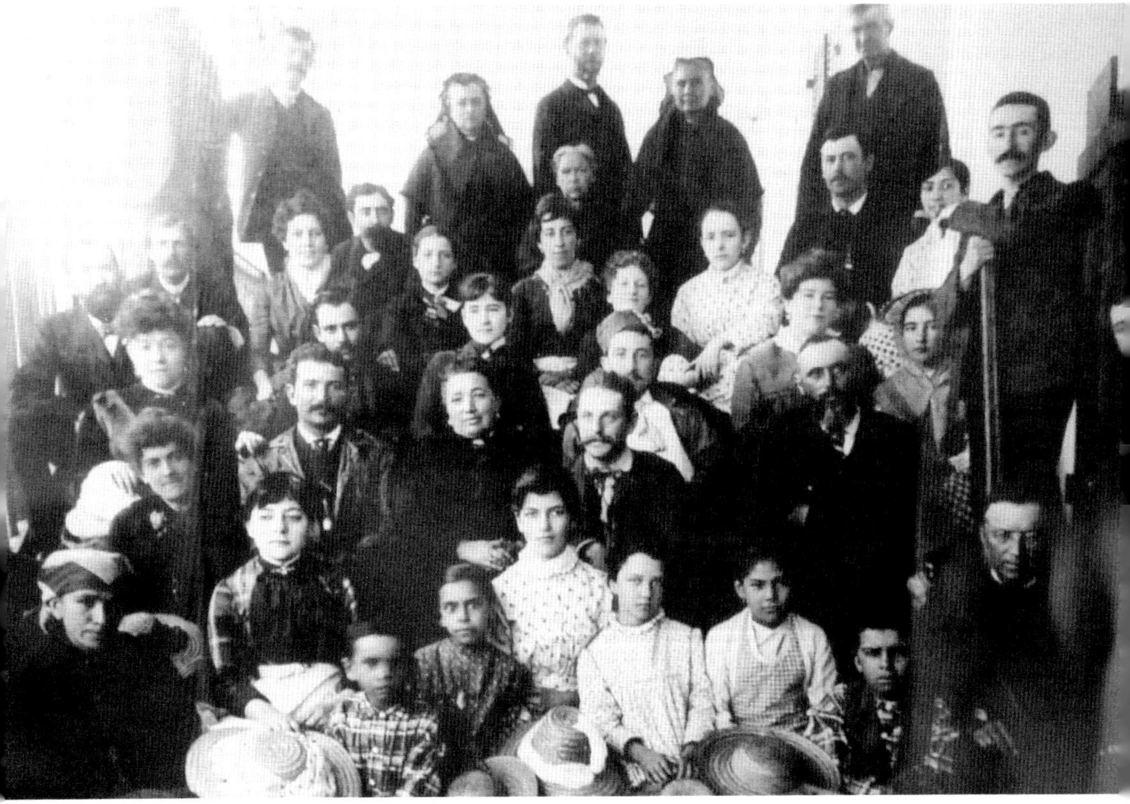

del Valle Family

All 48,612 acres of Rancho San Francisco were granted to Antonio del Valle in 1839 by Gov. Juan B. Alvarado in exchange for Antonio's exemplary military service. Rancho San Francisco runs from Valencia to Piru. Antonio died two years later, and the property was divided among his second wife, Jacoba, and the children from his two marriages. Antonio's oldest son, Ygnacio, inherited an 1,800-acre portion of the ranch and built a four-room adobe in 1853 on its western boundary at Camulos. His ranch comprised an area surrounding the former Indian village of Camulos, which means "juniper tree." He stocked the ranch with cattle and many fruit and walnut trees. This adobe became known as the Camulos Adobe, and it is now California Historical Landmark No 553. One day in 1842, Francisco Lopez, his ranch foreman, discovered gold on the property. This was before the gold rush at Sutter's Mill up north. This find spurred a minor gold rush, and many workers, including the del Valles, mined for gold. Rosary beads and jewelry were made from the gold they found.

After California became a state in 1850, the Land Grant Act of 1851 was an attempt to establish clear boundaries. All ranch owners had to provide legal documentation of their surveyed landholdings and the exact number of acres they claimed to own. Throughout a long, political career, Ygnacio was a part of the vigilante committee known as the Los Angeles Rangers, who dealt with the notorious Mexican bandits of the day. Under Mexican and American governments, he served as councilman, mayor, and state legislator.

This family portrait was taken in 1888 at Rancho Camulos. Mrs. del Valle is pictured in the top row, second from left. (Courtesy Rancho Camulos Museum.)

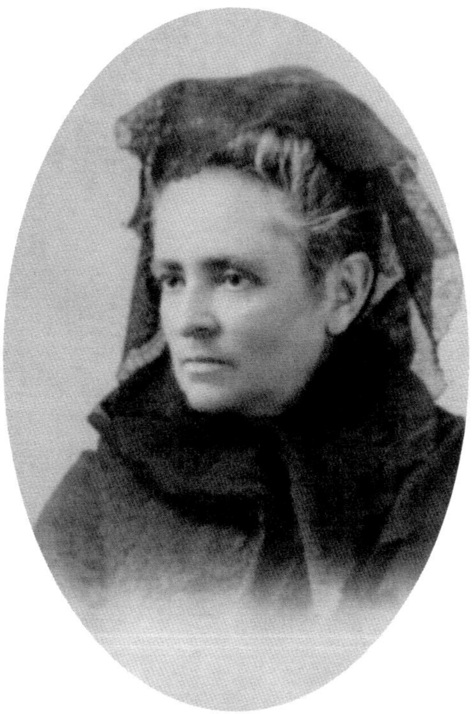

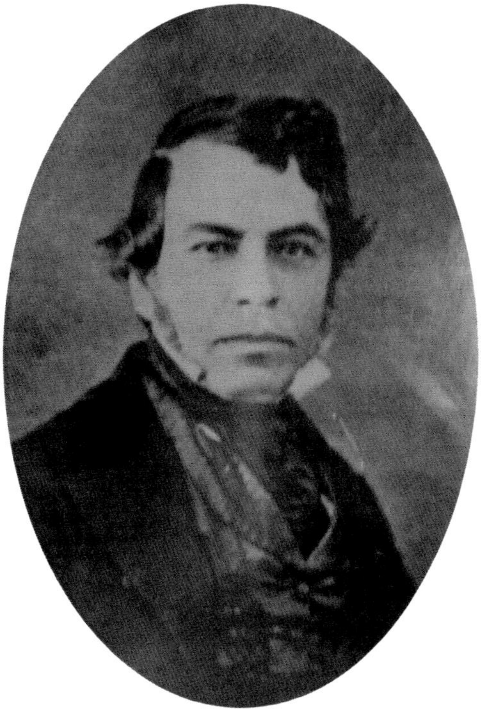

Ysabel and Ygnacio del Valle and the Chapel

Ysabel del Valle married her husband, Ygnacio, when she was 15. The couple had a Roman Catholic chapel built on their property, and Franciscan priests would visit the Chapel del Valle once a month since the old mission system had been dismantled. Many travelers stopped at Rancho Camulos on their travels to the San Buenaventura Mission or to the San Fernando Mission. Near the chapel, Ygnacio built a brick fountain, and his son Juventino planted a black walnut tree, which provided much shade for the family. Rancho Camulos was known as the "lost mission," and it was also a place of worship.

In 1880, Ygnacio del Valle died at age 72, and Ysabel assumed control of Rancho Camulos with the help of her three sons, Reginaldo, Juventino (Ygnacio's son by a different mother), and Ulpiano, who raised thoroughbred horses. The del Valles had a dozen children, of whom only five lived to adulthood. Ysabel would bring orphans to live at Rancho Camulos, and there were usually six additional children at the home. Doña Ysabel was living with her daughter Josefa in Los Angeles in 1905, and she passed away at the age of 68. She mourned her husband for 25 years and, before she died, had Ygnacio's coffin dug up at the Piru Cemetery and brought to her in Los Angeles. She was buried with him in his coffin. It has been told that when the funeral procession passed the Boyle Heights Orphanage, more than 300 children stood outside to pay their respects to Señora del Valle, whose work with the homeless became legendary. (Right, courtesy of Rancho Camulos Museum, Piru, California; left, photograph by Robert Ybarra.)

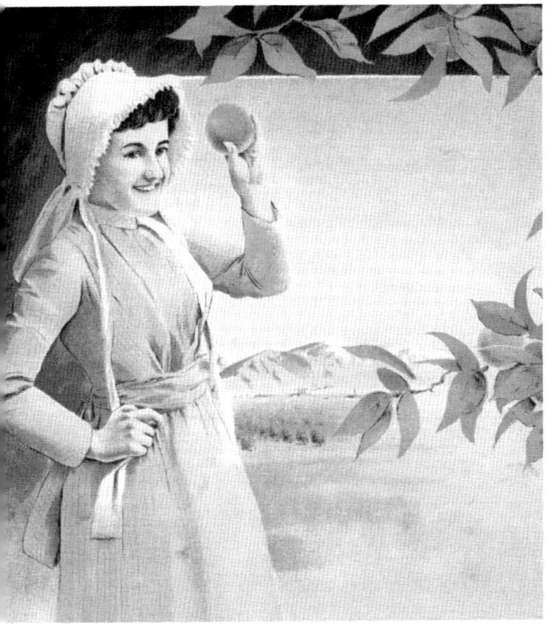

Ulpiano del Valle Citrus Label

By 1871, Rancho Camulos was producing 15,000 gallons of wine and brandy per year, and it would later publicize Helen Hunt Jackson's novel *Ramona* by bottling wine and labeling orange crates under the Home of Ramona label. The citrus groves consisted of 2,000 trees, 500 walnut trees, and 1,000 olive trees, and the returns were profitable. All the farming on Camulos Ranch was irrigated by the Santa Clara River, for water would be diverted into the great ditches running across the rancho. Portions of Rancho San Francisco were sold to Thomas Bard after the great drought of 1863–1864, which brought an end to the cattle era. Ulpiano was a founder and director of the Piru Citrus Association in 1914. The del Valles had planted the first citrus trees in the Fillmore-Piru area. The del Valle ranch supported 200 residents with the thousands of cattle, various fruits, walnuts, and acres of orange groves and vineyards. (Reproduced by permission of the Huntington Library, San Marino, California.)

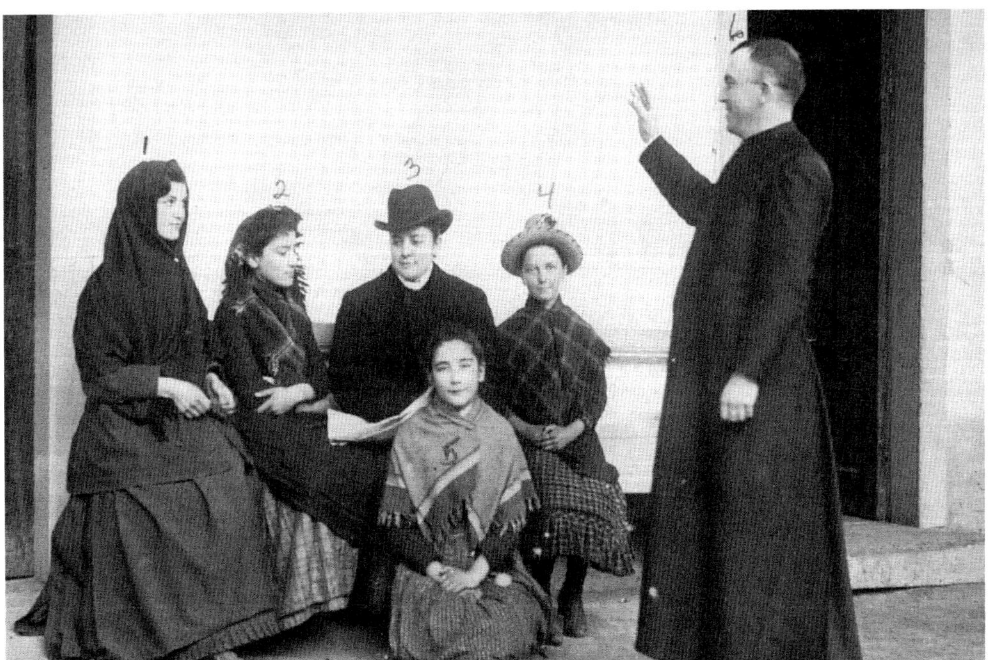

The del Valles and the Franciscan Priest

The Franciscan priests would come and celebrate Mass once a month before the town of Piru had built their Roman Catholic church. During these visits, the priests would join in the family celebrations and traditions, and the day would culminate with food and wine. The priests would always try to convert the local Indian population to Christianity. Pictured are Nena (1), Susanita (2), Ysabel (3), Natalie (4), and Enedina del Valle (5). The priest (6) is unidentified. (Reproduced by permission of the Huntington Library, San Marino, California.)

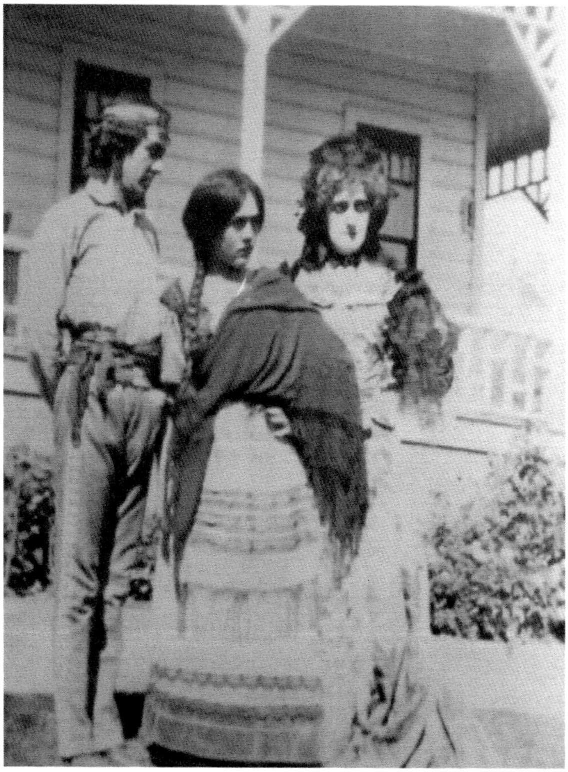

Mary Pickford and Helen Hunt Jackson's Story

D.W. Griffith, the famous Hollywood director, took Mary Pickford to Rancho Camulos, where she starred in the film *Ramona*. The film is available for viewing at Rancho Camulos as part of the docent tour. During filming, the actors, including Mary Pickford, stayed at the Piru Hotel in downtown Piru.

In 1884, Helen Hunt Jackson visited Rancho Camulos for only a few hours and became enthralled by the ranch. She based her book *Ramona* and the fictional Moreno Rancho on Rancho Camulos. It is well known that Don Coronel, a former mayor of Los Angeles, shared with Helen the personality traits of the various persons of the del Valle family. The day Helen Jackson made her visit, Ysabel del Valle and most of the family were not at home; therefore, Helen was dependent upon Don Coronel's descriptions. Don Coronel was a well-known authority on early Californio life in Southern California, and he was a frequent visitor to Rancho Camulos. He served as mayor of Los Angeles from 1853 to 1854, city councilman from 1854 to 1866, and state treasurer from 1866 to 1870. Don Coronel's stories influenced Helen to try to have the conditions of Native Americans improved. From him, she learned about the plight of the Mission Indians after 1833, during the time that the mission lands were sold and the Indian residents were dispersed. With the assistance of Indian agent and entrepreneur Abbot Kinney, they recommended massive government intervention and for the purchase of new land for schools for Native Americans. It was Jackson's dream that the book *Ramona* would bring attention to the plight of the Native Americans and that Congress would act. That did not happen, unfortunately. Helen Jackson passed away one year after her book was published. Rancho Camulos celebrates the days of the early Californios with their Ramona Days festival, which has become a tradition for Rancho Camulos Museum. Jackson's message is clear: she asks readers to look at the wrongs of the past in order to change the future and not repeat the same mistakes of maltreatment of the Indian. Rancho Camulos Museum is a US National Historic Landmark and is listed in the National Register of Historic Places. Pictured are Henry Walthall ("Alessandro") and Mary Pickford ("Ramona," center). *Ramona* tells the story of the white man's injustice to the Native Americans after mission secularization. (Courtesy Rancho Camulos Museum.)

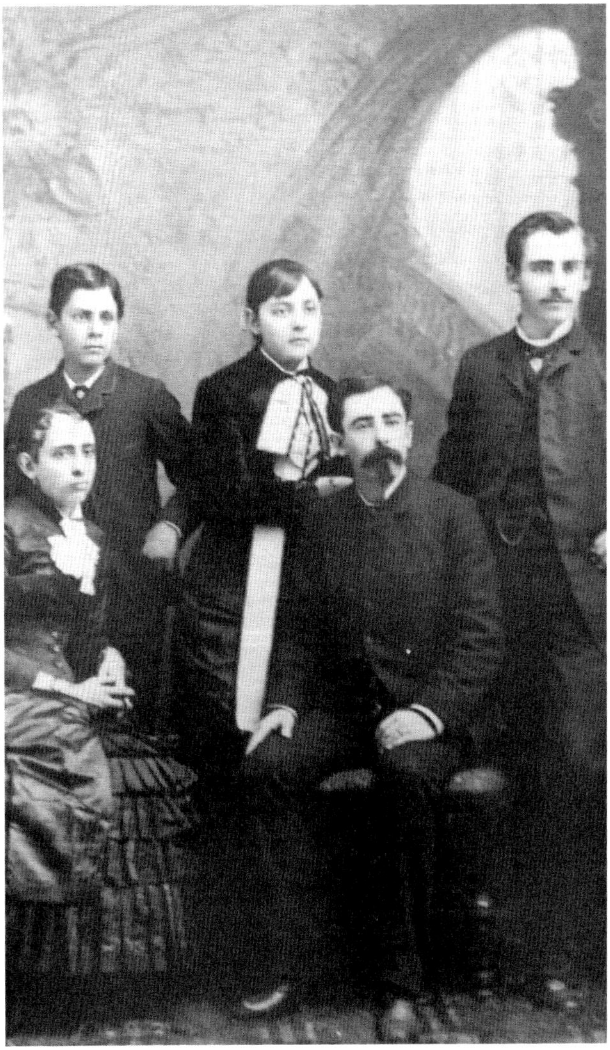

Reginaldo del Valle

Reginaldo was born in 1854 in the del Valles' home in Los Angeles. It was not until 1861 that the family moved to Rancho Camulos in Ventura County, and it was at Rancho Camulos that Reginaldo was tutored at home. He became fluent in English, French, and Spanish; later, he attended St. Vincent's Academy in Los Angeles for high school and graduated with honors. He attended Santa Clara University and, after passing the bar exam in 1877, he opened a law office. He joined the Democratic Party, beat his opponent in the election for state assembly, and he took his oath of office on January 2, 1880. There were only six assembly members from Southern California, and del Valle was the only Latino member. Pres. Woodrow Wilson appointed Reginaldo del Valle as his representative to Mexico in 1913, and in 1914, he was appointed president of the Los Angeles Public Service Board, later known as the Water and Power Commission, where he served for more than 20 years.

The University of California at Los Angeles will celebrate its 100th anniversary as a University of California campus. UCLA was built "in the place and stead" of the predecessor institution, the Los Angeles State Normal School, which had provided public higher education in California. The Los Angeles State Normal School was founded in 1881 for the preparation of elementary schoolteachers. Reginaldo Francisco del Valle was not mentioned, nor was he among the honored guests at a commemoration of UCLA held in 1930. Yet, as state assemblyman from 1880 to 1881 and state senator from 1882 to 1886, the bilingual, bicultural Los Angeles and Ventura County native of Mexican (not "Spanish") origin, Reginaldo Francisco del Valle was responsible for the establishment and funding of the Los Angeles Normal School, absorbed by the University of California in 1919 to become UCLA. The Los Angeles Normal School stands at Fifth and Grand Streets, the site of the current Los Angeles Public Library. The school was dedicated in 1882.

Reginaldo invited his friend Charles Lummis to stay at Rancho Camulos to recuperate from a mild stroke, and their friendship lasted until their deaths. Pictured from left to right are (seated) Mrs. Josepha R. (del Valle) Forster and Sen. Reginaldo del Valle; (standing) Ignacio del Valle Jr., Mrs. Ysabel (del Valle) Cram, and Ulpiano del Valle. (Courtesy of Rancho Camulos Museum.)

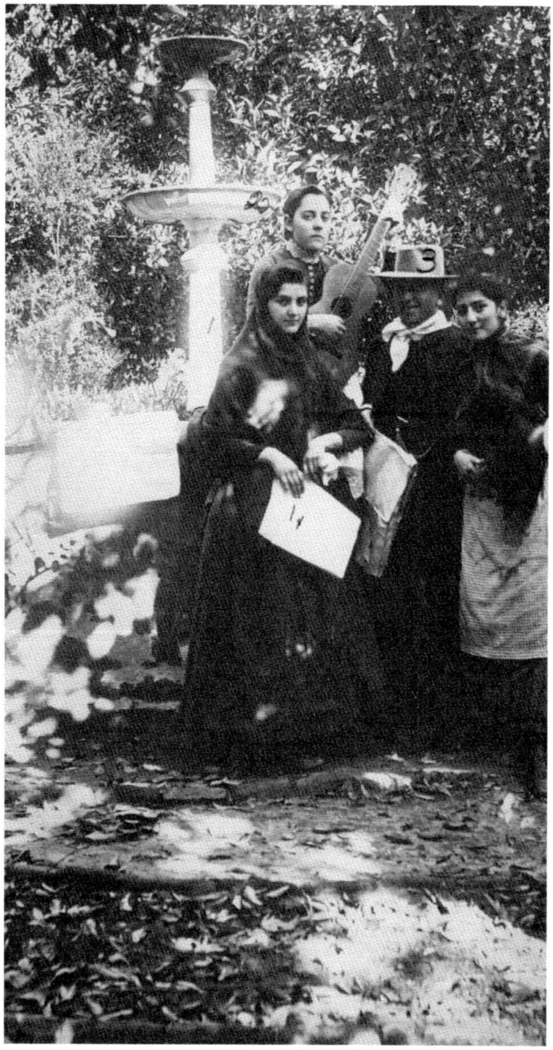

Charles Lummis

Charles was a pioneer photojournalist. He was the first city editor of the *Los Angeles Times*, advisor to Pres. Theodore Roosevelt, and the first preservationist in California. In 1887, he and Reginaldo were founders of the Landmarks Club, which was founded to advocate mission restoration. Charles was an advocate of preserving the Spanish heritage of California as well as Mexican and Native American traditions and customs. Los Angeles at the turn of the century was about the future and going forward—the "new Los Angeles" was what was in vogue. Historical preservation was not on the agenda. While he was staying at Rancho Camulos, Lummis took numerous photographs of the del Valle sisters and captured the life of the Californios on film. It was there that he fell in love with Susanita del Valle, who was 15 at the time. Charles was approximately 30 years of age and married. His wife, Dorothea, was a physician and quite accomplished. He promised he would divorce his wife, and when he did, he again pursued Susanita del Valle. However, Ysabel, Susanita's grandmother, would not allow the relationship to go forward.

During his many visits, he made wax recordings of the del Valle girls singing and playing the guitar. His collection includes numerous recordings and is now housed at the Braun Research Library Collection, Autry National Center in Los Angeles. After Helen Hunt Jackson's book *Ramona* was published in 1885, Charles wrote and published his own book, *Home of Ramona*, which told the story of Rancho Camulos as the setting for Jackson's book. This was published in 1888. During this same year, Charles gave Susanita leather-bound album with 83 blue-tinted photographs and several love poems. He inscribed the front cover page to Susanita, and her name was embossed in gold. In some of the photographs, he is seen dancing with her. The family would gather on the south veranda and hold their celebrations. In other photographs, Don Coronel is also pictured dancing and enjoying the festivities at Rancho Camulos. Charles was never excluded from the ranch, but his visits became less frequent. Susanita loved him and was heartbroken at 16. She did not marry until she was 35, when she wed a real estate broker from Los Angeles, Edson Carter. The following year, 1907, she and her baby died in childbirth. Pictured from left to right are (1) Nena del Valle, (2) Ysabel del Valle, (3) Charles Lummis, and Susanita. (Reproduced by permission of the Huntington Library, San Marino, California.)

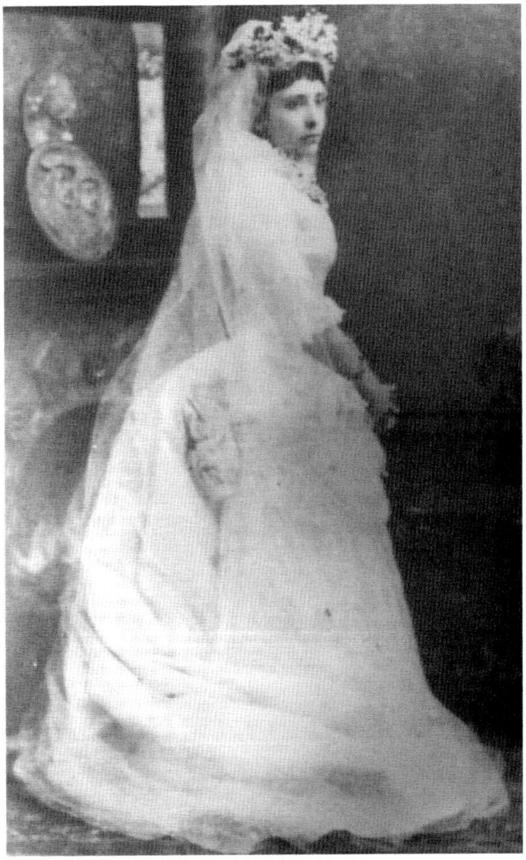

Josefa del Valle

In 1886, Josefa married Juan Fernando Forster, the son of John Forster, the English seaman who settled in California in 1833. John had married Gov. Pio Pico's sister, Ysidora Pico, in 1837, and he acquired 100,000 acres of land, including San Juan Capistrano Rancho and Rancho Santa Margarita, near Camp Pendleton in San Diego County. Juan Forster, the son, moved to Los Angeles in 1884 and built the Forster Block on Main Street. After he and Josefa were married, they built a house on Grand Avenue in Los Angeles where their two sons, Ygnacio Juan and Juan Fernando, were born. Juan Forster died in 1901 at the age of 56, three months before their second son was born. Josefa then took care of her mother, Doña Ysabel del Valle, and brought her to live with her at her home in Los Angeles in 1900. Josefa was very devoted to her mother. In 1903, Josefa and Susanita del Valle were dinner guests of Charles Lummis and his second wife, Eve, at the home Charles built, El Alisol, in Los Angeles. They spent time together sharing and reminiscing about the past. Susanita married in 1906 and died in 1907.

According to Charles's granddaughter Suzanne Lummis, Charles and Eva entertained lavishly and he expected his wife, Eva (Suzanne's grandmother), to prepare the food and to provide for all of his talented and wealthy friends. He would dangle his affairs under her nose until she could no longer remain married to him. She took her two older children, Turbesé, eight years old, and Keith who was four, and left Charles. Eva also left their child Jordan with his father. Although it was difficult for women to leave their husbands at the turn of the century as they were more dependent, Eva had a very good friend who helped her through this difficult time.

Phoebe Elizabeth Hearst helped Eva Lummis and took her and the children into her home. Phoebe's husband, George, had passed away in 1891, and Phoebe had a son, William Randolph Hearst, who became the successful publishing tycoon and businessman. Phoebe was an American philanthropist, feminist, and suffragist. She was a major benefactor of the University of California, Berkeley and its first woman regent. In 1897, she contributed to the National Congress of Mothers, which evolved into the National Parent-Teacher Association. In 1901, Phoebe Hearst founded the University of California Lowie Museum of Anthropology, renamed in 1992, the Phoebe A. Hearst Museum of Anthropology.

Frances Eve Douglas (1870–1969) was Charles Lummis's second wife, and she used the name "Eve" during their marriage. After their divorce in 1911, she used her maiden name of Douglas and sometimes "Eva," as well. (Courtesy of Rancho Camulos Museum.)

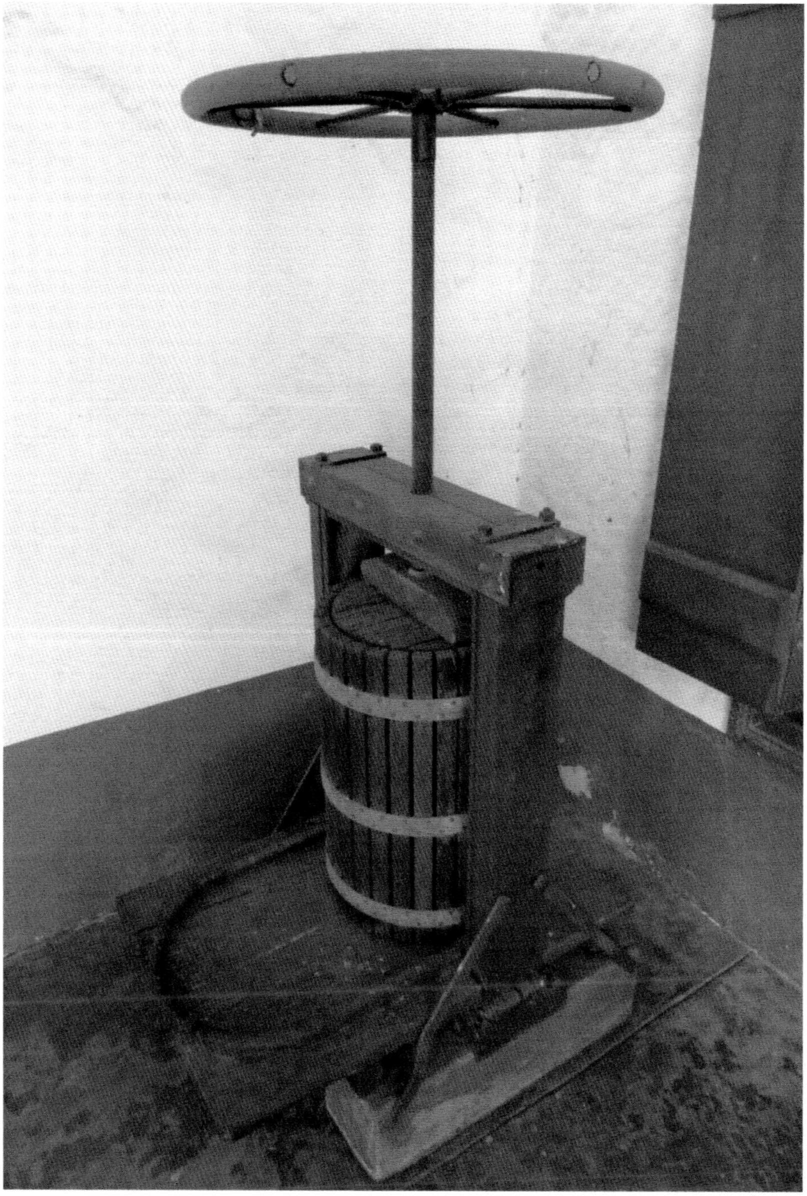

Dominguez Family–Donated Wine Press
Rancho Camulos was known for its fine brandies and wines, primarily between the 1870s and 1890s. The vineyards totaled 50,000 vines, which yielded 15,000 to 20,000 gallons of wine per year, and it produced 800 gallons of brandy. The primary agricultural product from Rancho Camulos was wine, and 90 acres of vineyards were planted in the 1860s. The fine wines and brandies were well known throughout Los Angeles and Santa Barbara. Ventura County had not been established yet, and the area was part of Santa Barbara County. In addition to oranges and grapes, the ranch produced almonds, walnuts, apricots, wheat, corn, and barley. Rose petals grown at Rancho Camulos were shipped to Europe to make perfume. The fountain is also significant because the family gathered around the south veranda and the fountain for its many celebrations. The fountain was first built in 1853. (Courtesy of Rancho Camulos Museum.)

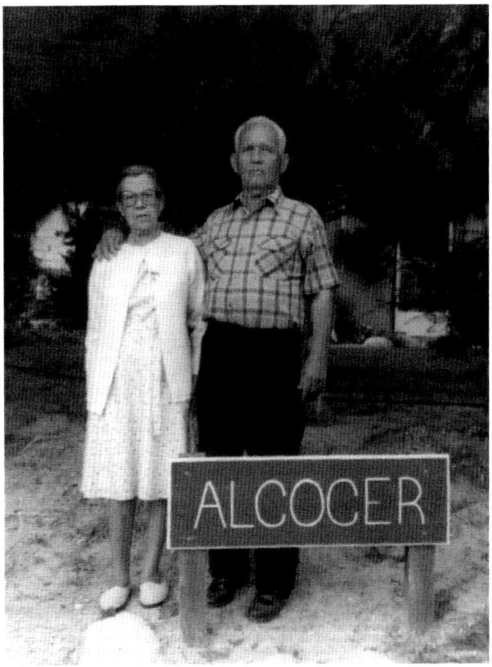

Moises and Maria Martinez Alcocer

Moises and Maria Martinez Alcocer were honored by Rancho Camulos as members of the "first families" of Rancho Camulos. The descendants of the original families who worked or lived on the rancho were all invited to participate and be recognized. Moises had parents who lived or worked on Rancho Camulos since the 1800s. Moises and Maria raised their seven children in Piru, and the children then attended Fillmore Junior High and all graduated from Fillmore High School. (Courtesy of Lucy Rangel family collection.)

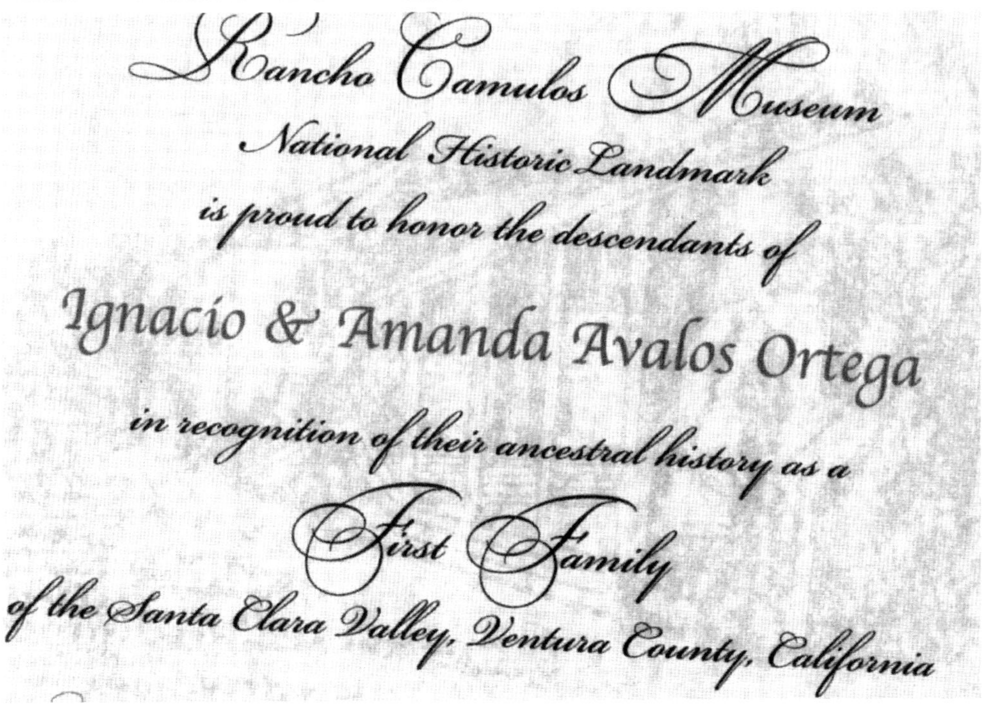

Rancho Camulos Museum
National Historic Landmark
is proud to honor the descendants of
Ignacio & Amanda Avalos Ortega
in recognition of their ancestral history as a
First Family
of the Santa Clara Valley, Ventura County, California

Ignacio and Amanda Avalos Ortega

Ignacio and Amanda were members of the "first families" of Rancho Camulos and are James Rangel's maternal grandparents. James Rangel married Lucy Alcozar; he was a firefighter, and she taught school in the Fillmore Unified School District for over 30 years. Today, Lucy serves on the Fillmore Unified School District Board of Trustees. (Courtesy of Lucy Rangel family collection.)

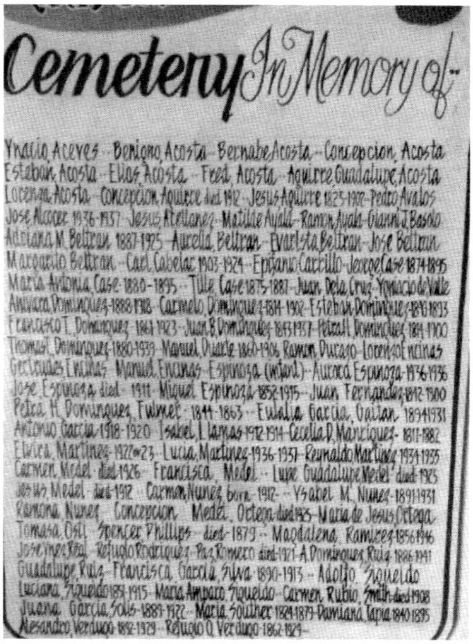

Individuals Buried at Rancho Camulos Cemetery

Among this list of names of many of the first families of Rancho Camulos is the name of Ygnacio del Valle. He was buried at the cemetery for 25 years until 1905, when his coffin was removed and taken to Los Angeles as requested by his widow, Ysabel del Valle, so they could be buried together upon her death. (Photographed by Robert Ybarra, courtesy of Rancho Camulos Museum.)

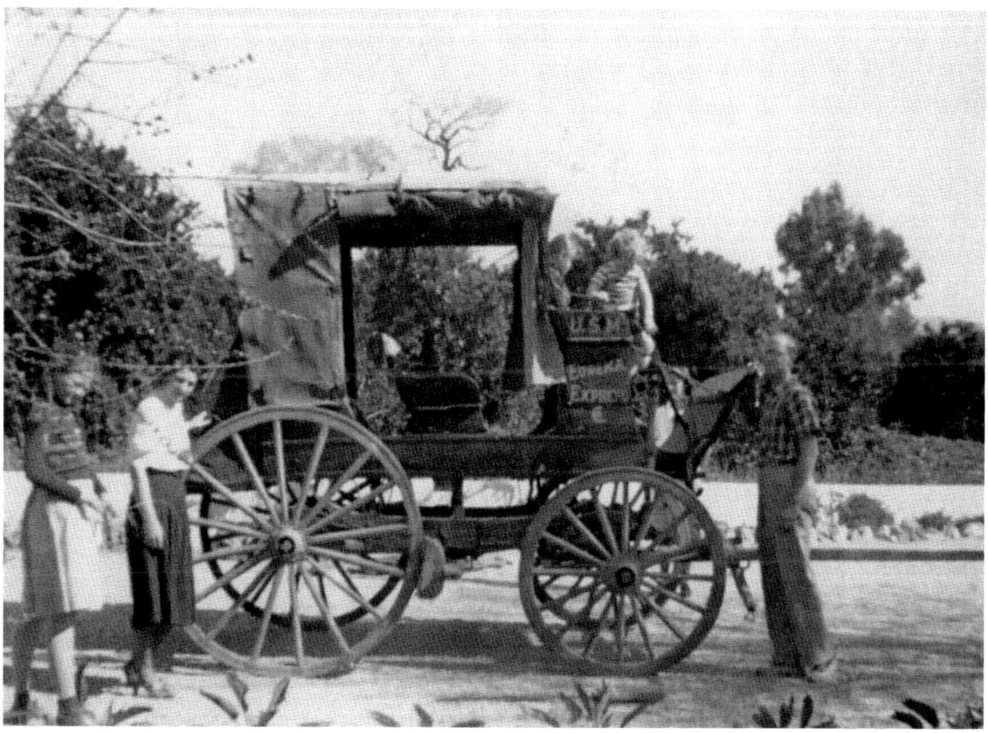

August Rubel and Family

The grounds are filled with flowers and plants native to the area, and on the northwest side is the large walnut tree that was planted in the 1860s by Juventino del Valle. August and Mary Rubel are pictured with their children in the carriage. In 1924, August Rubel purchased Rancho Camulos for $300,000 and added the schoolhouse for his children. The Rubel family still owns the 1,800-acre ranch. (Courtesy of Rancho Camulos Museum.)

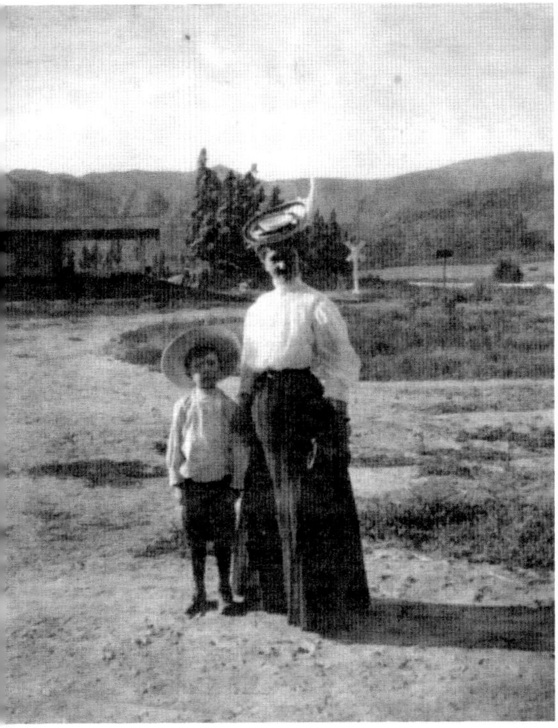

Rancho Camulos Train Stop

The del Valles urged the Southern Pacific Railroad Company to build a depot and to make a stop at Rancho Camulos in order to encourage tourism and to allow the del Valles to use the railroad to send their fruits and other products to the markets in Los Angeles. All of this was before refrigeration, and the fruit had to be packed and loaded for a quick delivery the same day in order for it to remain fresh. In addition to selling fruit to the Los Angeles markets, the del Valles sold their famous wines and brandy and various kinds of nuts and walnuts. (Courtesy of Kathy Corley Recicar family collection.)

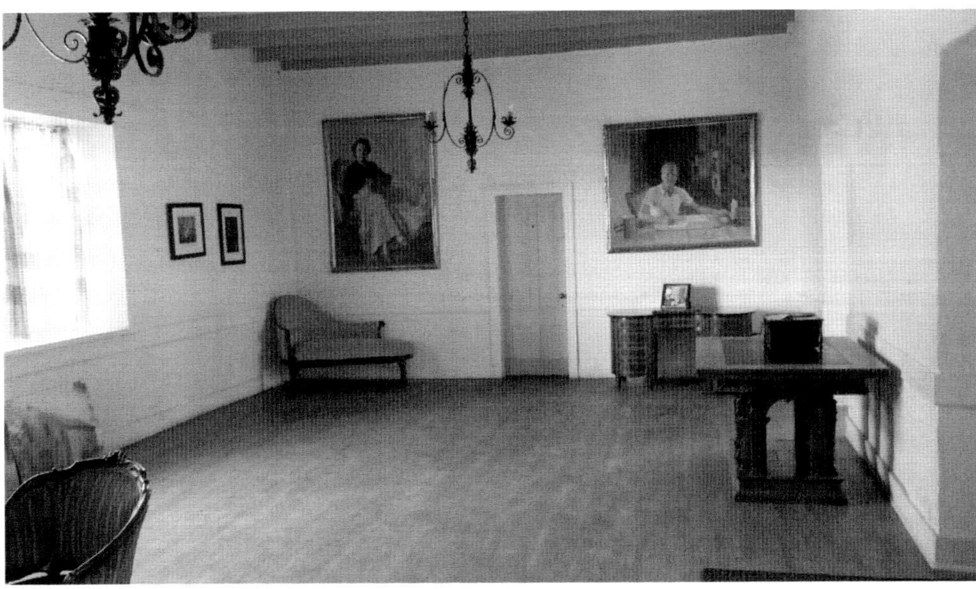

The Interior of Rancho Camulos

The Rubel family did not visit the ranch after their mother passed away, because her second husband, Edward Berger, was a recluse and did not want visitors stopping by unannounced. After the 1994 earthquake, in which one wall in his bedroom collapsed, he suffered a heart attack and was hospitalized. He later died in a nursing home, and the family took over the ranch. Now, part of it is a nonprofit organization. Paintings of Mary Rubel (left) and August Rubel (right) hang on the far wall. (Photographed by Robert Ybarra, courtesy Rancho Camulos Museum.)

CHAPTER TWO

Pioneers as Movers and Shakers

The city of Fillmore was named for Jerome A. Fillmore, who was the general superintendent of the Southern Pacific Railroad. Joseph D. McNab laid out the plots of land for the new community and hired William Mulholland to lay out the water pipes for water and irrigation of the crops. The railroad came through in 1887–1888, and the town was established in 1888 and incorporated in 1914. George Tighe was elected the first mayor of Fillmore, and he served until 1919. The community is a diverse one with many Hispanics and Anglos. The land grants were given to the Mexican landowners in good faith and were based on trust. The rules of the game changed in 1851 when the US government informed all landowners that proof of ownership was now required and that they would be expected to have the land surveyed and marked. Titles would have to be presented and approved. It was a difficult time for the Mexican landowners—many did not have such "proof," nor did they have all the land surveyed at this time. To complicate matters, the courts were ineffective and too slow to remedy all of the contested issues of land ownership. Then, the landowners began losing their acreage, or they lost their wealth fighting their battles in the courts. In came the homesteaders, and if they followed the guidelines, they claimed the land as their own and could begin cultivating and building on it. They could divert the water necessary to irrigate their crops. This is what the squatters attempted to do when they claimed land that T. Wallace More insisted he had paid for at the Santa Barbara auction. The US Land Commission decided in his favor, but their decision was later overturned. This allowed the squatters to homestead the open lands. Settlers came into the Fillmore-Bardsdale area, and a community was born.

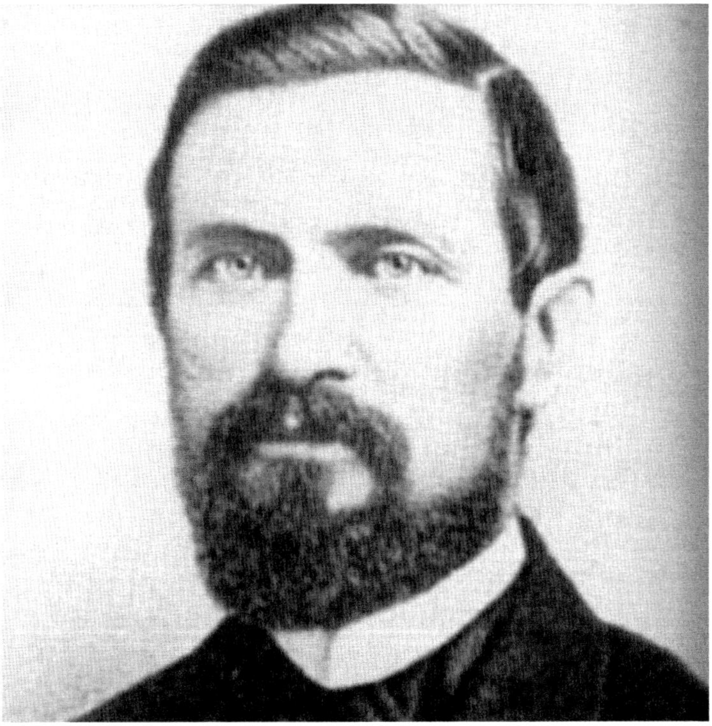

Thomas Wallace More

On March 24, 1877, in the early morning hours and under the cover of darkness, several masked men shot and killed Thomas Wallace More, the owner of Rancho Sespe. More and his brothers Henry and Andrew owned substantial holdings in California. Most of the property was obtained by purchasing Mexican land grants that had been given to many Mexican families prior to California becoming part of the United States. Included in these holdings were Rancho Santa Paula y Saticoy, Rancho Lompoc, Rancho del Purisma, La Patera, Santa Rosa Island, and Rancho Sespe.

In 1829, a resident of Santa Barbara by the name of Don Carlos Antonio Carrillo petitioned the provincial governor of Alta California for the tract of land known as Rancho Sespe. Not until Gen. Jose Figueroa became governor in 1833 was this confirmed and the concession ultimately granted. No grant was made for less than one square league, or approximately 4,428 acres. Some confusion arises from the fact that the file of official papers relating to the concession contains two copies of the official grant. Both have the same date of May 29, 1834, are signed by Governor Figueroa and the secretary, Augustin Zamorano, and list the conditions of the concession (that Carrillo must build a house and get the property surveyed), but one states the grant is for two leagues, while the other lists six leagues. On February 2, 1848, the United States acquired California under the terms of the Treaty of Guadalupe Hidalgo. Gold was discovered in Northern California, and gold seekers passed through the Santa Clara Valley on their way to find their fortunes.

In 1850, disturbing reports about the security of the existing land titles in California began to circulate among the ranchos. Boundary lines were called into question, and lawless men, squatters, and cattle thieves threatened the ranch owners. Extravagance and debt created havoc and brought about the collapse of the old Californio land system.

Don Carlos Carrillo died in 1852; his widow passed away a year later in February 1853. Then, in April 1853, the Land Commission confirmed the original petition of Carlos Antonio for Rancho Sespe. It was approved for six square leagues, or 26,000 acres. A few months after this decision, the probate court of Santa Barbara ordered the estate held by Josefa Carrillo to be sold at auction. (Courtesy of the More Mesa Homeowners Association.)

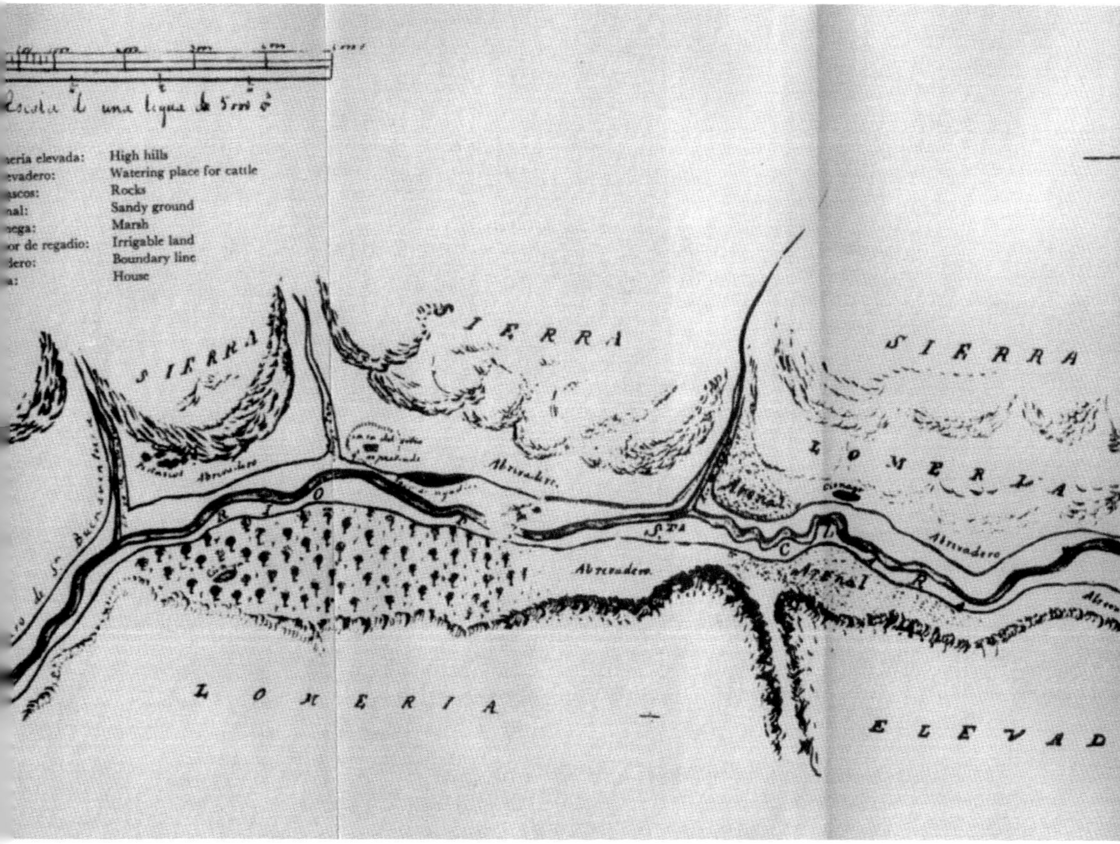

Map of Rancho Sespe

The public auction was advertised as follows: "Of the Rancho San Cayetano being the whole of the rights to said rancho of the late Josefa Castro de Carrillo, deceased . . . It comprises six leagues of land (confirmed by the United States Land Commission)." The successful bidders were the More brothers, who paid $17,500 for 13/14 of the land. A year later, they purchased the remaining one-fourteenth for $1,000. This averaged about 70¢ an acre. During the severe drought of 1862–1864, Thomas and his two brothers, Henry and Alexander, dissolved their partnership. Henry and Alexander received the island of Santa Rosa in exchange for Rancho Sespe, and Thomas also received a small ranch in Goleta. This made Thomas the principal title holder of Rancho Sespe.

After the California Gold Rush and the Civil War, settlers were looking for a new life and a new place to live, and they attempted to settle on and claim land directed in the Homestead Act of 1862. The newcomers, known as squatters, settled along the Sespe Creek and Santa Clara River, which was near Thomas More's ranch house. The squatters argued that the grant deed he purchased was for only two leagues and not six and that they had the right to the land and the water. The dispute was in the courts, and that system was too slow and ineffective to resolve the issue. Thomas remained living in Rancho Sespe with his wife, Susana, one of the daughters of the famed Ortega family in Santa Barbara.

One day, T. More, his son-in-law Charles Storke, and others built a canal to divert the scarce water from the Santa Clara River and Sespe Creek to his land. There was a confrontation, and F.A. Sprague, one of the squatters, had his rifle when he confronted More and they argued. (Reproduced by permission of the Huntington Library, San Marino, California.)

Susana A. Hill More

Susana Hill More married T. Wallace More on June 1, 1853. She was the daughter of Daniel Hill (1797–1865) and Rafaela Sabina Luisa Ortega (1809–1879). Her mother was Jose Francisco Ortega's granddaughter; hence, Susana was his great granddaughter. Capt. Jose Francisco Ortega founded the San Francisco presidio and assisted in founding Mission Santa Barbara. He was a California pioneer, and in 1795 Gov. Diego de Borica granted him 26,529 acres in Santa Barbara County. Susana and T. Wallace More had four sons and a daughter, and their daughter Mattie married Charles A. Storke. It was Charles who assisted the More descendants with business transactions after T. Wallace More's murder in 1877 and after the death of Susana More in 1879.

On the night of March 23, 1877, and into the early hours of March 24, seven men allegedly met at Frank Sprague's store at Rancho Sespe, donned gunny sacks as masks, and made their way to the More house. At that hour, all were asleep, including Jim Tot, the cook; his foreman, George Ferguson; and two employees, Juan Olivas and Santiago Reveal. Two or four of the masked men positioned themselves at the gate of the corral, while the other three went to the Mores' barn and set it on fire. Soon, all were awakened by the noise of the horses and smelled the smoke. They rushed out to save the animals. After More retrieved some harnesses, he came out into the open area, where he was shot. As he tried to struggle to his feet, three of the masked gunmen walked up to him and pumped numerous rounds of rifle and shotgun lead into his head. The masked men fled the scene. More was dead. The cook said there were five masked men, while others reported seeing seven. Only the perpetrators knew for sure. This group of settlers was in a dispute with Thomas over the land and water rights. Thomas had purchased six leagues of land, but the courts claimed it was only two leagues that he had bought and that the rest was public domain. The squatters attempted to claim the remaining land, which resulted in More's assassination.

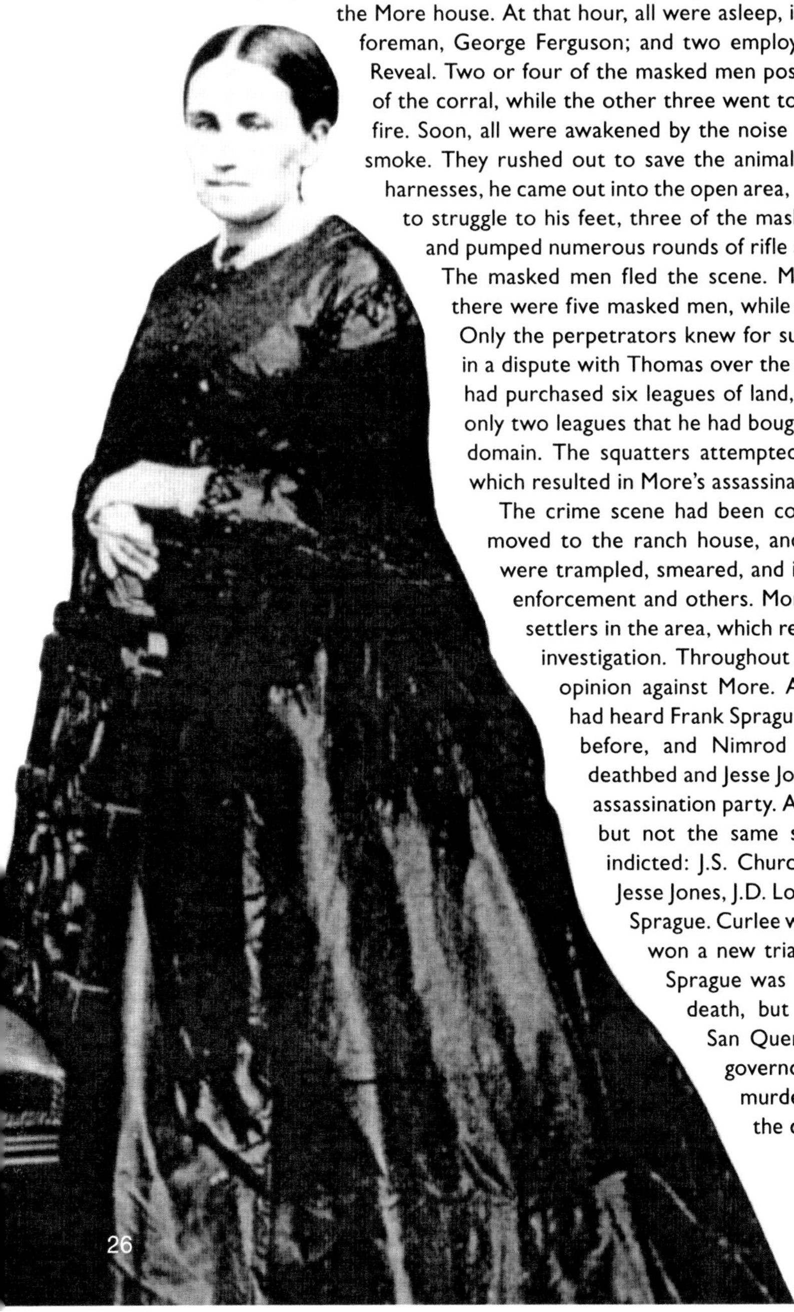

The crime scene had been contaminated. More's body was moved to the ranch house, and the perpetrators' footprints were trampled, smeared, and intermingled with those of law enforcement and others. More was disliked by most of the settlers in the area, which resulted in a slow and ineffective investigation. Throughout the valley, there was a biased opinion against More. Austin Brown claimed that he had heard Frank Sprague plan the murder three weeks before, and Nimrod Hickerson confessed on his deathbed and Jesse Jones claimed to be a part of the assassination party. All three named seven suspects, but not the same seven. Eventually, seven were indicted: J.S. Churchill, John Curlee, W.H. Hunt, Jesse Jones, J.D. Lord, Charles McCart, and Frank Sprague. Curlee was found guilty, though he later won a new trial and he was acquitted. Frank Sprague was found guilty and sentenced to death, but after serving seven years in San Quentin, he was pardoned by the governor and released. The More murder was known as the crime of the century. (Author's collection.)

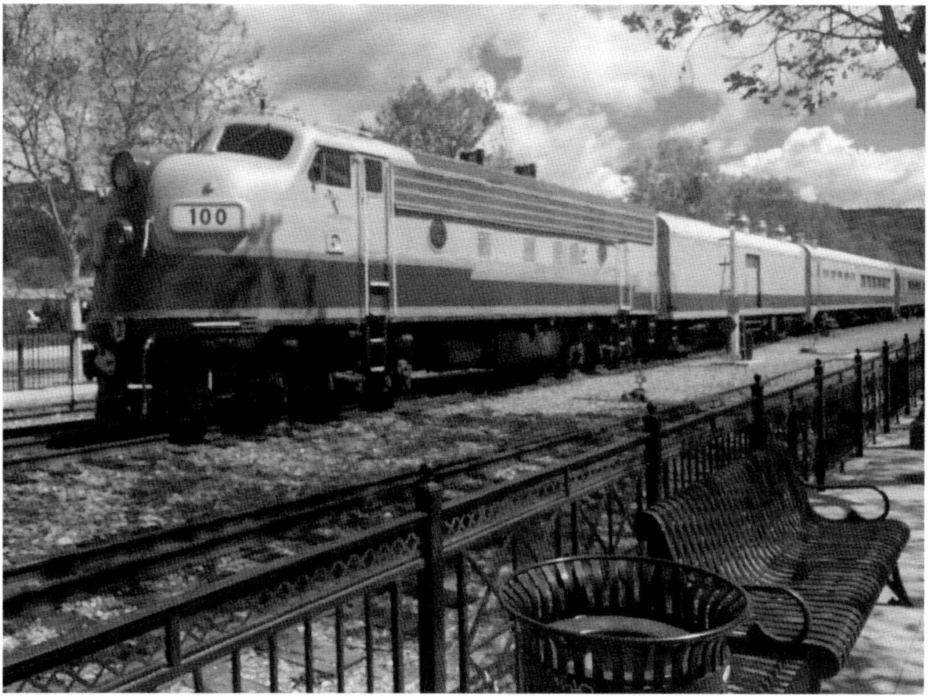

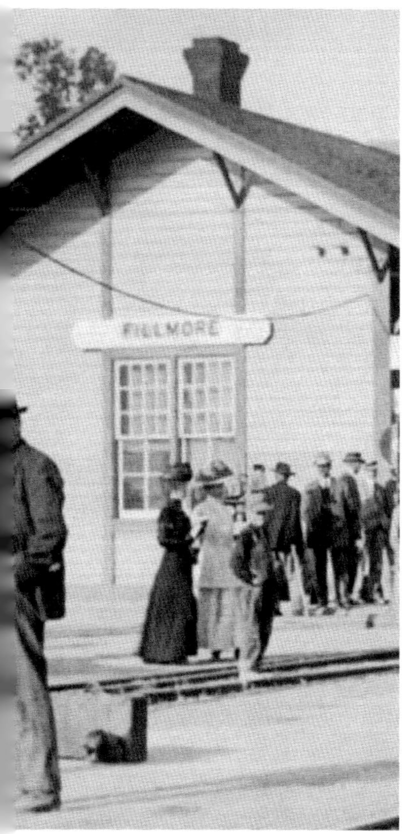

Jerome A. Fillmore

Jerome A. Fillmore was the general superintendent of the Southern Pacific Railroad when they were building the line that connected Santa Paula, Fillmore, Piru-Rancho Camulos, and Castaic. There was a distance of exactly eight miles between the towns. Jerome liked the community of Fillmore and decided a town should be established around the railroad site. This was in 1888, and by 1890, oranges, lemons, and other goods were transported by train to Los Angeles. The train depots were laid out at exactly eight miles apart from each previous city. Joseph D. McNab, who founded the Sespe Land and Water Company, had laid out the town, which would soon become the city of Fillmore.

Together with the Southern Pacific Railroad Company, Sespe Land and Water promoted the newly formed town of Fillmore. In 1885, William Mulholland was hired by Joseph D. McNab and the Sespe Land and Water Company to lay out the water pipes for irrigation of the crops. As part of his compensation, he was granted 20 acres on Sespe Creek. Jerome Fillmore liked the area, and he worked with McNab to promote the town of Fillmore. Today, the depot is part of the Fillmore Historical Museum, and within the depot is a grand mural painted by former art teacher John Brothers of Fillmore High School; it depicts a vintage Central Avenue as a colorful and new town with a bustling business district. (Photograph by Robert Ybarra, courtesy of Fillmore Western Railway and D. Wilkinson.)

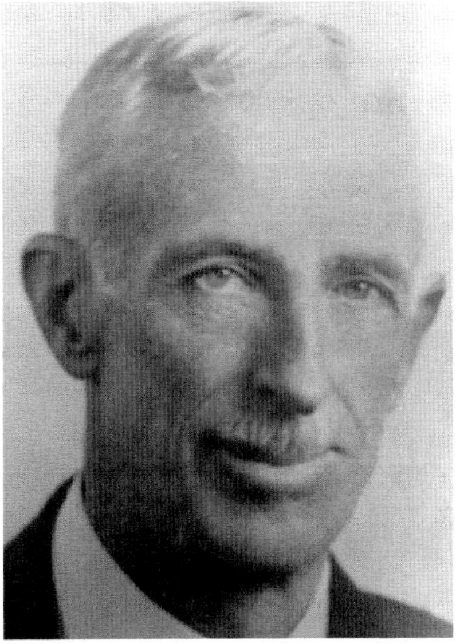

George Tighe

George served as the city's first mayor from 1914 to 1919. He was the stationmaster for the Southern Pacific Railroad and he managed Tighe's General Store on Central Avenue. In addition to that, he was very active in the community of Fillmore. He also served as president of the Fillmore State Bank, which was built with the Sespe sandstone on the face of the building. It had been quarried and taken through the Sespe area into the city of Fillmore for this purpose. Members of the board of directors were William Shiells and Hugh Warring. The city of Fillmore had a fire on Main Street, and many of the new businesses had to move. They relocated around the corner to Central Avenue. (Courtesy Bob Cox family collection.)

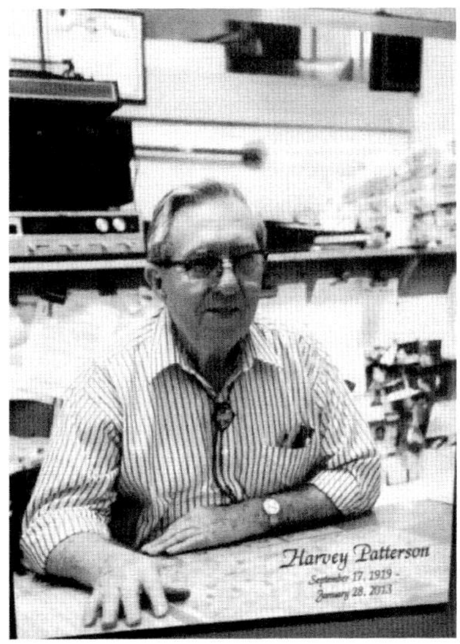

Harvey Patterson, Patterson Hardware

Businesses relocated to Central Avenue after the fire on Main Street. One of the businesses to recently celebrate its 100-year anniversary is Patterson Hardware. Harvey Patterson took over the family business and served the community of Fillmore well during his tenure. Harvey and Emma raised their children, David Patterson, Patricia Tompkins, Nancy English, and Michelle Patterson, in Fillmore. Today, Michelle Patterson manages the family business. Patterson Hardware has supported the community and youth sports programs over the years. (Courtesy Patterson family collection.)

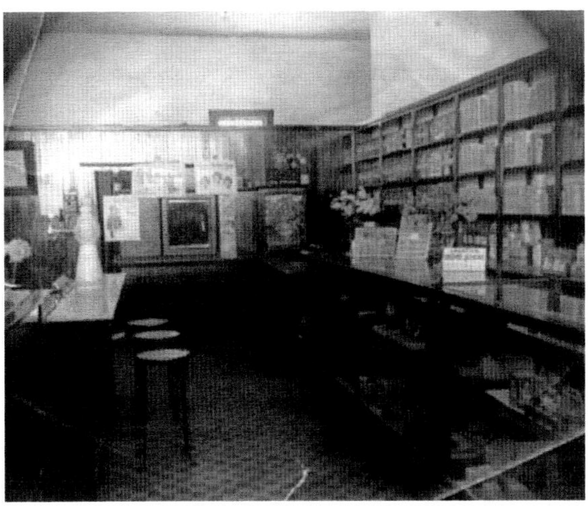

Dr. Ira Hinckley and His Drugstore

Dr. John Hinckley was the first physician for the city of Fillmore from 1890 to 1902. His son Ira was the first dentist in Fillmore and ran the drugstore, which was in the front of his dental office. It later became Clough's Pharmacy. Lawrence Hinckley, Dr. Ira Hinckley's son, and his wife, Mildred Hinckley, a minister, transformed their home into the Artists' Barn. The Barn hosted many well-known artists and is Ventura County Cultural Heritage Landmark No. 59. (Courtesy of Bob Cox family collection.)

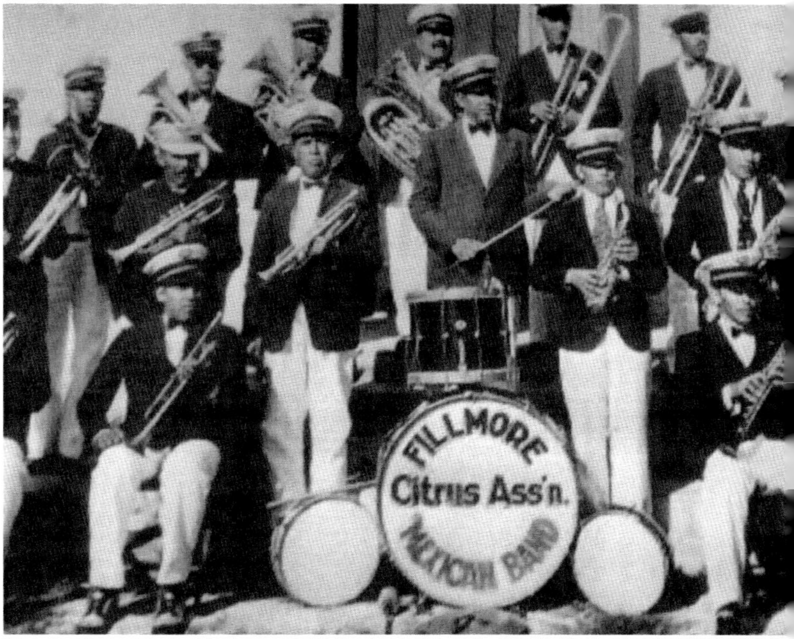

Dolores "Lolo" Sánchez and the Mexican Band
Baseball teams and group bands were organized to encourage the labor force to take part in activities during their leisure time on weekends. The players enjoyed the competition of playing the teams in neighboring towns and labor campsites. (Courtesy M. Ramirez family collection.)

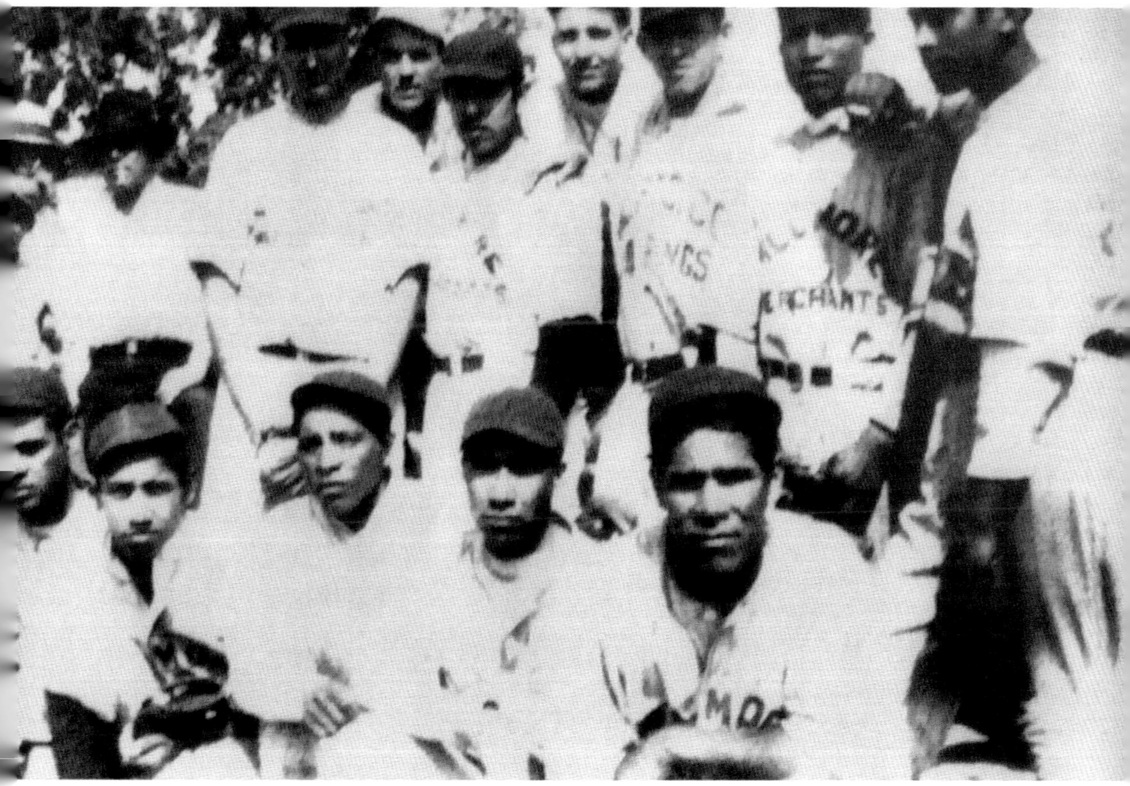

The Fillmore Merchants Baseball Team
Here is a team photograph showing some of the labor force during their spare time. (Courtesy of M. Ramirez family collection.)

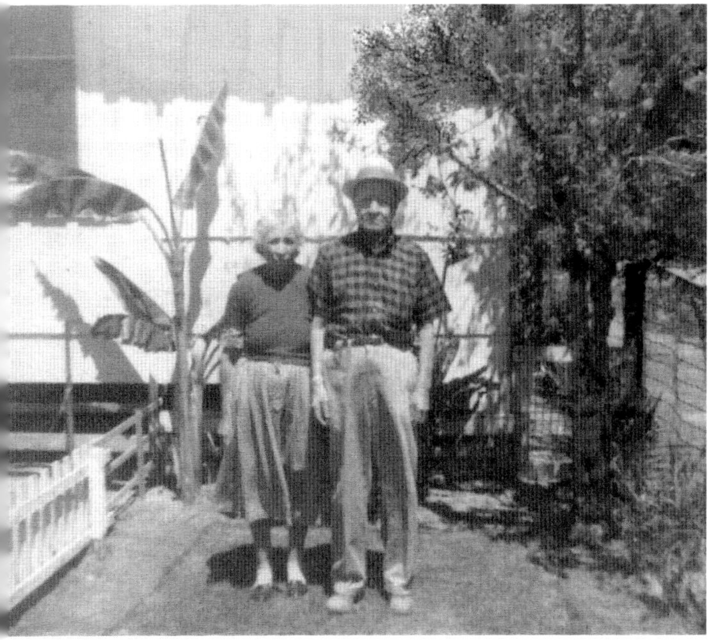

Rancho Sespe and Mr. and Mrs. Mendes

Mr. and Mrs. Mendes worked for the Spaldings on Rancho Sespe and lived in the worker housing provided by the ranch. The Spaldings provided for their labor force and had two bunkhouses built for their single workers. Mr. Mendes tended the Spaldings' famous rose garden and the landscaping adjacent to the family home. Mrs. Mendes assisted Mrs. Spalding with the housekeeping and general assistance. (Courtesy of the Mendes family collection.)

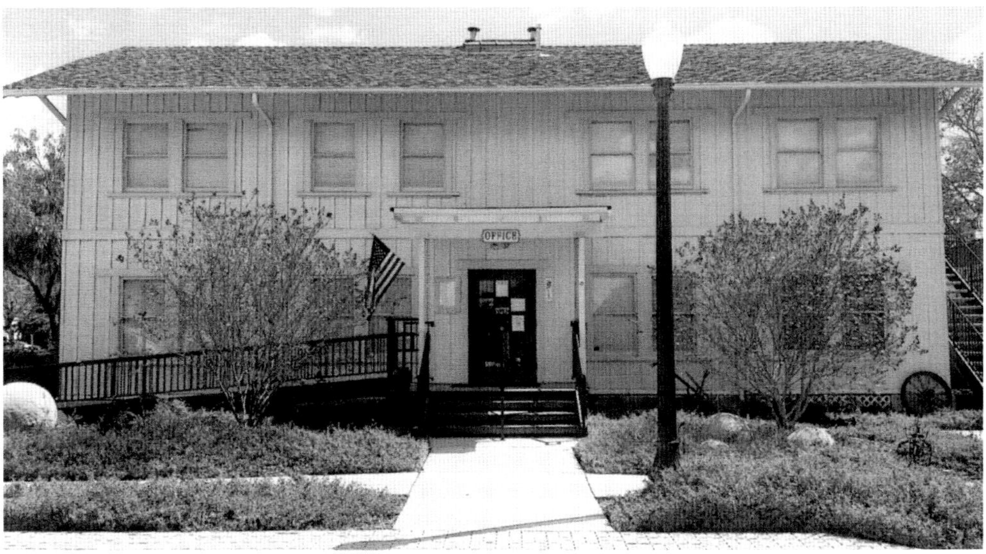

The Sespe Bunkhouse

Morton B. Hull purchased the Rancho Sespe property from the More estate in 1888. His daughter Eudora Hull inherited the property. She married Keith Spalding, and together they cultivated the land and fostered the growth of the citrus trees on its many acres. They hired the architectural firm of Green and Green to design a bunkhouse for their workers on the ranch. It was well known that the bunkhouse was for single, white males only, and they lived there while working for the Spaldings at Rancho Sespe. There was a separate housing area for workers of other ethnic backgrounds. It was common practice to segregate the workers, and this was also done at nearby Limoneira Ranch. Two bunkhouses were built, and one of them currently houses the Fillmore Historical Museum near the city hall and city park area off of Central Avenue. By 1910, Rancho Sespe had become the world's largest lemon orchard. (Photograph by Robert Ybarra.)

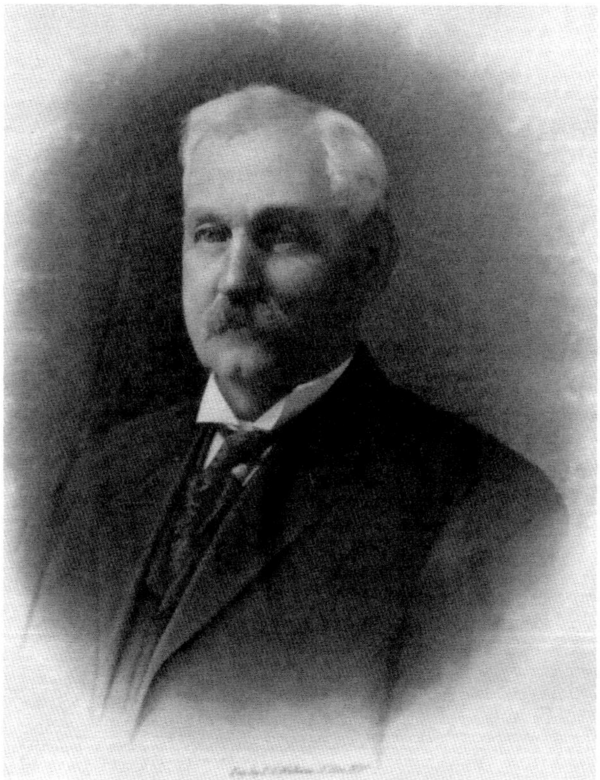

William Shiells

The Shiells Company donated the parcel of land on Central Avenue for the City of Fillmore to build a public library, the Veterans Memorial Building, and the Veterans Youth Building for the community to use. William and his brother James were very generous to the city and to the people of Fillmore. If something was needed in the community, the William Shiells Company would provide for it, or William would take care of it personally.

William T. (Bill) shared how his grandfather William Shiells Sr. was a good neighbor and friend to the del Valle family at Rancho Camulos. Before selling the ranch in 1924, the del Valle family offered it to William Shiells prior to his death, but he explained that he had enough land investments, so they sold the land to August Rubel. August Rubel had been the owner of the Billiwhack Dairy on Aliso Canyon Road in Santa Paula. He moved his family to Rancho Camulos in Piru, California, and the Rubel heirs own the property to this day.

William (Bill) explains that his grandfather and two uncles—James and Francis—brought in Texaco Oil. Texaco leased the land in Shiells Canyon, off of Guiberson Road in Bardsdale, to drill for oil. William Shiells Sr. was elected to the Ventura County Board of Supervisors, and he was a founder and director of the Fillmore State Bank. Later, the bank became the Bank of Italy and after that it was sold to the Bank of America. William and his brother James came to Santa Barbara County in 1872. Ventura County was a part of Santa Barbara County until 1873. William and James worked together on a farm near Carpinteria until 1879. William ventured alone into Ventura County and was once again joined by brother James in 1884. The two brothers acquired 1,200 acres near Fillmore. They planted oranges, lemons, and walnuts on the property, and much was devoted to stock raising. In 1910, they leased 880 acres to the Montebello Oil Company, and the company struck oil. Many people who came to the Fillmore-Piru-Santa Paula areas from Oklahoma after the Dust Bowl worked in the oilfields. The Fillmore area has provided employment opportunities in the citrus and oil industries since the early 1900s. (Courtesy of Shiells family collection.)

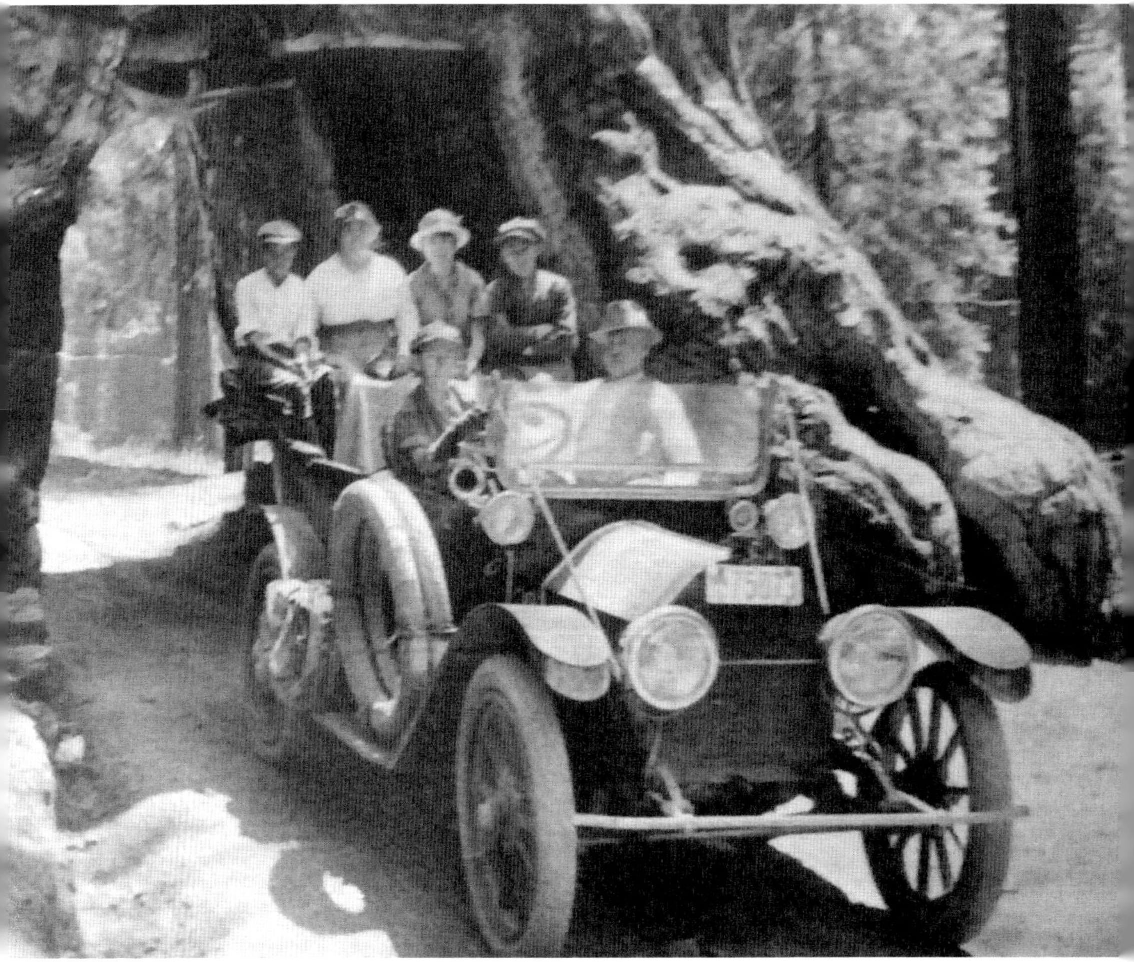

William Shiells and Family

In addition to being a family man, William was a director of the Fillmore State Bank and president of the Fillmore Improvement Company, and in 1914 he was elected Ventura County supervisor. He was a Mason and a member of the Knight's Templar. He married Sarah Thompson in 1893, and together they had four children: Helen (Kimble), James Francis, William Jr., and Lester.

Sarah Shiells paid to have the church that Mary Bard had gifted to the City of Fillmore in 1933 moved and rebuilt in its current location, on the corner lot on Saratoga and Second Streets. This was something Sarah Shiells was so proud of doing, and she enjoyed attending services at the "chocolate church" on Saratoga Street. The film *The Thornbirds* featured the church. William also helped fund and build the Methodist church in Fillmore. His grandson, also William, recalls his days as a Boy Scout leader for Troop 406 when they would hold their meetings at the Veterans Youth Building. William retells the story of how proud his grandmother Sarah Shiells was to pay to have the Fillmore Episcopal Church moved from the Thomas Bard Estate of Berylwood to its present location in 1933. The locals referred to it as "Little Chocolate Church" because of its rich chocolate color. Although he was a Presbyterian, Shiells helped raise funds for the Methodist church in Fillmore and for other religious causes. (Courtesy of William Shiells family collection.)

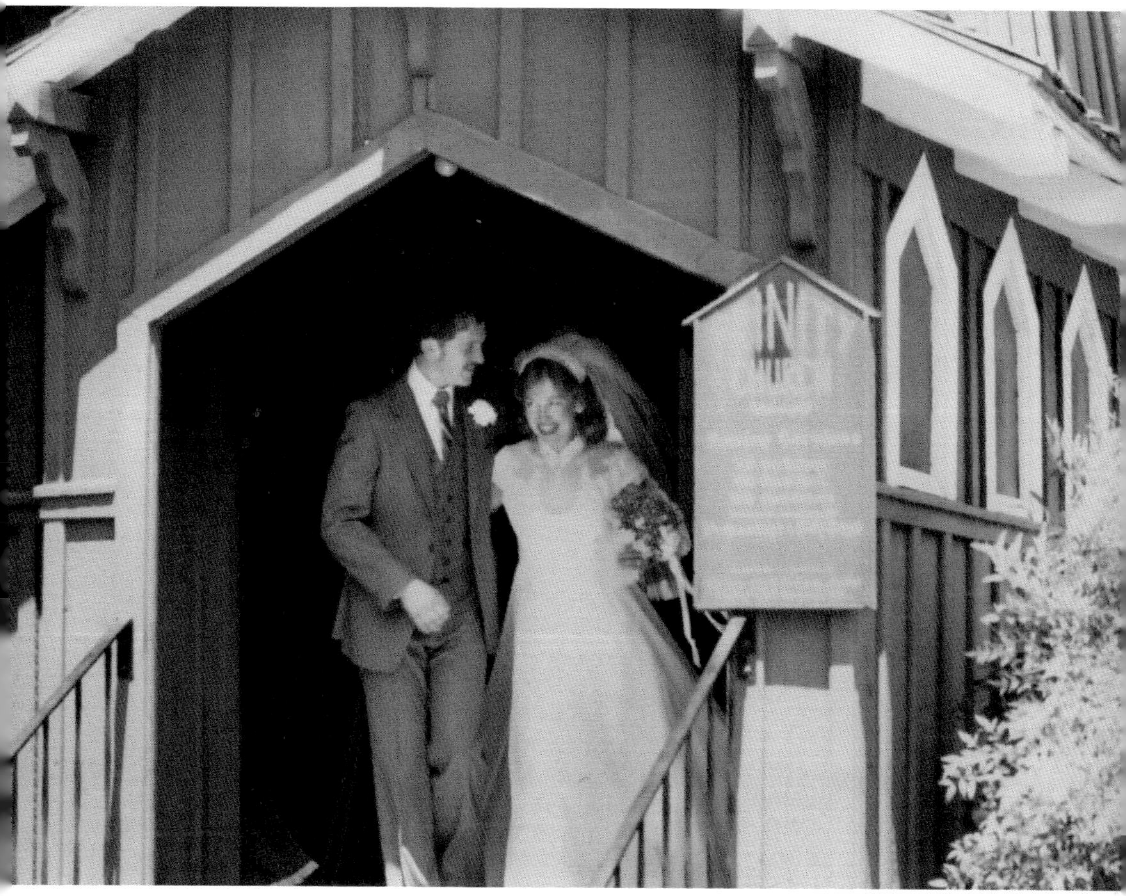

Richard Arnold and Susan French-Arnold

One of the pastors of the Episcopal church was Rev. F. Kenneth Barta. Known as "Father Ken," he had a strong, positive influence on the youth attending his parish. One of those individuals was Susan French. She is the youngest daughter of Dr. and Mrs. William French. Susan and her older sister, Cathy, both graduated from Fillmore High School. Susan and Richard Arnold were married by Father Ken in the Episcopal church in what is definitely a fairy tale come true. She is a writer for the Mondavi Winery, where her husband is the wine master. (Courtesy of the Susan French-Arnold collection.)

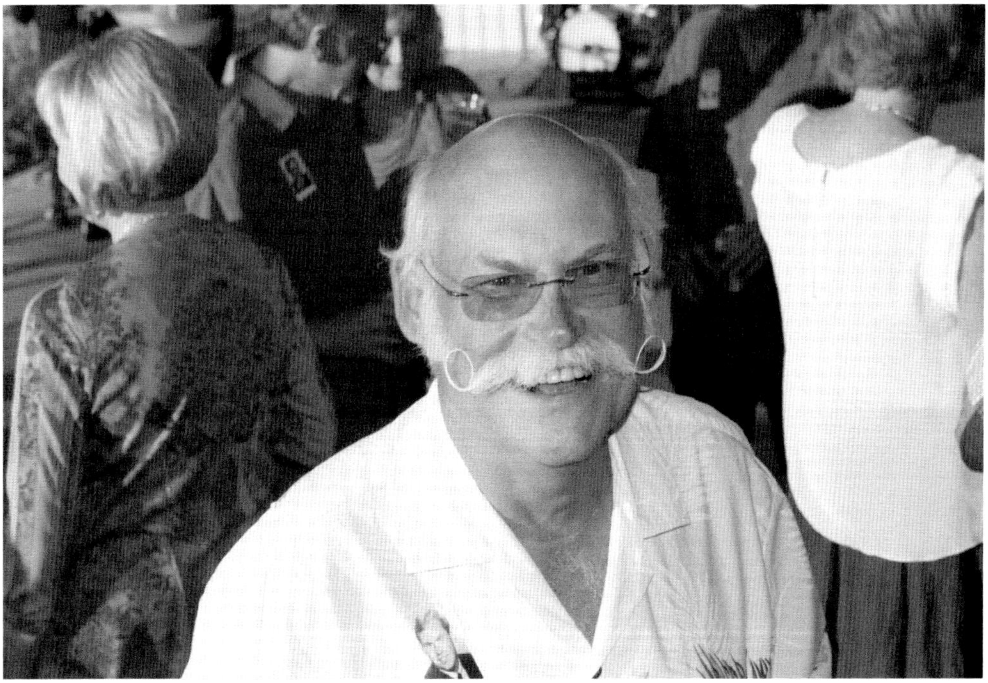

Oz Arundell and the Arundell Family
Oz is also a product of Fillmore schools, and he divides his time between Alaska and Fillmore. He and his wife support all projects and the scholarship fund for Fillmore Unified School District. The Arundell family members were also early pioneers in the community of Fillmore. Art Arundell, one of their sons, grew up to become the librarian in Fillmore, and he served for 28 years. His sister Nadine married Albert Graham, and both were teachers in the Fillmore Unified School District. Ruth Arundell Bryce, another Arundell descendant, married Fred Bryce, former councilman and mayor of Fillmore. Shanna Bryce is their daughter. (Courtesy of Ed Epperheimer.)

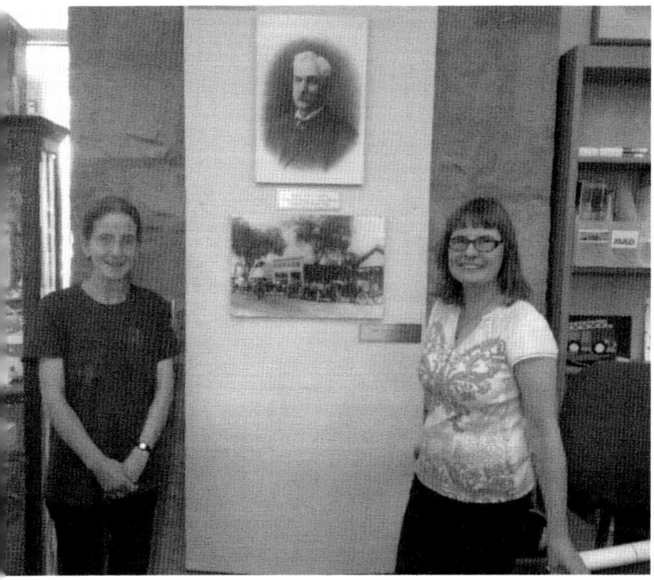

Art Arundell and Kathy Kushnell
Art Arundell assisted the Fillmore Historical Museum in organizing old photographs, and he worked tirelessly on the city's bicentennial in 1988. He enjoyed reading, particularly about history. He was a familiar face around town and was always one to engage in conversation. Today's librarian, Kathy Kushnell (right), maintains a very well-stocked library for community residents and works with her assistant, Harriet (left). The library is maintained as part of the Ventura County Library System. (Author's collection.)

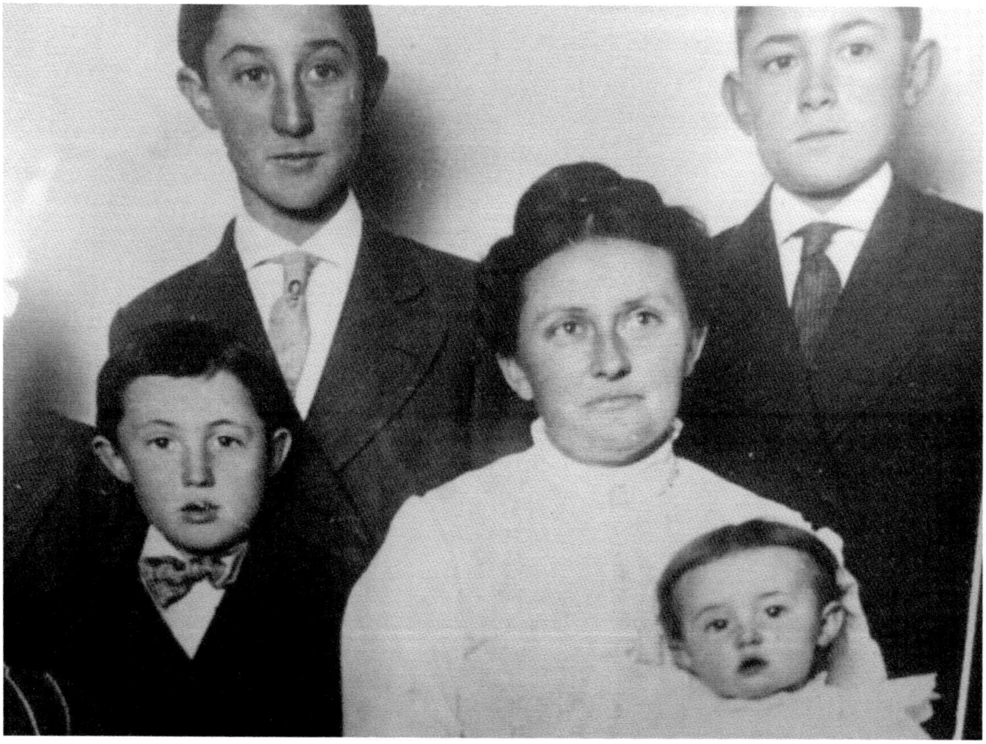

Mosbarger Family

William Mosbarger came to California in 1901 to work for the Limoneira Company as a teamster. Mary Jane was a housewife, raising five boys and a girl in Fillmore. All the Mosbarger children attended Fillmore schools. While others ate, Mary Jane would hover over the table, snatching up an empty plate just as soon as a person was finished; when they quit eating, Mary Jane would sit down and eat. Glen and Cliff were very close since they were only two years apart in age. Glen graduated in 1915 with his two friends Jim Haynes and Leon Harthorn. Glen purchased a laundry business, while Cliff Mosbarger enlisted in the Navy during the World War I and served until 1919. Con stayed at home during the war years to help his father, and he enjoyed spending his leisure hours at the Fillmore Pool Hall, which was managed by Jim and Jack Ipswitch. Orley took over a laundry route and was an avid tennis player. He would play with Glen Phillips, Ernie Milton, and Willard Foster. Ernie Mosbarger was quite an athlete while attending Fillmore High School. He played on the high school basketball team, which won the 1926 Southern California Basketball Championship. Vivian, the only girl, was very active in clubs and programs at Fillmore High School. She was well known as an excellent cook. (Courtesy of Dick Mosbarger family collection.)

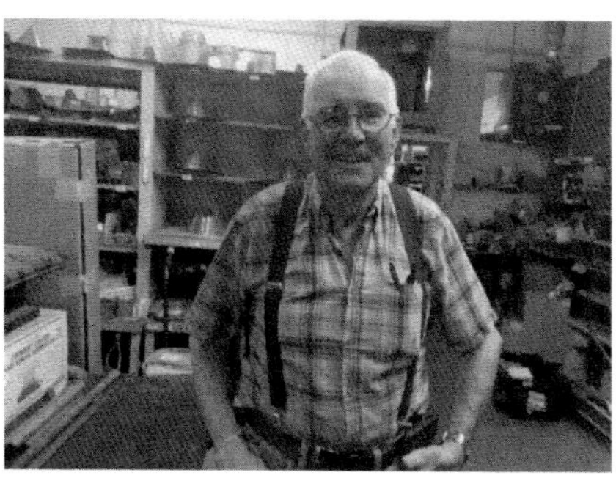

Dick Mosbarger

The Fillmore Future Farmers of America (FFA) were guided and advised by Dick Mosbarger (Glen's son and Mary Jane's grandson). He taught school for years until his retirement. Many students received awards for their prize livestock and other projects they pursued as part of the FFA group activities. (Courtesy of Dick Mosbarger family collection.)

The Deardorff Family

It was Benjamin Deardorff and Caswell Elkins who diverted the water from Pole Creek through the outlying acreage of Fillmore—today's Blaine Avenue—so they could use it to irrigate their fruit trees. Texaco later put an oil refinery in the area. The Deardorff family was also very influential in establishing the community of Fillmore. Deardorff's daughter Stella married Rudolph A. Fremlin. (Courtesy of Bob Cox family collection.)

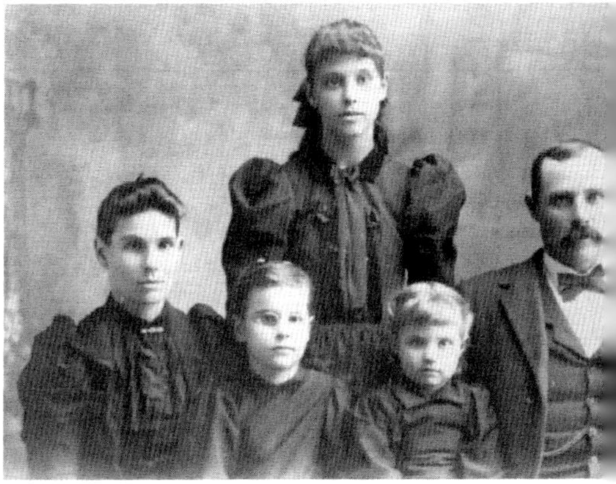

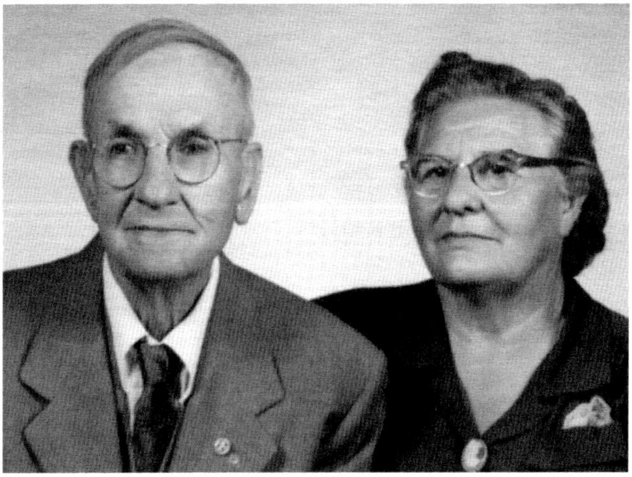

Rudolph Fremlin Family

It was Rudolph Fremlin who developed Foothill, carving out Foothill Circle and selling the parcels of land for $100 each. When Queenie Tieltsort's husband took ill and went to the Bard Hospital in Ventura, it was Rudolph who paid for the medical bills. He did so in exchange for acreage on Foothill that he later developed. He permitted Queenie to live in her home for the remainder of her life. (Courtesy of Bob Cox family collection.)

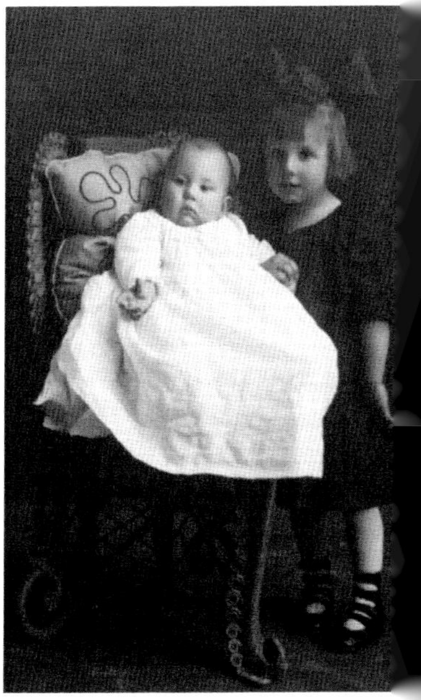

Fremlin Children

Rudolph and Stella Fremlin had five children—Vera, Guy, Lois, Janet, and Ray. Ray was born in an apricot orchard in Bardsdale, where his family lived. In 1923, the family moved to Sespe and Fillmore schools, and Ray graduated from Fillmore High School in 1932. Vera and Guy were educated in London, England, where their father, Rudolph, had gone to school. The others attended Fillmore schools. Vera returned to Fillmore and became an educator, teaching in the Fillmore school system. Ray graduated from Ventura College in 1935 and from Stanford University in 1938 with a degree in engineering. He worked briefly at the Texaco Refinery in Fillmore from 1939 to 1941. Ray served as an officer in the US Navy from 1946 to 1956 and at the US Naval Missal Test Center in Point Mugu from 1956 to 1973. Ray also worked for Lockheed Aircraft from 1973 to 1981. He joins the many notables who made an impact upon the Fillmore community. Pictured are Guy Fremlin (baby) and Vera. (Courtesy of Bob Cox family collection.)

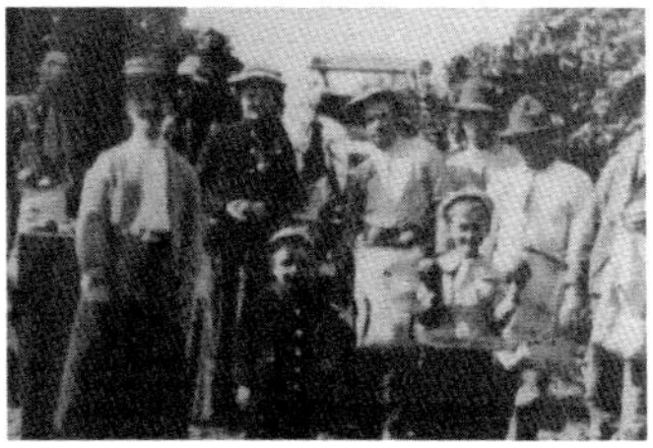

Julius Balden

Julius Balden owned the land where the former Ford dealership was built; he also grew citrus in the Fillmore area. Julius settled in the area with his wife, and they raised their family in Fillmore. He purchased 20 acres of land along the south side of Highway 126, where he cultivated Valencia oranges. He was a well-known horticulturalist, and he loved and appreciated plants and trees. It has been shared within the family that he planted the palm trees along Central Avenue in the early 1900s. Those palms have since been removed, but many older photographs show the palm-lined Central Avenue, which was Fillmore's main business district. This photograph shows the Balden family in 1910. (Courtesy of Kristine Hyatt family collection.)

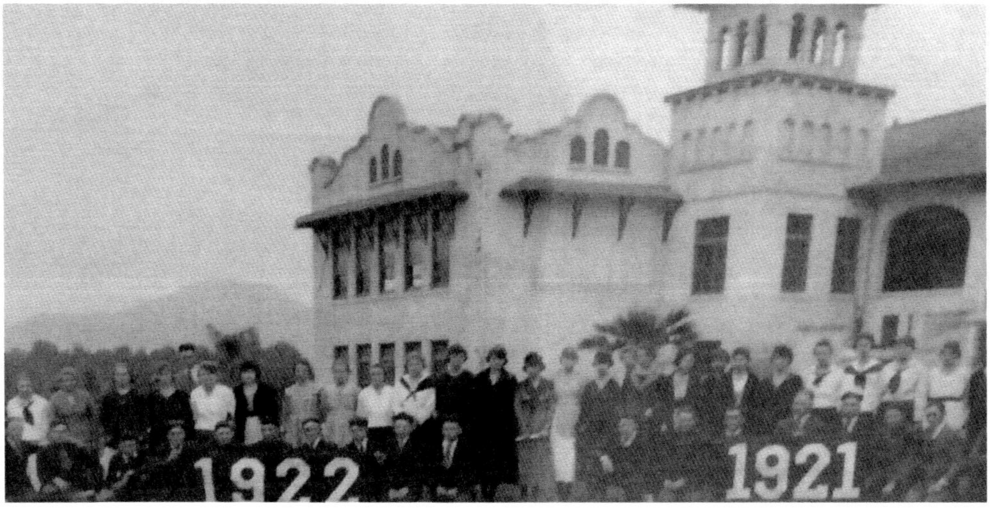

Harold Balden

Harold Balden (pictured behind the "2" in "1921") built his home on the corner of Second and Saratoga Streets. He managed the family business (Balden Ranching Company) and the citrus orchards. He contributed a great deal to the community of Fillmore and to the business community. He helped establish the first shopping center in Fillmore. He hired Gene Wren to work on the ranch and supported all of the scouting efforts Gene attempted to do. In this image, he is pictured in front of Fillmore High School. (Courtesy of Kristine Hyatt family collection.)

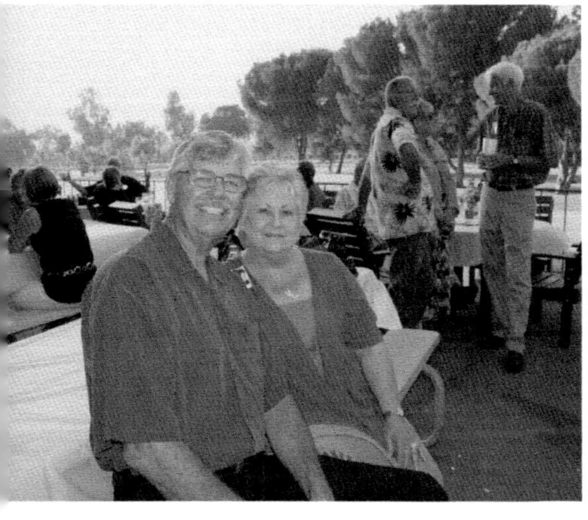

Mike and Kris Hyatt

Kris Jaynes Hyatt is a direct descendant of Julius Balden, and her grandfather was Harold Balden. She recalls many good times at her grandparents' home and all of the memorable family gatherings. She is the daughter of Ted and Barbara Jaynes. Mike and Kris both graduated from Fillmore High School, and they continue to support the community of Fillmore and the business community. Mike served in Vietnam and is part of the Ventura County Sheriff's Department Search & Rescue unit. (Courtesy of Kristine Hyatt family collection.)

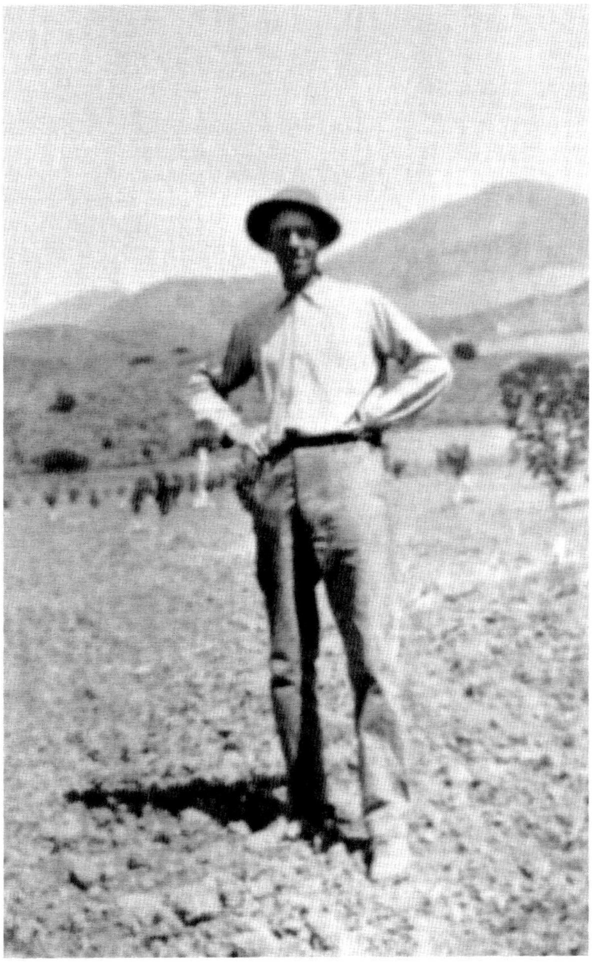

Clifford Hardison and the New Lemon Seedlings
Hardison Ranch, known as La Campana I, produced many acres of oranges and lemons on its acreage. Hardison Ranch and Rancho Sespe landowners would work cooperatively along with the other citrus ranch owners in Bardsdale and, later, Piru. They formed the Fillmore Citrus Association. The Hardison family owned many acres of citrus groves in the Fillmore, Santa Paula, and Saticoy areas. Clifford Hardison, Domingo Hardison, and Wallace Hardison were all related. Wallace Hardison was the cofounder of the Union Oil Company with his business partners Lyman Stewart and Thomas R. Bard.

Elvira Wiklund was the daughter of Charles and Cecilia Wiklund, who farmed near the north end of Sespe Avenue (now Grand Avenue). In addition to farming oranges, lemons, and olives, Cecilia Wiklund shipped crates of live chickens to Los Angeles restaurants from the Sespe Railroad Depot. Elvira attended the newly opened Fillmore High School, traveling there daily by horse-drawn buggy and accompanied by fellow Sespe resident Edith Moore (now Jarrett). Elvira's brother Albert Wiklund was in the first graduating class from Fillmore High School. Before that school opened, he attended Santa Paula High School. He boarded in that town during the week since the trip from Sespe to Santa Paula was too far for daily travel.

Sespe was more of a separate community from Fillmore in the early 1900s, with its own depot for freight and passengers on the railroad. It had its own store, post office, church, park, and two grammar schools. Elvira and the other children in the Sespe area attended elementary school located in area known today as Grand Avenue. (Courtesy of Hardison family collection.)

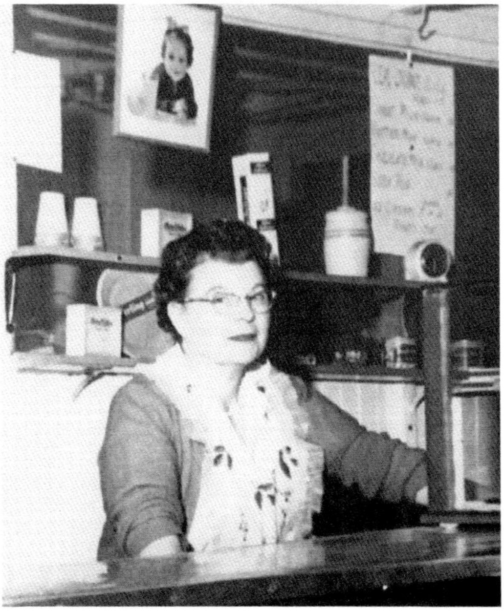

The Hardisons Open the Sanitary Dairy
Clifford Hardison came to the Sespe area to serve as foreman on the family's ranch, where he supervised the clearing, terracing, and the first plantings of the citrus trees on the property. Later, he acquired his own first, small acreage near Kenny Grove Park, and he planted lemons on his land. A freeze destroyed those trees, so he replanted more cold-tolerant oranges. He was an orange grower for nearly 70 years. He and Elvira Wiklund married in 1914, and in 1916 they acquired land along the newly built Telegraph Road, where they started the Sanitary Dairy. When the dairy started in 1916, it was named to reflect the strict procedures that ensured clean, wholesome milk—a real issue in the 1900s. The milk was delivered to customers very fresh—twice daily after the morning and afternoon milkings. Most homes lacked refrigeration in the early 1900s. Refrigeration was developed after World War I, with ammonia being used as the cooling agent; now, Freon is used. Elvira Hardison operated a roadside stand at the dairy until 1956. Sales included milk and dairy products, homemade sandwiches, candies, and a special item, the freshly squeezed orange juice that she made with fruit from their orange groves. A small gas station was nearby, and there was a picnic area for customers. Elvira is pictured here at the dairy roadside stand on its last day of operation in 1956. (Courtesy of the Hardison family collection and Tom Hardison.)

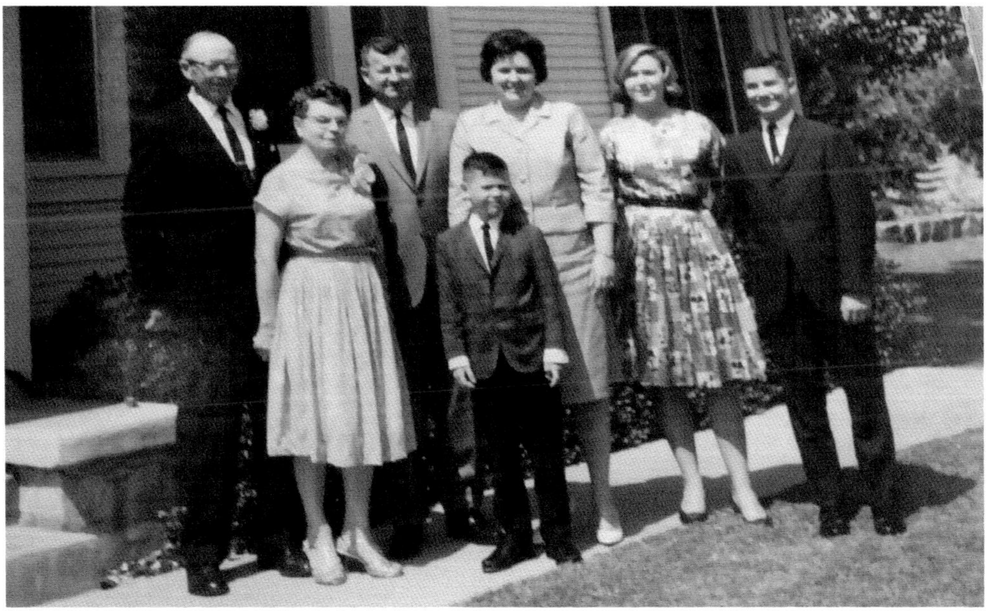

Clifford and Elvira's 50th Wedding Anniversary
Celebrating Clifford and Elvira's 50th wedding anniversary, the Hardison family took time out for a photograph. They are, from left to right, Clifford, Elvira, Russell, Betty, Geraldine, and Tom, and in front is Philip Hardison. (Courtesy of Hardison family collection.)

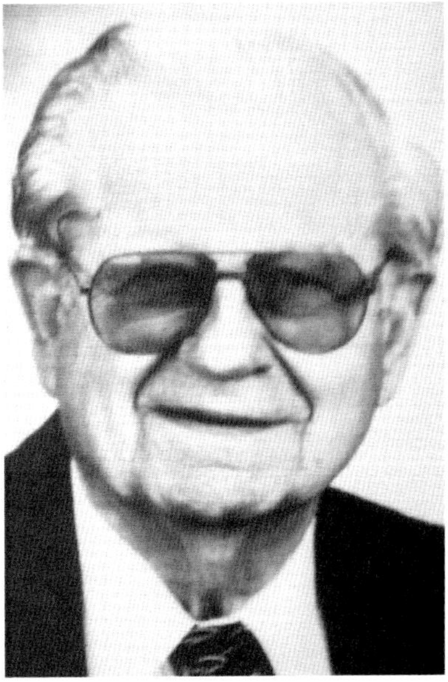

Russell Hardison

Russell Hardison, son of Cliff and Elvira, attended local schools and acquired the Sanitary Dairy when he returned from the service after World War II. The dairy employed at least 60 people while in operation. Hardison operated the dairy from the same location until 1977, when shifting consumer patterns made it difficult to continue home-delivery operations, and most small-scale dairies gave way to the larger operations based elsewhere. Russell and Betty Hardison had three children: Thomas, who attended the University of Santa Clara, Geraldine, who was a teacher by profession, and Philip, now deceased, who was an architect interested in historical preservation. (Courtesy of the Hardison family collection.)

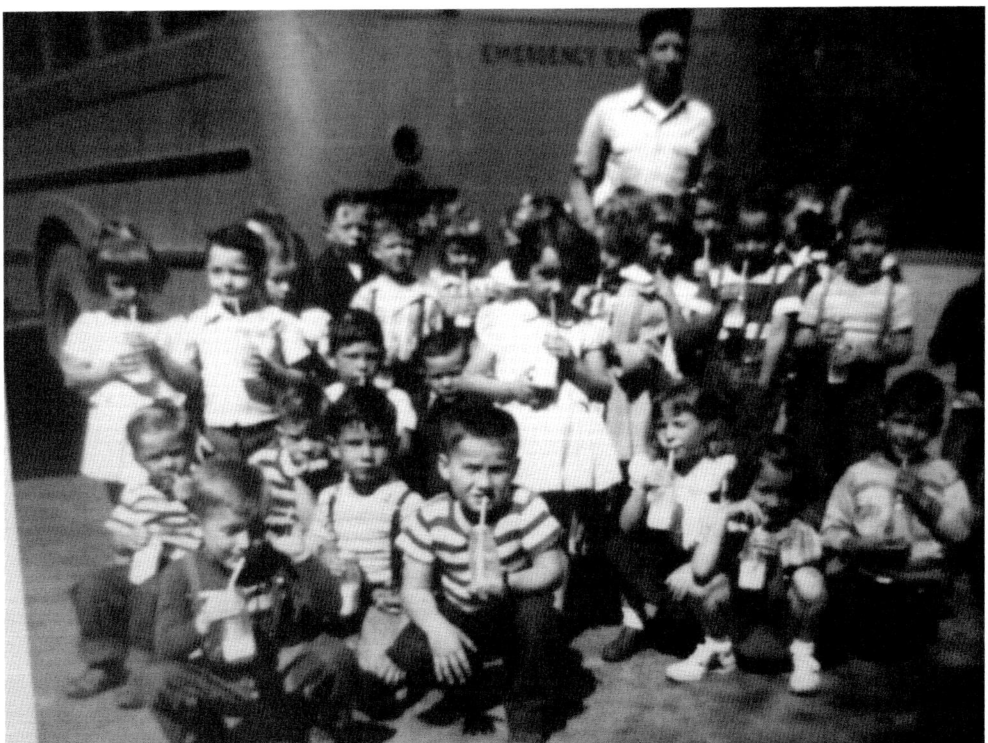

Sanitary Dairy Field Trip

This photograph shows a Sanitary Dairy field trip for kindergarten children from Fillmore's Sespe School. They each have their own milk fresh from the cows at the dairy. This was a traditional field trip for all elementary school children attending Sespe, Mountain View, and, later, San Cayetano schools. (Courtesy of Hardison family collection.)

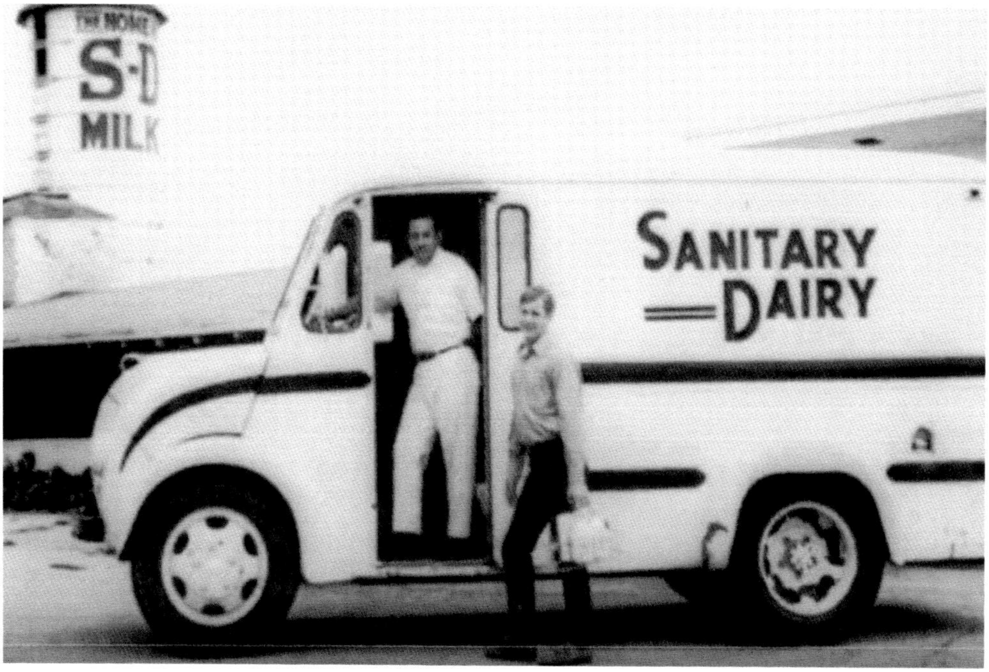

Paul Conaway

Paul Conaway (pictured inside the truck) was the milkman everyone knew around town, for it was Paul who delivered the fresh Sanitary Dairy milk to local businesses, restaurants, and Fillmore schools. He would begin his milk run at approximately 4:00 a.m.; then, he would deliver milk to the local school grade school. Paul was a member of the Lions Club International, and he was active in coaching little league. Carol, his wife, is a registered nurse, and together they have remained active in the community. Paul and Carol reside in Fillmore, where they remain close to their children and grandchildren. Also pictured is Wayne Sampson, who assisted Paul as a high school student. (Courtesy of Hardison family collection.)

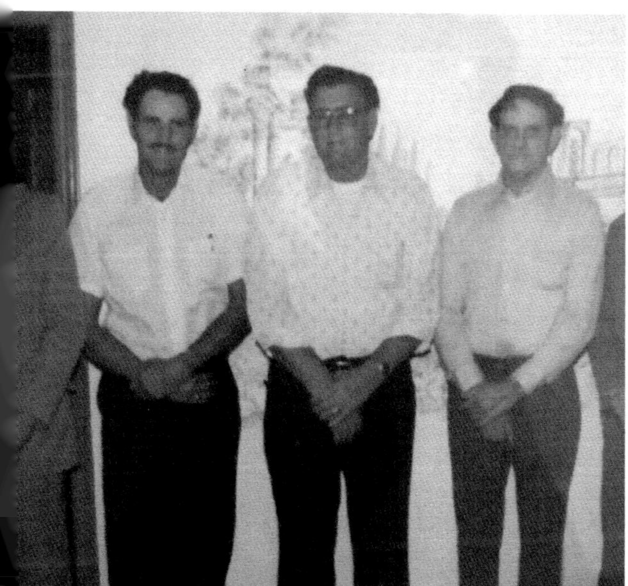

Ellis Van Noy

Ellis Van Noy (third from left) and his brother A.J. (second from left) used their crane service to do projects for the city. Ellis moved the canons to the present site on the City Plaza Park. Another canon was moved to the Veterans Memorial Building. Ellis donated much of his time and effort to assist the city of Fillmore. His four girls attended Fillmore schools, and now their children are Fillmore students. Ellis was married to Barbara Van Noy for a number of years, until his death. (Courtesy of Barbara Van Noy family collection.)

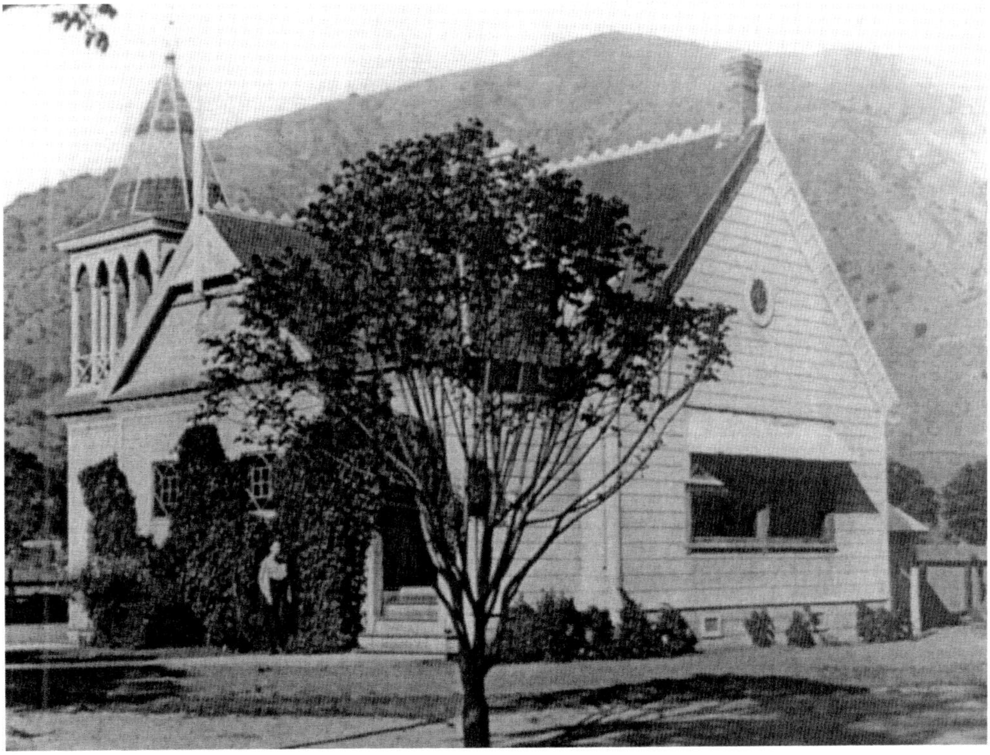

Elvira Wiklund and Edith Moore Jarrett

Elvira Wiklund is pictured in front of Sespe School, one of the grammar schools in the Sespe area. Elvira attended elementary school here when she was a young girl, as did many other children in the Sespe area, which is known today as Grand Avenue. Elvira Wiklund is standing in front of this school. Elvira was an enterprising businesswoman, and she assisted her husband, Clifford, when he decided to open the Sanitary Dairy. (Courtesy of Hardison family collection.)

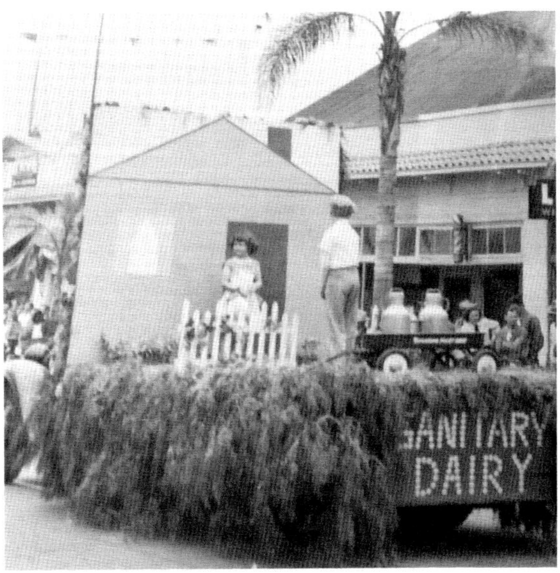

Sanitary Dairy Float

Geraldine Hardison sits on the Sanitary Dairy float with Wayne Sampson during a Fillmore Festival parade in the late 1950s. (Courtesy of Hardison family collection.)

CHAPTER THREE

Bardsdale and Piru Notables

In January 1887, Bardsdale was established by real estate developer Royce G. Surdam (1835–1891) on 1,500 acres of the old Rancho Sespe land grant that he purchased from his business associate Thomas R. Bard, in whose honor he named the town.

Chambersburg Avenue is named for Thomas Bard's hometown of Chambersburg, Pennsylvania. Money was scarce in the small farming community, and they had circuit-riding pastors for six years since they did not have a permanent building for a church. Thomas R. Bard donated two lots for the church and parsonage; in addition, he purchased two stained-glass windows for the north and west walls of the church. The building of the church unified the community, and they donated time and labor by digging and building. The community members dug out the basement and hauled the Sespe brownstone used for the foundation. The county cultural heritage board says the clapboard church is the only example of Carpenter Gothic in the Fillmore-Bardsdale area. In 1979, it was declared a county landmark, and it was placed in the National Register of Historic Places in 1986. Much of Bardsdale still resembles what it looked like back in 1900. There are groves of avocado trees, which have replaced orange trees for the most part, and groves of lemon trees. The Elkins Golf Course is on the southeast corner, and the Bardsdale Cemetery is still used by Bardsdale and Fillmore residents. There are numerous descendants of early families who still live in the community—George King's grandson Monty Winkler and his wife, Maio, reside in the family home, as does Bernice Michel, who married Harold Michel, a descendant of Jacob Michel.

Piru is also a small, unincorporated community with a rich history dating back to the 1800s. As of the 2010 census, it had a population of 2,063. Piru, though small, is steeped in history, and many of the residents are descendants of the first families of Rancho Camulos. Their ancestors lived on Rancho Camulos or worked for the del Valle family. The name *Piru* comes from the Tataviam Indian word for the tule reeds, which grow along Piru Creek. These reeds were used to weave the baskets that Tataviam people made for carrying materials and for cooking. The community of Piru was founded in 1887 by David C. Cook, the publisher of religious books from Illinois. He purchased the Temescal Mexican land grant from the sons of Ygnacio del Valle. He brought his family west to create a "Second Garden of Eden," and he was hoping to improve his health. Cook built his first home on Main and Center Streets. In 1890, he constructed his permanent home, the lavish Queen Anne–style mansion known as the Piru Mansion. Lake Piru is the recreational area behind the community of Piru, and many go boating there and enjoy the picnic areas with their families. Besides the del Valle family, Hugh Warring, Chester Warring, Harry Lechler, Donna Chessani, Jose Nuñez, and the Alcocer and Dominguez families left a lasting impression upon Piru.

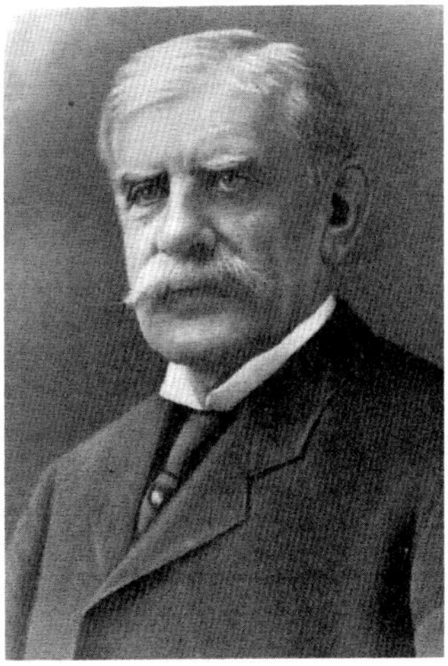

Thomas Bard

Thomas Bard purchased land from the del Valle family and from the More brothers' surviving heirs after T. Wallace More's murder. After his former business associate Royce Surdam passed away on September 2, 1891, Thomas Bard bought most of his Bardsdale land holdings. Bard knew T. Wallace More's son-in-law Charles A. Storke. Charles had married More's daughter Mattie, and they had one son, Thomas Storke. Charles Storke attempted to assist the heirs with business transactions involving the More estate. (Courtesy of Santa Clarita Valley Historical Society.)

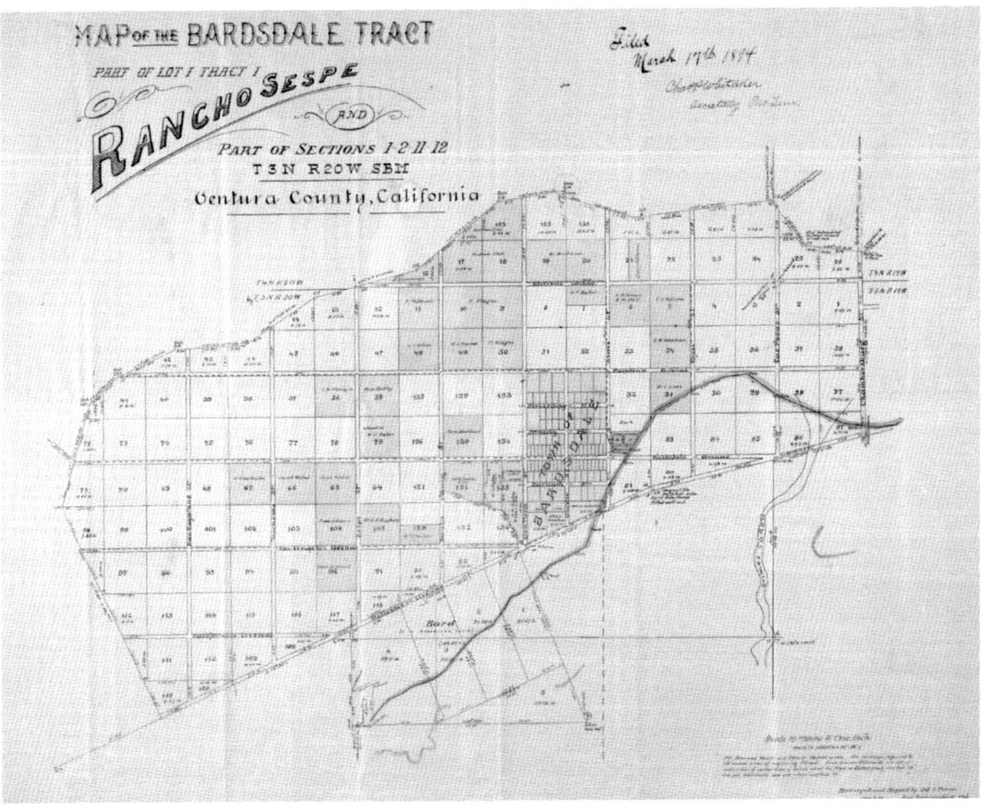

Map of Bardsdale, 1894

Bardsdale was established in 1887 by Royce G. Surdam on 1,500 acres of the old Rancho Sespe grant that he purchased from business associate Thomas R. Bard, in whose honor he named the area. On March 22, 1887, Surdam began running train excursions from Los Angeles to the Fillmore Station to see Bardsdale, which he claimed was the "Eden of Southern California." On June 8, 1889, the Bardsdale schoolhouse, built by O.J. Goodenough, was accepted by the trustees. Minnie Taylor was the first teacher in the new schoolhouse. She began teaching in August 1889 at a salary of $60 per month. (Reprinted by permission of the Huntington Library, San Marino, California.)

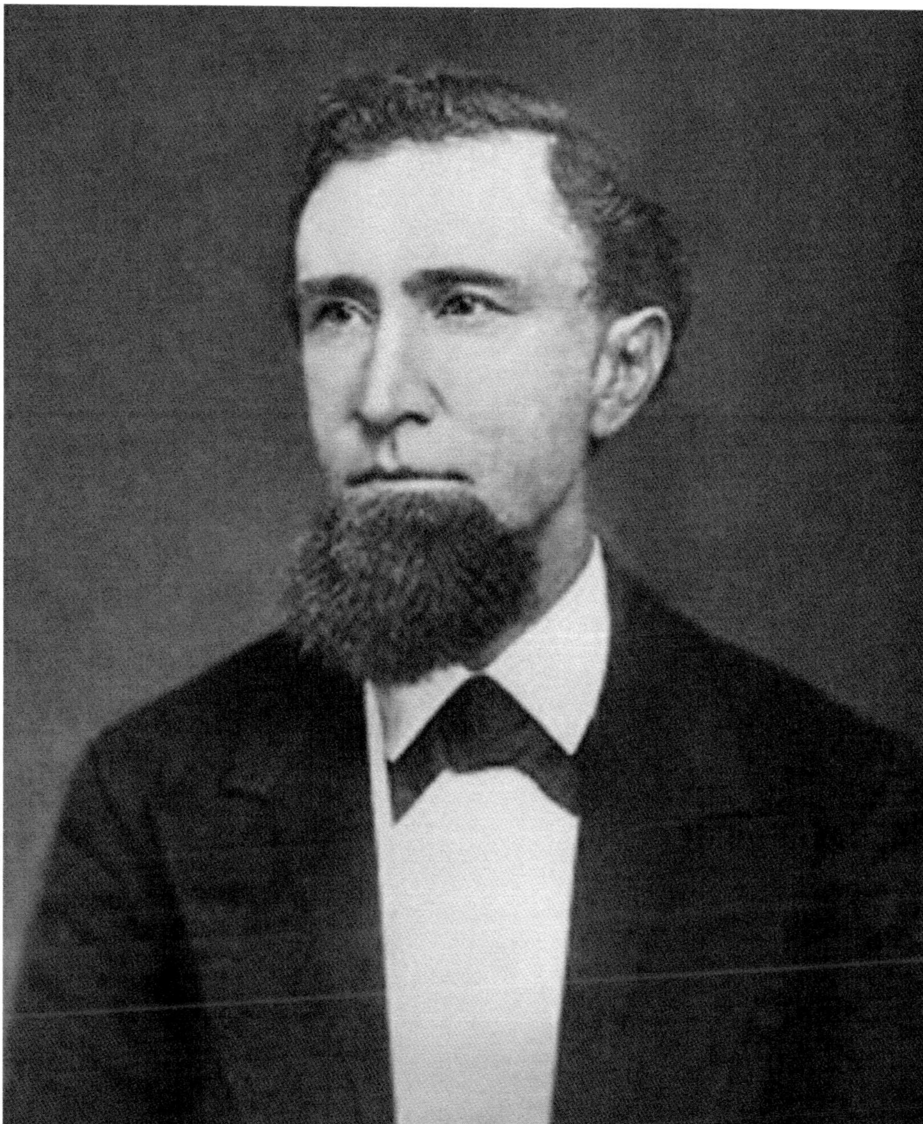

Royce Surdam

The US Post Office Department established the Bardsdale Post Office on May 18, 1887, and Royce Surdam was appointed as the first postmaster. He would deliver the mail into the town of Fillmore twice a day. The new Bardsdale Post Office was built in 1892, and the small wooden structure, about 10 feet square, currently sits on the property of the Fillmore Historical Museum in the city of Fillmore. It was described as one of the smallest post offices in the state of California. The Bardsdale Post Office was discontinued on May 15, 1906. That same year, the Bardsdale Methodist Church was founded, and the Bardsdale Cemetery Association was established on June 1, 1895. The cemetery district shareholders were R.F. Robertson, Mary Phillips, Robert Strathearn, Martin Stoll, R.J. Ealy, A.S. Strobridge, J.D. LeBard, C.C. Elkins, Edward Meser, B.S. Clayton, C.J. Michel, F.G. Hutchinson, and E. Robert Dunn. On March 22, 1887, Surdam began running train excursions from Los Angeles to the Fillmore Station to see Bardsdale, which he claimed was the "Eden of Southern California." (Courtesy of Santa Clarita Valley Historical Society.)

George and Hattie King

George King came to California at the age of 21 and to Ventura County in 1894. He settled in Piru, where he lived for six years, and he was employed as a farmworker and as a part-time clerk in a general merchandise store for C.J. French. In the meantime, he invested in five acres of land in Bardsdale, where he planted a citrus grove. He made it his permanent home in 1900. George succeeded J.R. McKee as manager of the late Senator Bard's interests at Bardsdale until the property sold in 1910. He was secretary of the South Side Improvement Company, an organization that installed a complete water-pipe system in Bardsdale. Later, along with Judge Elkins, Senator Bard, and others, they made it possible to install the Cienega water system, which brought water to the citrus fruits on 500 acres of south Bardsdale. George King was instrumental in forming the Fillmore Union High School District, and he became the first president of the Fillmore Union High School Board. He was also a trustee of the Methodist church in Bardsdale. In Piru, California, he was married in October 1896 to Hattie Virginia Busick. Hattie came to Ventura County when she was 12 years of age, and after the death of her mother, she made her home with her aunt Mrs. S.A. Guiberson in Bardsdale. She was educated in the Ventura County schools and was a dressmaker. The Kings were the parents of two children, Oona Caroline and Agnes Blanche, both graduates from Fillmore High School. Oona is the oldest child. From left to right are Oona, Hattie, George, and Agnes. (Courtesy of Montgomery and Maio Winkler family collection.)

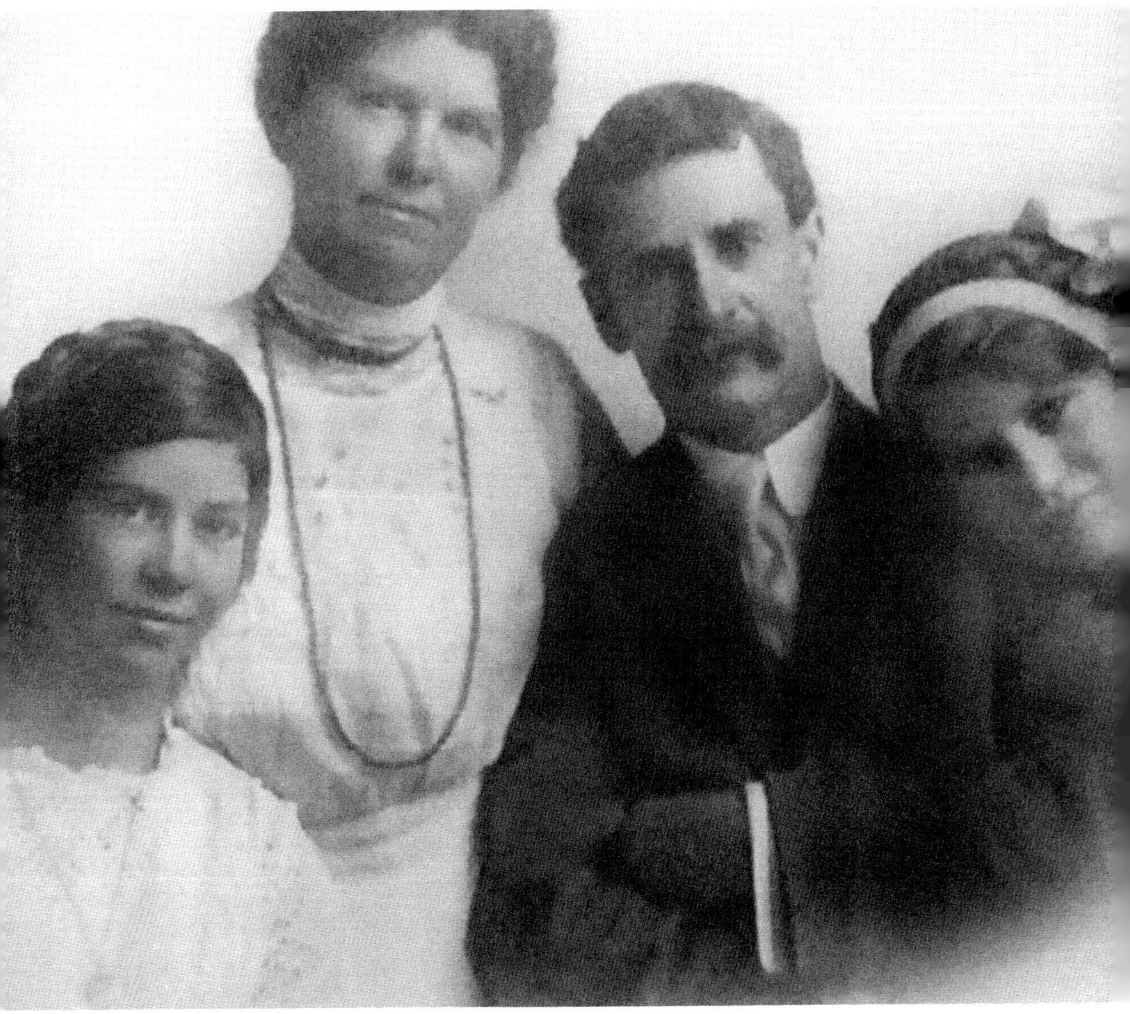

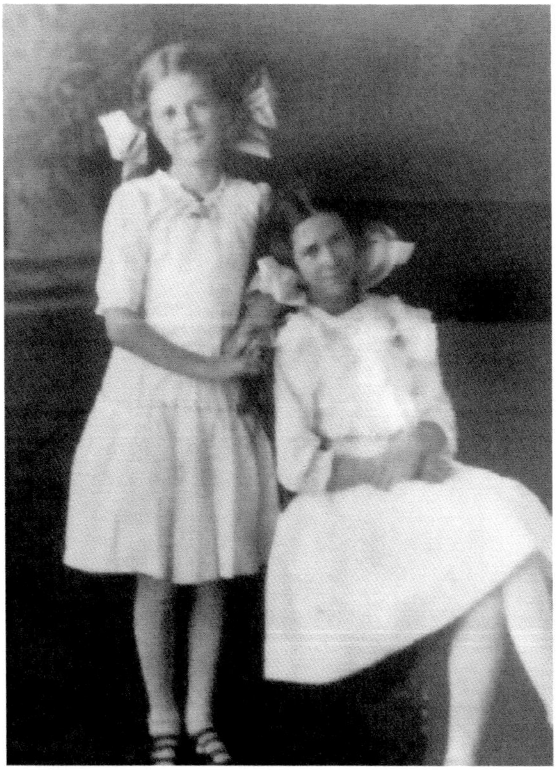

Oona Caroline and Agnes Blanche King

George and Hattie King had two daughters: Oona Caroline (seated at right), the oldest, and Agnes Blanche (standing at left), the youngest. Agnes is Montgomery Winkler's mother. The photograph below shows Hattie King with her youngest daughter, Agnes, among the citrus trees. (Both, courtesy of Montgomery and Maio Winkler family collection.)

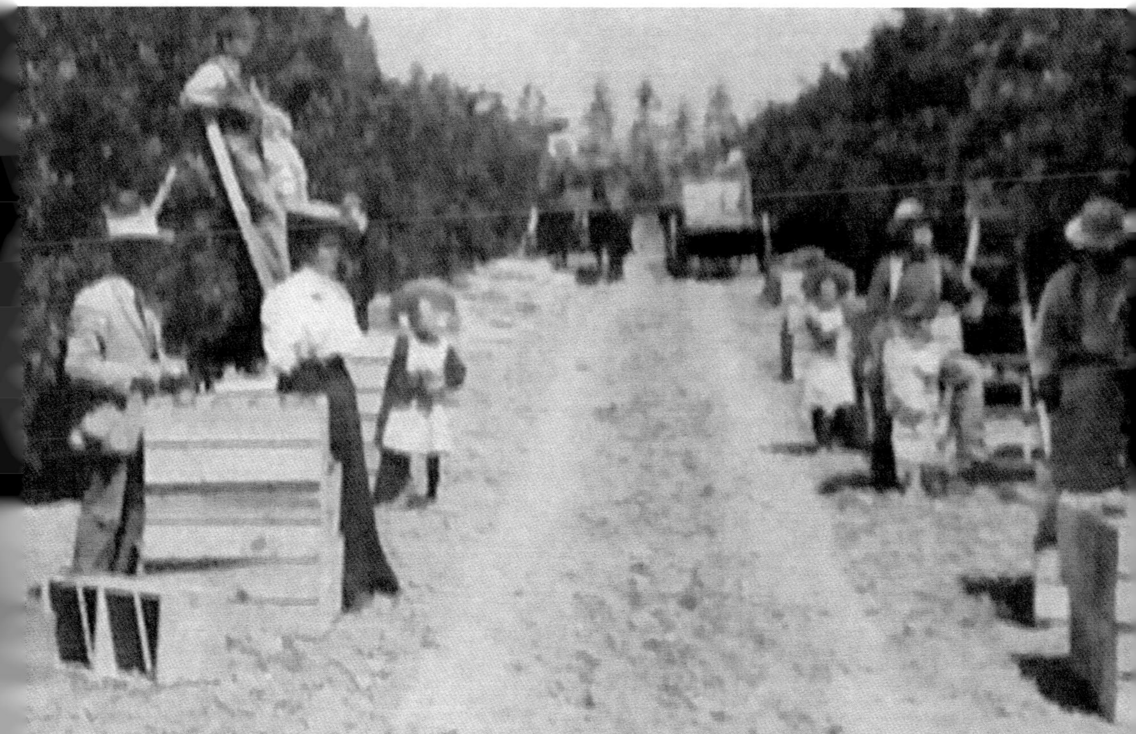

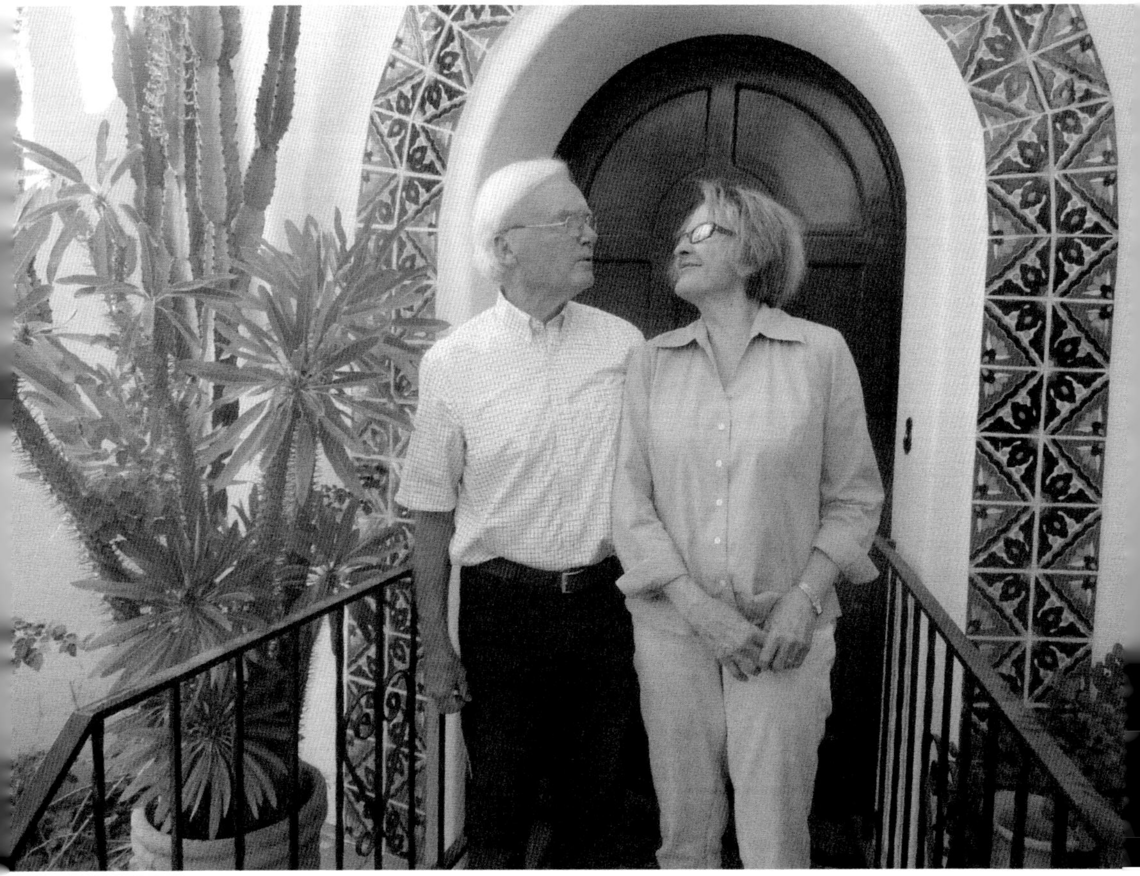

Montgomery "Monty" and Maio Winkler

Monty, as he is known by friends in Bardsdale and Fillmore, served as Congressman Teague's assistant in Washington, DC, and then served Congressman Lagomarsino during his tenure in Washington. Maio and Monty Winkler met while they were attending George Washington University in Washington, DC. Monty was a graduate student there, and the rest is history.

Monty Winkler is the grandson of George and Hattie King of Bardsdale. The story that is frequently told is that the young George King left Kansas and made his way to Fillmore. Soon, he was a land agent selling plots in the community of Bardsdale, and by the late 1920s, he purchased one of the plots of land for himself. Today, that plot of land sitting across the Santa Clara River is still in the King family. Monty and his wife, Maio, maintain the ranch, which mostly grows avocados. Monty was born in 1932, and his father died when he was four years old. His mother took a teaching position outside of the area, and Monty moved back to Bardsdale and lived with his grandparents. Eventually, his mother returned, and his early life revolved around the ranch. He and his wife, Maio, occupy the family home today and enjoy ranch living. After graduating from Fillmore High School and Whittier College, Monty went to Washington, DC, to attend graduate school at George Washington University. He found a job as assistant to Congressman Charles Teague, who represented Ventura County. He served Congressman Teague, then his successor, Rep. Robert Lagomarsino, for 22 years. Monty remained in the nation's capital for another decade serving as a lobbyist for agriculture. During this time, he married Maio, and they raised three sons.

During his time in Washington, DC, Monty also represented the California Avocado Commission and was successful in opening doors to global markets. In the past few years, Monty and Maio have planted more than 6,000 avocado trees and have removed the orange trees. (Author's collection.)

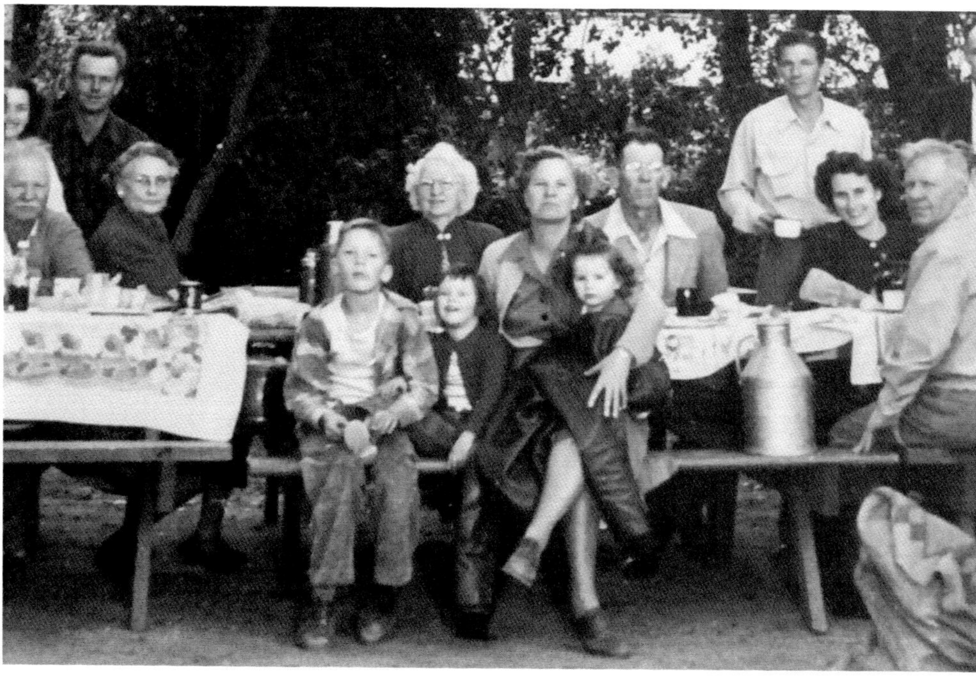

The Michel Family

Jacob Michel was one of the very first to purchase acreage in Bardsdale. His family still owns the land, and they cultivate the citrus orchards that Jacob and his son Charles managed. Later, it was Harold Michel, Charles's son, who managed and cultivated the land. Now Harold's wife, three daughters, and their families manage the ranch. The home where Harold grew up was built for Chester Michel. Now, Harold's family retains ownership, and his wife, Bernice, still resides there. The home has been declared a historical landmark. (Courtesy of Harold Michel family collection.)

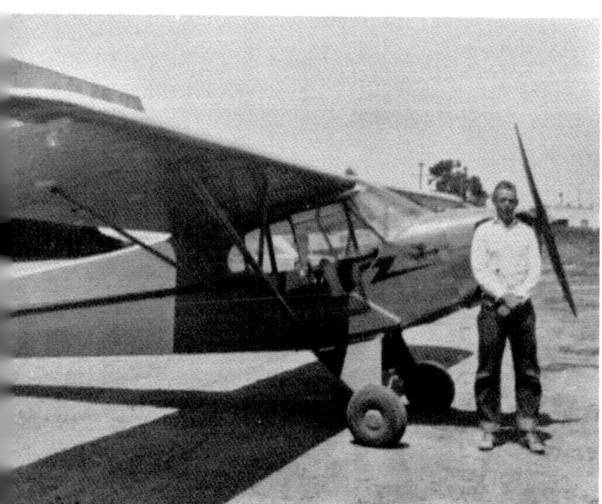

Harold Michel

Harold Michel was a third-generation family rancher in the Santa Clara Valley and a graduate of Fillmore High School and Ventura Community College. He was a member of the Bardsdale School District Board of Education, and he worked for Texaco Oil Company and the California Department of Water Resources while maintaining the family ranches. Harold enjoyed flying and earned his pilot's license at the Santa Paula Airport. He served his country during World War II when he entered the US Army and joined the 3rd Division in Europe. After the war, he married Bernice Blythe on July 27, 1946. Bernice, a successful seamstress, would sew while attending to her girls. They had three daughters, Sandy, Elizabeth, and Martha. Today, Bernice Blythe Michel still resides in the family home, which has been designated a Historical Landmark. (Courtesy of Harold Michel family collection.)

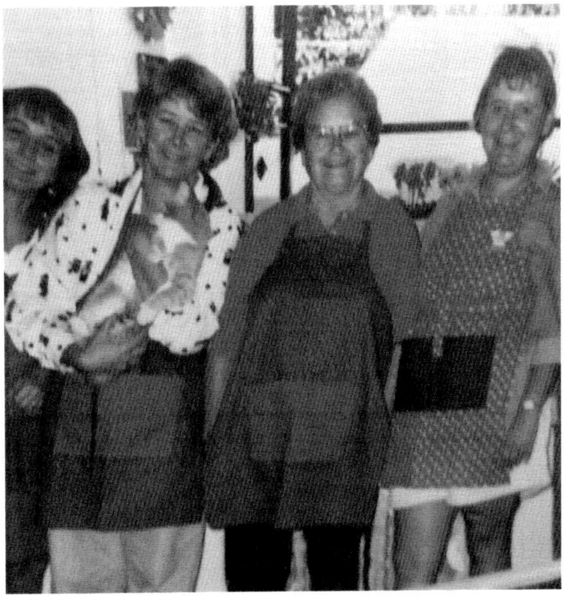

Michel Girls

Harold and Bernice had three daughters, Sandy, Elizabeth, and Martha. The girls attended elementary school in Bardsdale; they then attended Fillmore Junior High and Fillmore High School, as all the young people did from Bardsdale and Piru. The Fillmore Unified School District bused the students into Fillmore each year. Elizabeth Michel said, "It was difficult leaving familiar surroundings to go to school in Fillmore. We didn't know everyone and everything was so new to us. It was a difficult adjustment, but soon we made friends and we eventually adjusted." Pictured from left to right are Martha, Sandy, Bernice, and Elizabeth. (Courtesy of Harold Michel family collection.)

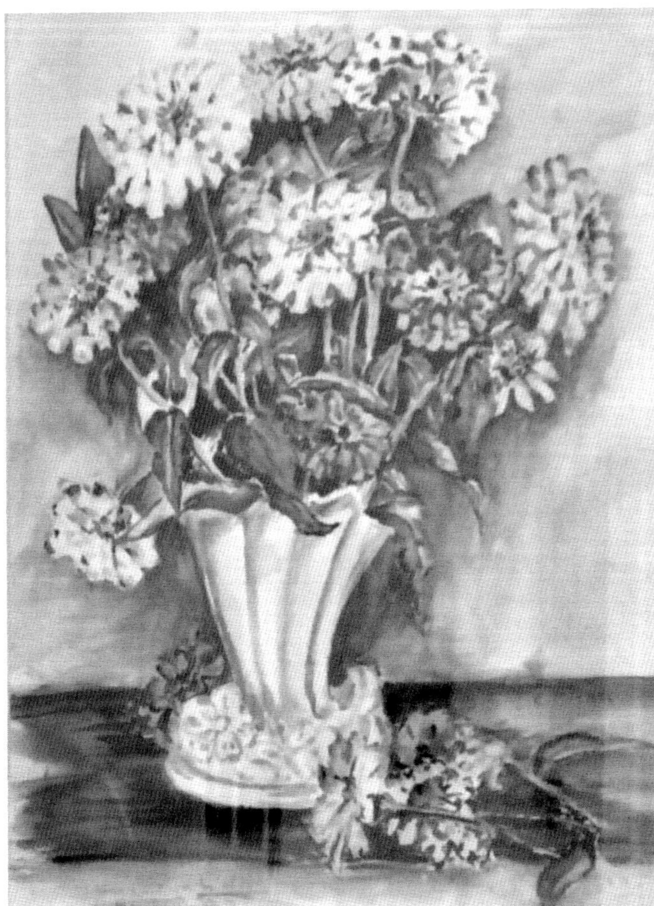

Esther Michel

Esther Michel enjoyed painting and drawing. Here is one of her original works. It hangs in the living room of the Michel home in Bardsdale. Esther was married to Charles and she was Harold's mother and grandmother to Harold's three daughters. (Courtesy of Harold Michel family collection.)

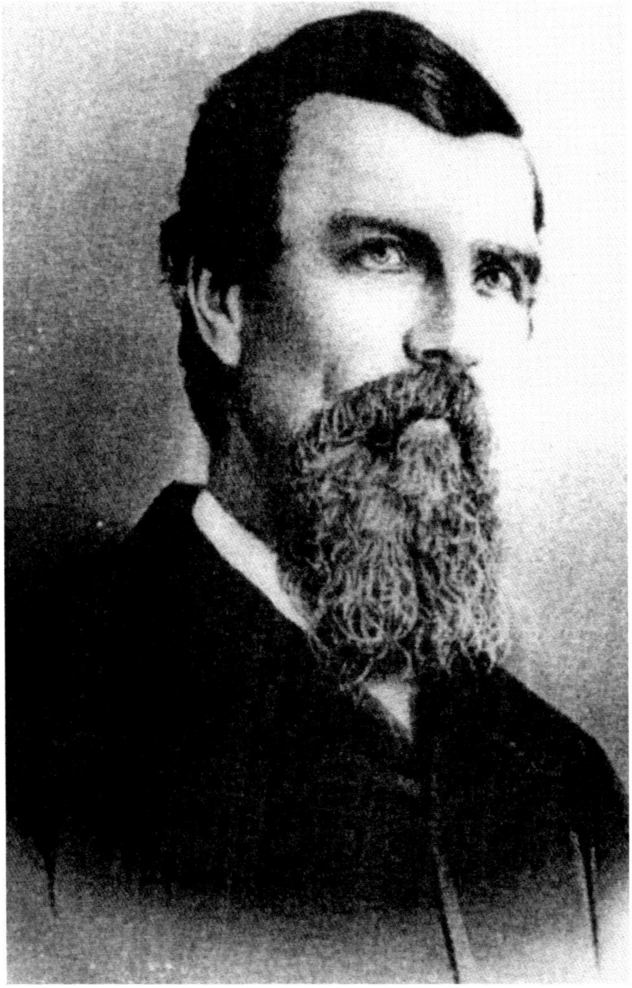

O.J. Goodenough
In 1861, O.J. Goodenough enlisted in the Union army, and from 1862–1863, he was a wagon master for the government, which meant he carried supplies to various western posts. This was before any railroad transportation. He left government service in 1863 and farmed in Ventura County from 1883 until his death in 1895. He contracted and built some of the first buildings in Fillmore and Bardsdale, including the first school in Bardsdale, and he was one of the founders of the Fillmore Presbyterian Church. O.J. Goodenough married Zedora Tietsort, and they had five children: Mrs. R.A. Holley, Mrs. Harry Hiller, Glen C., Earle O., and Edgar D. Edgar Goodenough attended Fillmore schools until 1883, when he became an employee of his father's ranch. He was the chain man for the civil engineer engaged in subdividing Rancho Sespe. Afterward, he worked at the stone quarry in Sespe Canyon. Edgar Goodenough purchased land in the Sespe Canyon and in Fillmore. Later, he and Mr. Stowe subdivided and sold land under the name of Stowe-Goodenough subdivision. This was the first subdivision put on the market in Fillmore. He served as a supervisor of roads in Fillmore from 1903 to 1906, and he was director of the Fillmore Irrigation Company.

Behind Bardsdale School was another building that was used for church functions, bazaars, and dances. This was also where Rev. John Guiberson would preach to his congregation on Sundays. Bernice Michel shared that it was a beautiful building and that all of the young people would go there and dance and have a great time. (Courtesy of Santa Clarita Valley Historical Society.)

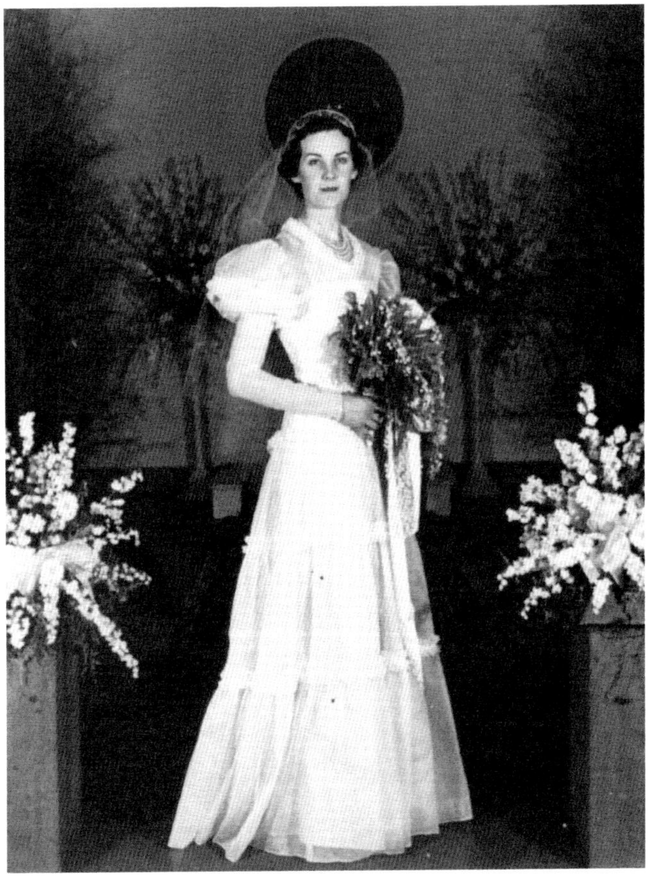

Elizabeth Munger Blanchard

Elizabeth Munger Blanchard was born on March 18, 1917, to John Pinkerton Munger and Ella Wileman Munger of Bardsdale. Elizabeth's family moved to Santa Paula when she was 11 years of age. At Santa Paula High School (class of 1933), she served as student body vice president and editor of the yearbook and also worked on the school newspaper. In addition to being a member of various clubs and organizations, she was a member of the California Scholarship Federation. She attended Holmby College in Los Angeles for two years and then returned to Santa Paula and married Eliot McClelland Blanchard, grandson of Santa Paula founder Nathan Weston Blanchard. Together, the couple attended Stanford University. Eliot received his law degree, and Elizabeth earned her bachelor of arts degrees in journalism, economics, and history. When World War II broke out, Eliot joined the Navy and served in the Pacific. It was during this time that Elizabeth provided a home for a young lady, Minnie Ybarra, who cared for Eliot and Elizabeth's two boys, Jim and John Blanchard. Elizabeth was Minnie's positive influence while Minnie was growing up because Minnie's mother passed away when Minnie was very young. Elizabeth served on the county Juvenile Justice Commission for 22 years and served on the Santa Paula Elementary School Board of Trustees for 17 years. There were numerous honors bestowed upon her throughout her many years of philanthropy. She served as president of the board of directors of the Museum of Ventura County, and as a docent. Elizabeth was elected foreperson on the Ventura County Grand Jury as well. Her brother John Munger became the first dermatologist in Ventura County, and this is something she was always very proud to share. She was selected as the Santa Paula Chamber of Commerce Citizen of the Year in 1983 and was honored as grand marshal for the Santa Paula Festival. She loved life and she always made time for others. (Courtesy of Betsy Blanchard Chess family collection.)

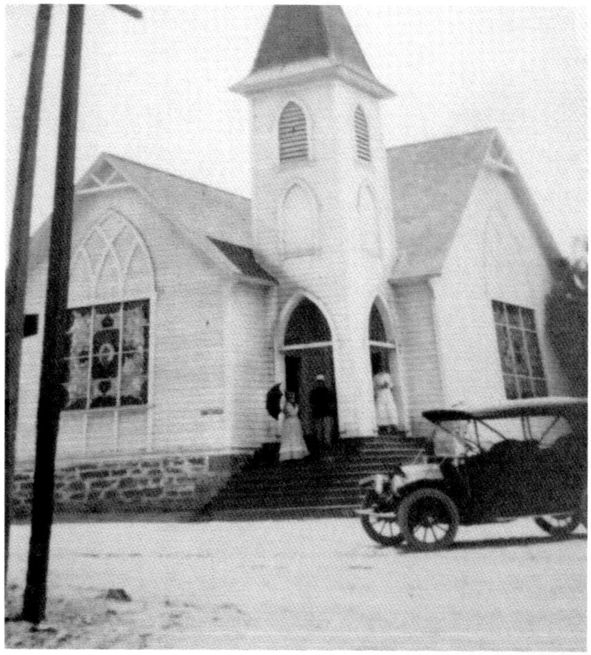

Bardsdale Methodist Church
In 1898, a new church was built on the corner of Bardsdale Avenue and Ventura Street near Robertson's store. It was constructed on two lots donated by Thomas Bard, who also contributed the stained glass windows. It is known as a historical landmark today. The church united the community of Bardsdale because they would use the location as a gathering and meeting place. Various festivities were held there as well. (Courtesy of Harold Michel family collection.)

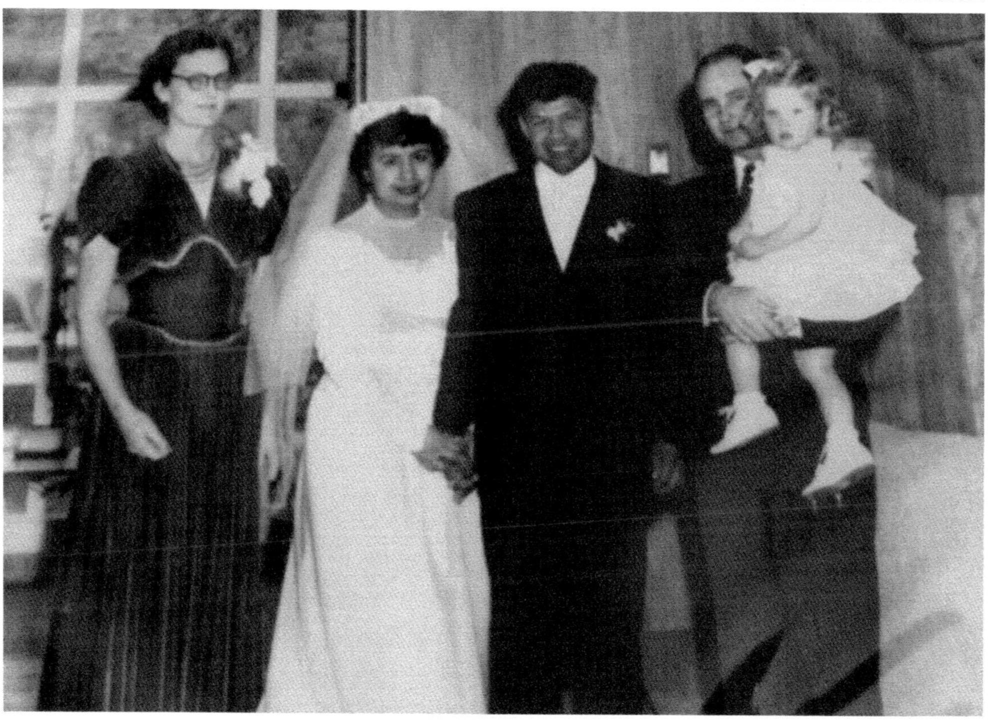

Eliot and Elizabeth Blanchard Family
Elizabeth is on the left, newlyweds Minnie and Woody are in the center, and Eliot Blanchard is on the right, holding a very young Betsy Blanchard. The Blanchard family continued to influence Minnie and Woody throughout their lives in the most positive ways. For Minnie, who grew up in foster care until she met Elizabeth Blanchard, it was a nurturing she relied upon. (Courtesy of M. Ybarra family collection.)

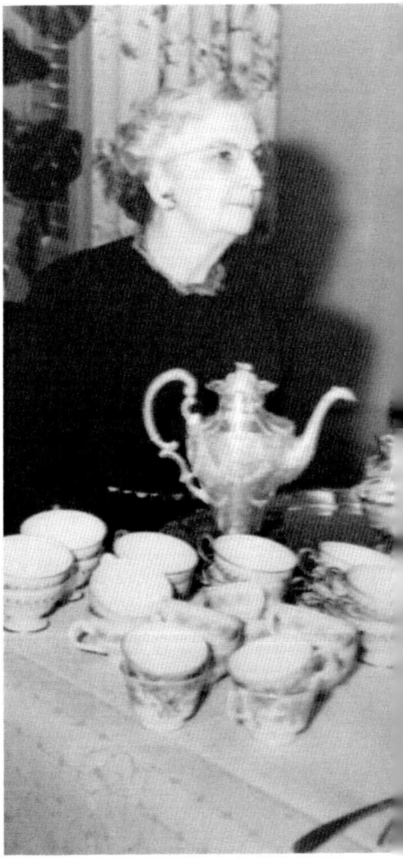

Ella Wileman Munger

Ella and John Munger settled in Bardsdale after their marriage and had two children, Elizabeth Munger (now Blanchard) and John Munger. The family moved to Santa Paula in 1927. John R. Munger was born in December 1915 in Bardsdale and graduated from Santa Paula High School in 1932. He attended Ventura College, where he played football and basketball, and he transferred to Stanford University and graduated in 1937. John was proud of the fact that he played football at the Rose Bowl for two years. He earned his medical degree from the University of Southern California, but World War II broke out before he could complete his medical training, so he enlisted in the Army and became a flight surgeon and was stationed with the 790th Bomb Squadron of the 8th Air Force in England. Following the war, he successfully completed a dermatology residency program at Los Angeles County-USC Hospital and became the first physician specializing in dermatology in Ventura County. (Courtesy of M. Ybarra family collection.)

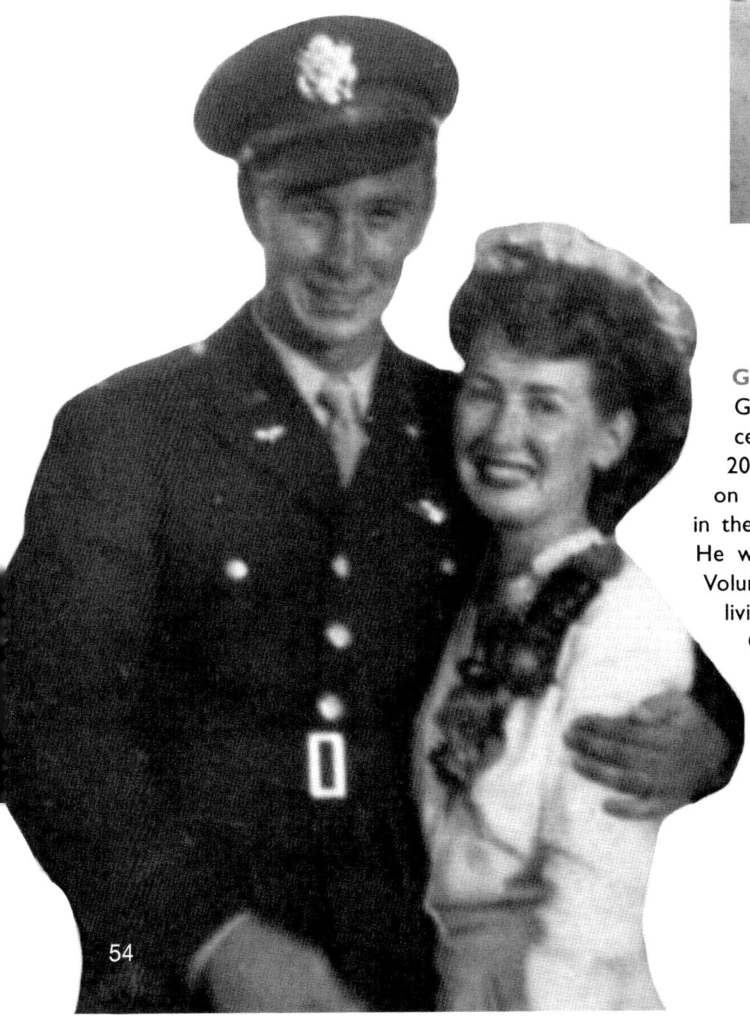

George and Lawanda Campbell

George and Lawanda Campbell celebrated their 71st anniversary in 2015, and this photograph was taken on their wedding day. George was in the Air Force and flew B-17 planes. He was the fire chief of the Fillmore Volunteer Fire Department (longest-living fire chief) and was co-owner of Campbell's Auto Repair with his son Roger. Lawanda was a librarian at Fillmore High School for many years. (Courtesy of Harold Michel family collection and Kathy Campbell.)

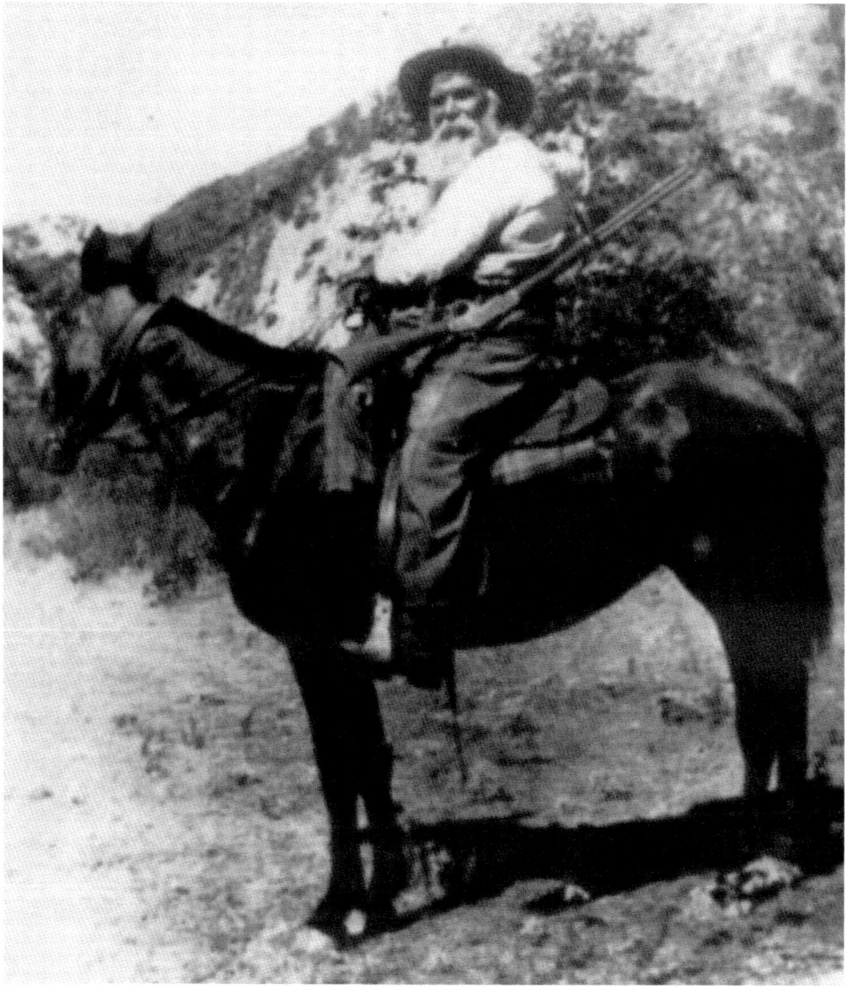

Piru and Dominguez Family

The Tataviam lived primarily at the northern portion of the Santa Clara River east of Piru Creek, and the high ground west of Piru Creek was the western boundary that separated the Tataviam from the Chumash. This also included Hopper Canyon, which is on the western border of Dominguez Ranch. Tataviam roughly translates to mean "people facing the sun." Sickness and diseases brought by Europeans decimated the Indian population in the Santa Clara Valley by the time the Mexican men traveled northward to settle the ranch lands. These men were the first Californios. Carmelo Dominguez, a Yaqui Indian, and his wife, Petra Dominguez, settled at Rancho Camulos from Sonora, Mexico. Carmelo and Petra had 10 children, and Francisco, who was seven at that time, was the youngest. Carmelo worked on Rancho Camulos for 50 years until his death in 1902. He and Petra are buried at Rancho Camulos Cemetery. Carmelo's sons grew up and worked on the ranch as well. Lupe Dominguez, Francisco's youngest child, remembers her grandmother, Petra, as a flamenco dancer. The Homestead Act of 1862 allowed the Dominguez brothers to acquire land of their own, and they renounced their Mexican citizenship and became naturalized citizens of the United States in order to own the land. The Dominguez brothers homesteaded their land; Juan received his homestead patent in 1881, Miguel in 1890, Francisco in 1891, and Francisco Morales, Dolores's husband, received his in 1892. Benjamin Reasoner, a beekeeper, homesteaded his land at the base of Dominguez Canyon in 1890, and his wife homesteaded land in 1900. (Courtesy of Michele McKinley family collection.)

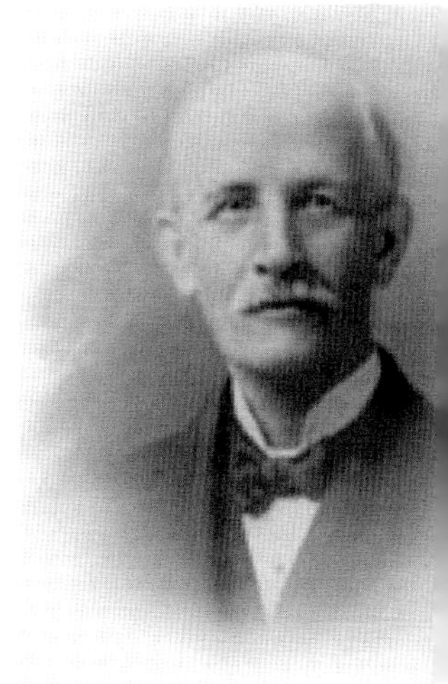

David Cook

In 1887, David C. Cook acquired 89 acres of land from Camulos Ranch, which was to become the town of Piru. David attempted to have the Southern Pacific Railroad build a depot in Piru, but that did not happen. He built his family's first home, which later became the Piru Hotel. In 1890, the "Piru Mansion" was constructed for the family in the Queen Anne style. The Cooks moved into their new home, and after several years, David decided to move back to the Midwest to pursue his publishing business. The Piru Mansion is designated as Ventura County Landmark No. 4 by the Ventura County Cultural Heritage Board. In 1981, the it burned to the ground but was rebuilt. The late Philip Hardison, an architect, had taken more than 400 photographs of the mansion as part of his senior thesis in college, and the mansion was rebuilt following the details chronicled in the images. (Courtesy of Missy Pennington Cervantez family collection.)

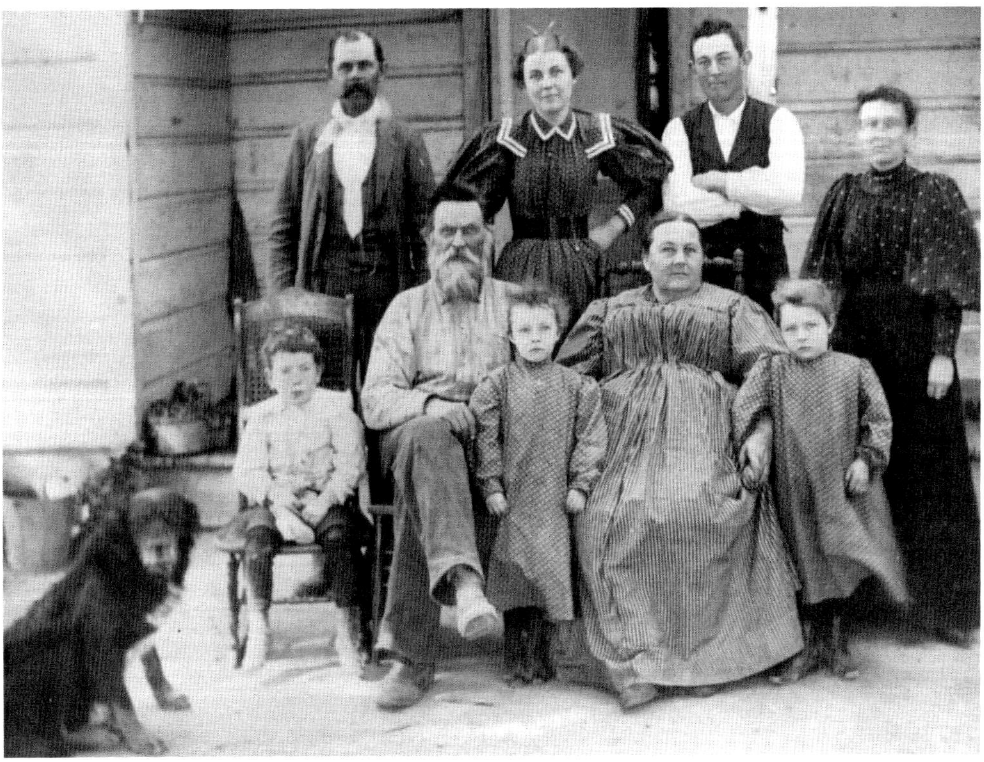

B.F. Warring

B.F. Warring came out west by way of the Isthmus of Panama when he was 24 years old. He contracted Panama fever on his voyage before finally arriving in San Francisco. From there, he traveled to San Jose, where his sister lived. In September 1869, he moved to Ventura County, where he laid claim to 160 acres of land known as "Buckhorn Ranch." The land had been claimed as belonging to the part of the Sespe land grant owned by T. Wallace More, but after B.F. Warring contested this in the courts for over 10 years, he was successful in obtaining a US patent and was named the owner. It was his home until his death on July 1, 1903. He and his wife, Missouri Dorcas Easley, had five children. (Courtesy of Missy Pennington Cervantez family collection.)

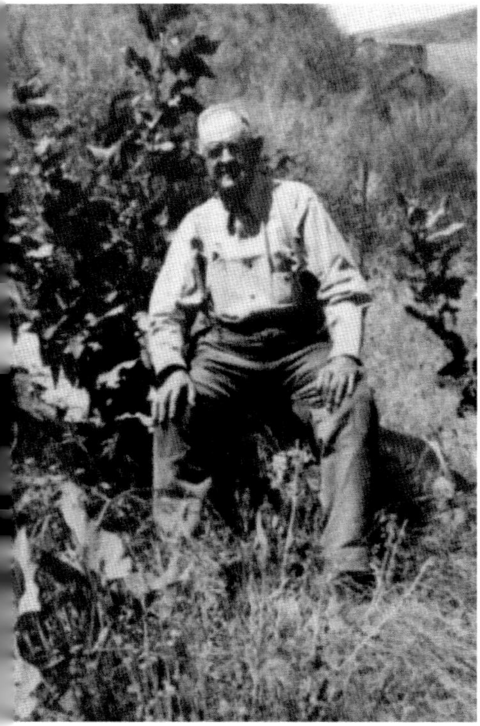

Hugh Warring
Hugh Warring purchased the Piru Mansion from William and Addie Ramsay in 1912. Warring served on the Ventura County Board of Supervisors and on the board of the Ventura County Cooperative Association, as well as the Piru Citrus Association. He was one of the first to grow citrus in the area and was instrumental in building the packinghouse for the Piru Citrus Association. He also served as a trustee for Fillmore Union High School, was a stockholder in the Fillmore State Bank, and served as a member of the Benevolent and Protective Order of Elks and the Masonic Order. On January 20, 1969, the Piru Mansion was designated as a Ventura County Landmark. Hugh Warring had four children with Alice Conaway, and they lived happily for 15 years until her death. In 1903, he married Orie J. Eaton in Piru. They had two children, Benjamin F. and Chester Arnold. Hugh Warring owned the Piru Water System and was instrumental in designating the Piru Fire District as Fire Station 28. He agreed to install fire hydrants when the fire district assigned Piru a pumper. (Courtesy of Missy Pennington Cervantez family collection.)

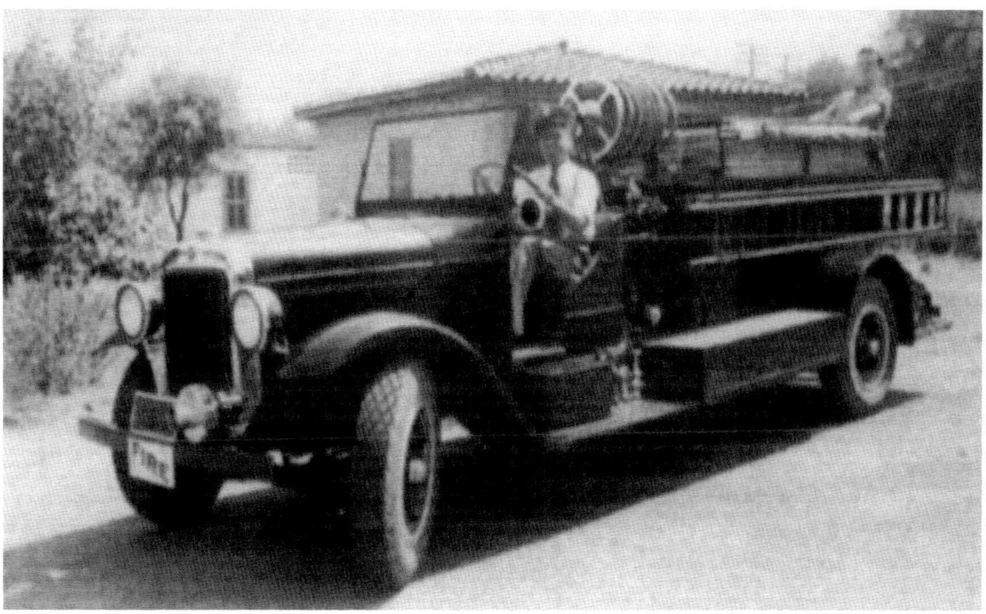

Frank Bowdie
Frank Bowdie was Piru's fire chief in 1928 when the district took charge of the Piru Fire Department. Frank Bowdie operated a gasoline station, where he also lived, at 4072 Center Street (which was then Highway 126). In 1931, district personnel built a firehouse on Market Street, and it was in use as Piru's fire station until 1950. Today, the fire station is on Church Street. The property was sold to the fire district for $500 by Harry Lechler's father. (Courtesy of Missy Pennington Cervantez family collection.)

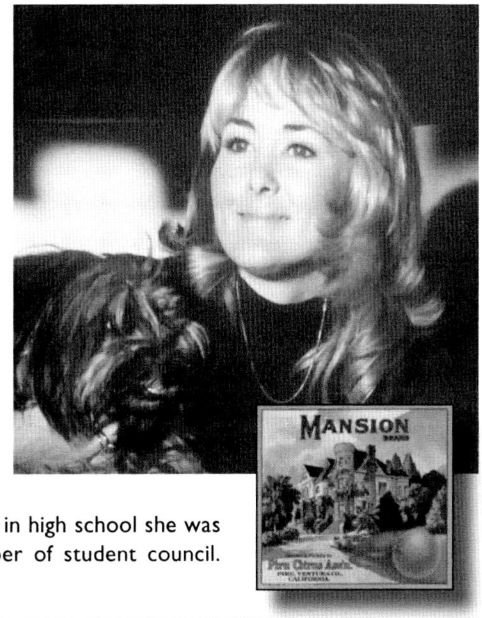

Sandy Warring, Growing up in the Mansion
As soon as Hugh Warring purchased the Piru Mansion, and before he moved into it, he had indoor plumbing installed. There were three bathrooms built inside, and the outhouse was no longer used. Hugh also purchased a pipe organ for the Piru church, and it was installed in 1935. The organ was housed in the wall behind the church's altar; the keyboard remains intact, but the pipes need to be placed in the wooden racks. In a magazine interview in the 1930s, Hugh spoke about the time he was a musician in a band that called themselves "the Buckhorn Ranch Band." At the age of 21, Hugh bought his first 50 acres of farmland, which bordered the Buckhorn Ranch. Hugh's granddaughter Sandy lived at the mansion, and she was a product of Piru and Fillmore schools. She was very active in her community, and in high school she was a cheerleader, homecoming princess, and a member of student council. (Courtesy of Sandy Warring family collection.)

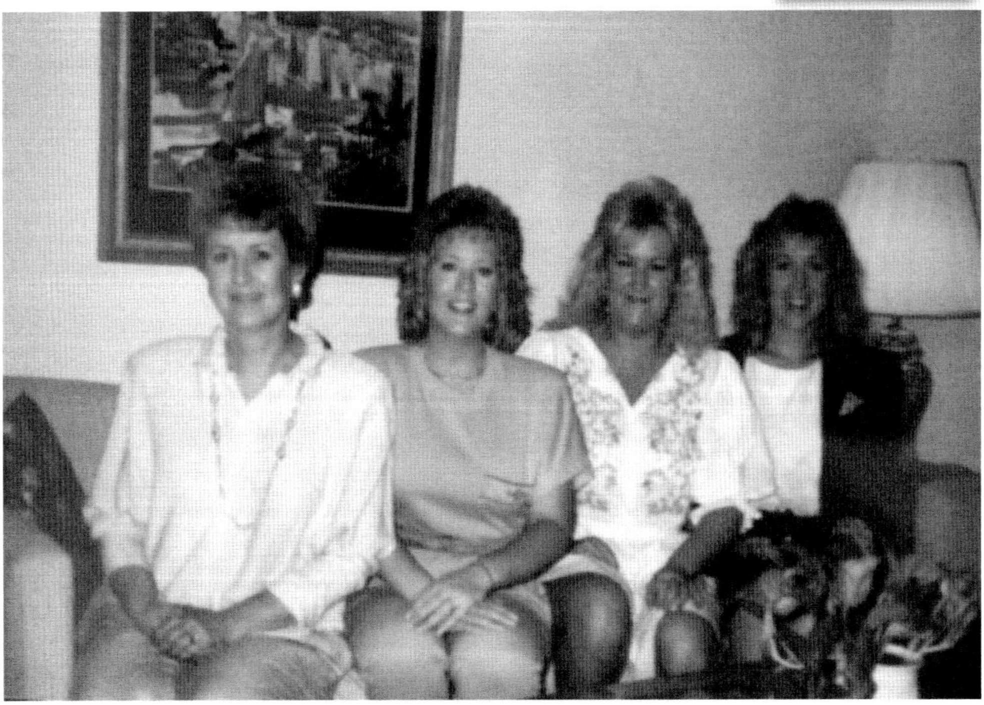

The Warring-Pennington Girls Celebrate a Family Holiday Together
The Pennington family is a close one, and after their mom passed away, sisters Stacy, Missy, and Kathy have become closer than ever. Missy is also putting together a family-history scrapbook, and all family members are participating. Their grandfather's legacy is one they share with their children. Pictured from left to right are Honor Susanne Warring-Pennington, Melissa Suzanne Pennington-Cervantez, Stacy Ann Pennington, and Honor Katherine Pennington-Petouglu. (Courtesy of Missy Pennington Cervantez family collection.)

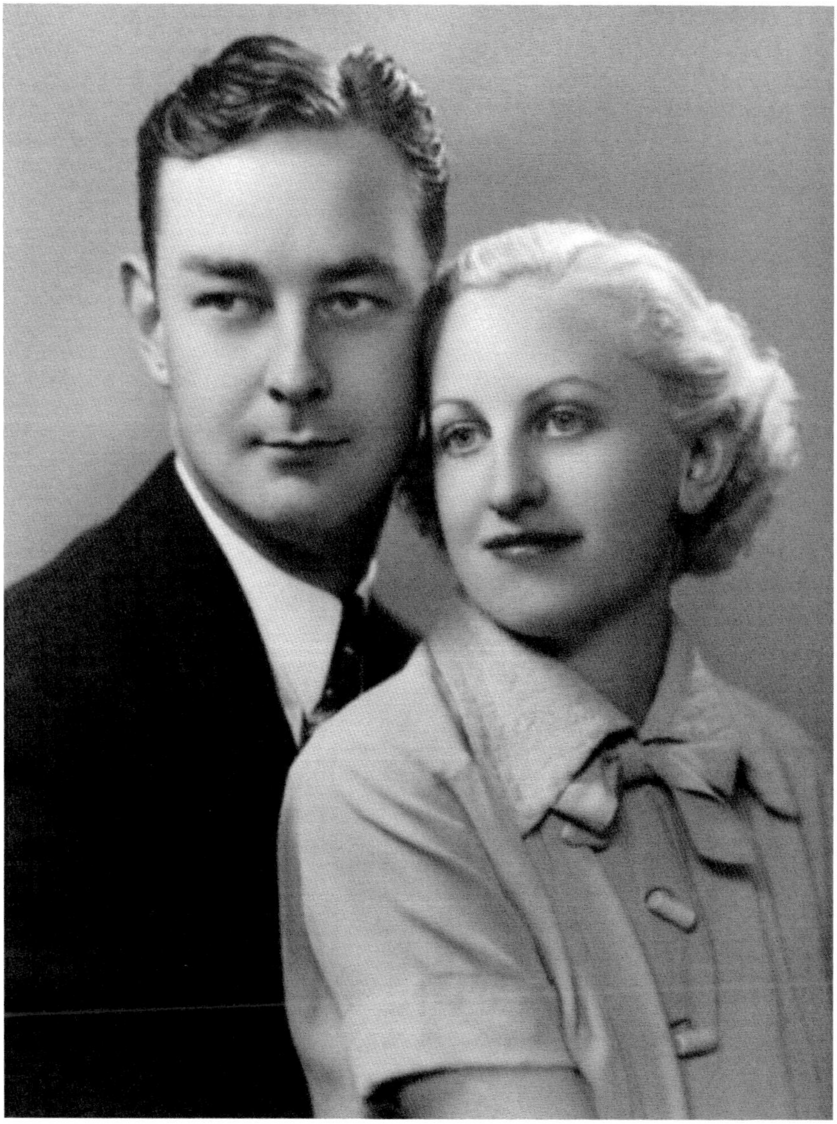

Chester and Honor Warring
There were once two separate water companies in Piru: Domestic Water Company and Piru Water Company. One irrigated the farmlands, and the other served residents. The Warrings merged the two companies since they owned 100 percent of the stock in both companies. Warring Water Service Inc. served the water needs of the community in Piru then as it still does today. Hugh's son Floyd eventually took over the business. Hugh's eldest son, Edwin, was appointed general manager over all enterprises: Fruit Rancho and Warring Water. Lester (another son) took over the management of Buckhorn Ranch. Tragically, Chester and his wife, Honor, were killed in a car accident on Highway 126. One of the first responders shared that when he and others were attending to him, Chester unselfishly told them to "help my wife" first. Chester died shortly after, and Honor succumbed to her injuries the following day in the hospital. The drunk driver who had crossed over the highway and hit the Warrings was killed instantly. The Warrings' children, Richard and Susie, were awarded ownership of the ranch. The family members who kept control of the Piru Mansion eventually sold it to the Newhalls in 1968. (Courtesy of Missy Pennington Cervantez family collection.)

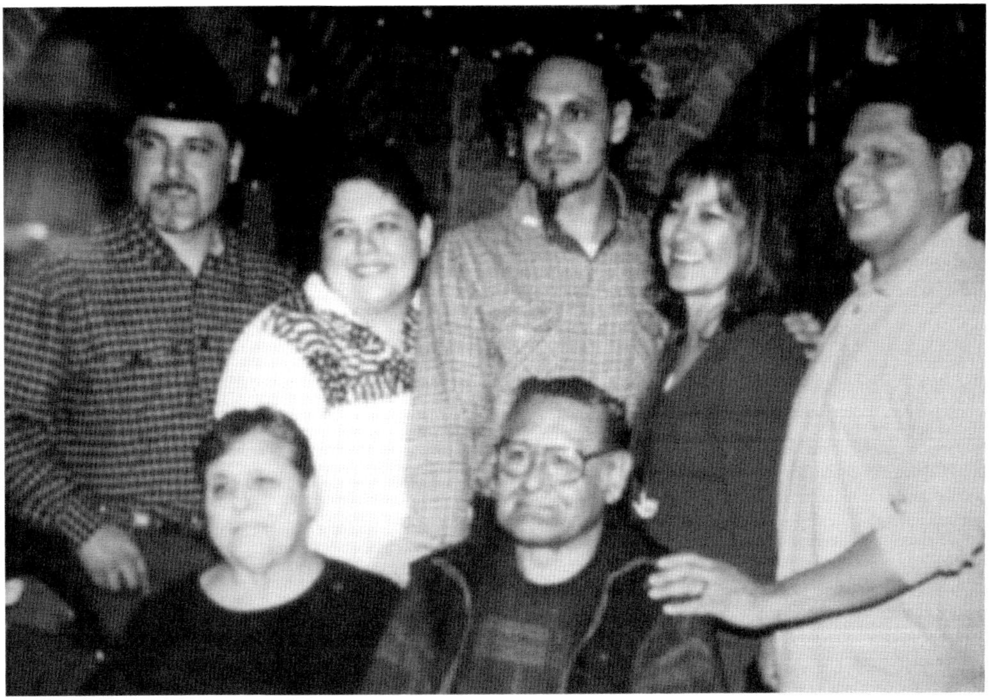

Dominguez Family Descendants

The Dominguez family can trace its history back seven and eight generations. They have shared their oral histories with the Ventura County Museum of Art and History, and these accounts are available for anyone to check out and listen to or read. Rosalind Dominguez (now Ybarra) remembers when they attended the Temescal School, which was close to the river. All the children attended school there. The Dominguez family maintains contact with one another via social media, but they also have family reunions where they make the effort to see one another and reconnect with family. This is a trend happening across the country—families are making the effort to connect and share. The Dominguez family is included in the historical first families of Rancho Camulos Museum. From left to right are (sitting) Rosalind and Lupe Ybarra; (standing) Michael, Michelle, Darrin, Lani-Kay, and Damian Ybarra. (Courtesy of Michele McKinley family collection.)

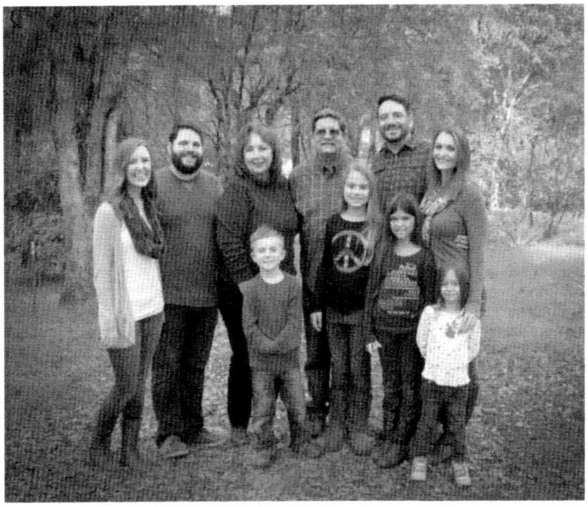

Dominguez Family Reunion

The Dominguez family holds family reunions regularly, and they continue to chronicle their family history. The children attend Piru Elementary School, then transfer to Fillmore schools. (Courtesy of Michele McKinley family collection.)

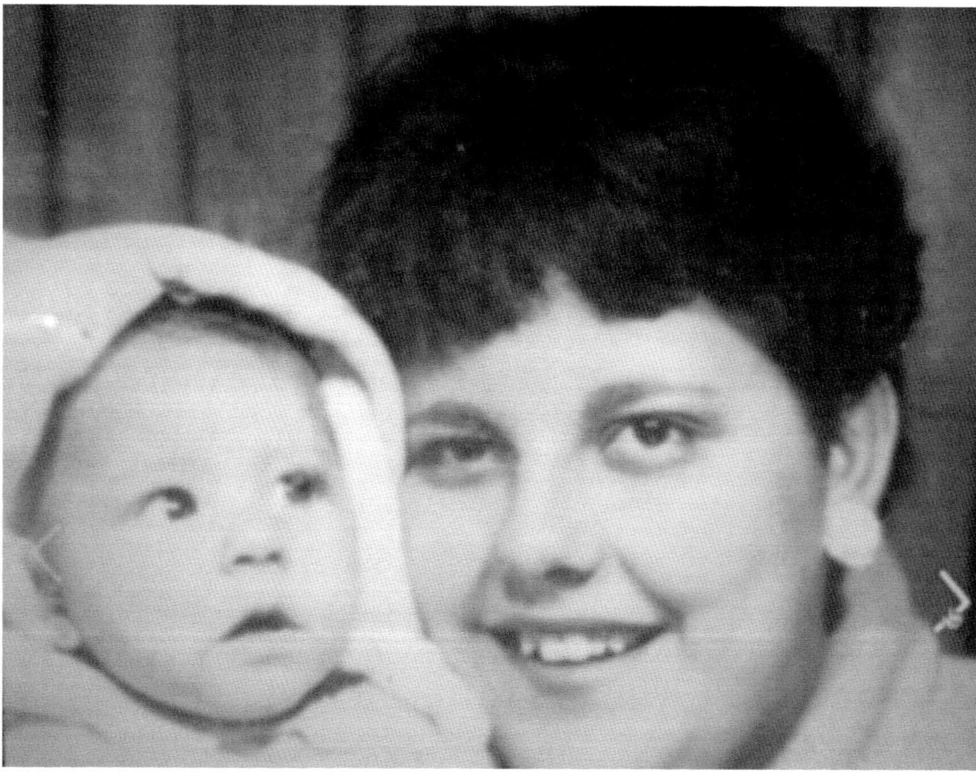

Rosalind Dominguez Ybarra and Michelle Ybarra (McKinley)
Lupe Ybarra married Rosalind, and they lived in Piru with their growing family. They had five children: Michele, Lani Kay, Darrin, Damian, and Michael. Lupe recalls that when the children were growing up, attending elementary school in Piru was convenient because the community was not very large, and the school was close to their home. When they had to attend Fillmore Junior High and Fillmore High School, it was not very convenient. Fillmore Unified School District provides busing to and from school, but if the students wanted to participate in after-school activities or sports, parents had to arrange for their own child's transportation. Lupe explains that he would take the his sons and the neighbor's son to school early in the morning, at 6:00 a.m., and at the end of the day, they would wait for him to take them home. Parents worked together to make certain their children had transportation. (Courtesy of Michele McKinley family collection.)

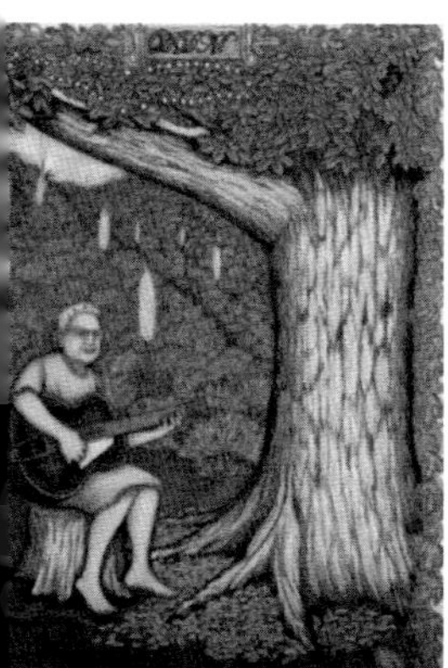

Darrin Ybarra
Darrin Ybarra is a product of Piru Elementary, and he graduated from Fillmore High School in the early 1970s. He pursued his passion for painting and decided to honor both his paternal and maternal grandmothers through his art. This piece depicts his grandmother Petra Dominguez playing her guitar. The family would gather around after dinner, or just get together and sing. She taught them many Mexican ballads, and they learned to sing in Spanish as well as in English. The Dominguez family is one of the first families of Rancho Camulos. Darrin's family donated the Dominguez wine press to Rancho Camulos Museum in the interest of preserving authentic historical artifacts. The Dominguez family would assist in the winemaking from 1860 to 1890; later, they tended the land and sheared the sheep. (Courtesy of Darrin Ybarra.)

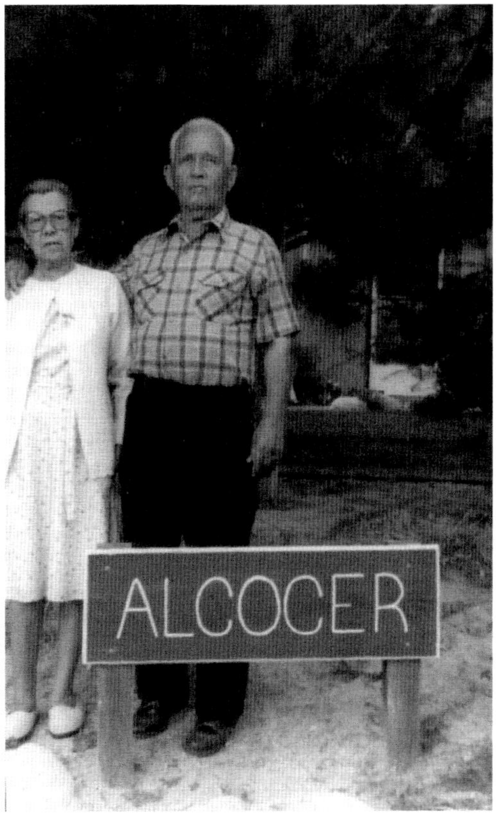

Moises and Maria Alcocer

Moises asked Maria Martinez to marry him while they were in Mexico. They were secretly married by a Catholic priest on June 16, 1928, in a cave in Huanimaro, Mexico. This was during the time the Catholic priests were being persecuted by the government.

Moises and Maria had eight children; their first, David Alcozar, was born in 1929. The hospital changed the spelling of their name to *Alcozar*—so some of their children are known by this spelling. Their third child, "Little Joe," died of pneumonia when he was a year old. He is buried at Rancho Camulos Cemetery, and the cross marking his grave was made by his older brother David, crafted out of cement and marbles. The Rancho Camulos family and workers called Moises "Monchie," and his main job at Camulos Ranch was to trap gophers and to irrigate the orchards. The orchards consisted mainly of walnut and orange trees at that time. Monchie worked seven days a week, up to 10 hours a day, and he was paid 25¢ per gopher. At the end of the workday, he would bring in the gopher tails for August Rubel to count, and he would be paid accordingly. (August owned Camulos Ranch from 1924 until his death; then his wife took over the day-to-day operations.) They would burn the tails each day. Moises bought a Chevy Luv pickup truck with his gopher money and also made a down payment on his house and paid his taxes. On weekends, Moises would take his boys with him to Camulos to pick walnuts. At lunchtime, they would make a fire in the orchard and eat their mother's homemade burritos—chorizo con huevos, frijoles y arroz, or nopales con carnitas in chile sauce. Sometimes, the whole family would go on these work outings, and they learned how to work hard.

During World War II, August Rubel served in the American Field Service, and he was killed in Tunisia in 1943 when the ambulance he was driving ran over a land mine. Moises and Maria maintained a garden at their Piru home, and Moises grew corn, chile peppers, bell peppers, cucumbers, carrots, lettuce, tomatoes, and fruit trees. He enjoyed providing food for his family from his garden. (Courtesy of Lucy Rangel family collection.)

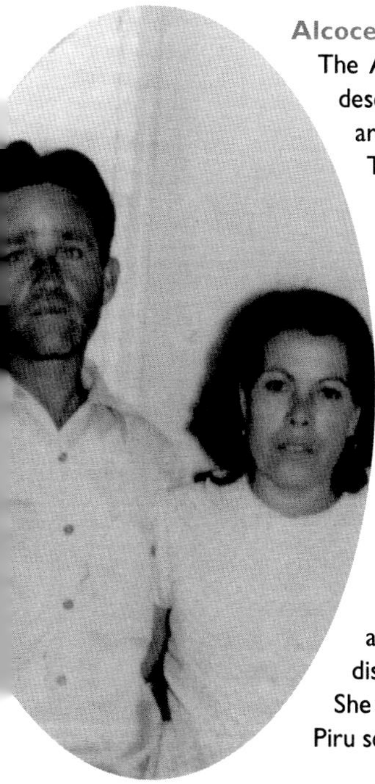

Alcocer Family

The Alcocer family has been influential in the shaping of Piru's history. Their descendants are Moises Alcocer and Ignacio and Amanda Avalos Ortega, who are members of the first families of the historical Rancho Camulos Museum. Their children are Steve Alcocer, Danny Alcozar, Lucy Alcozar Rangel, Connie Alcocer Drusen, Joe Alcozar, Esther Alcocer Gurrola, and David Alcozar.

The Alcozar boys attended Piru and Fillmore schools as well. They would go with their father, Moises, to pick walnuts and other fruits at Rancho Camulos. Moises told them the story of when the St. Francis Dam broke (Moises had been a rescuer). He shared that "the residents of the Santa Clara River had no warning and the police drove with their sirens trying to desperately warn the people of the impending danger." After the flood, he and a group of men went searching for survivors and victims, and they found many bodies buried in the mud with hands sticking out. There were dead animals and livestock tangled in the tree branches. Bodies of some of their relatives were found a few days later. The house and surrounding buildings at Camulos Ranch escaped the floodwaters as a bank of trees caught the debris and channeled the water away. The only damage was a loss of the lower orchards near the Santa Clara River. It was after this disaster that Moises traveled to Mexico to ask Maria Martinez to marry him. She did, and they returned to California. Pictured below are students from the Piru school. (Both, courtesy of Lucy Rangel family collection.)

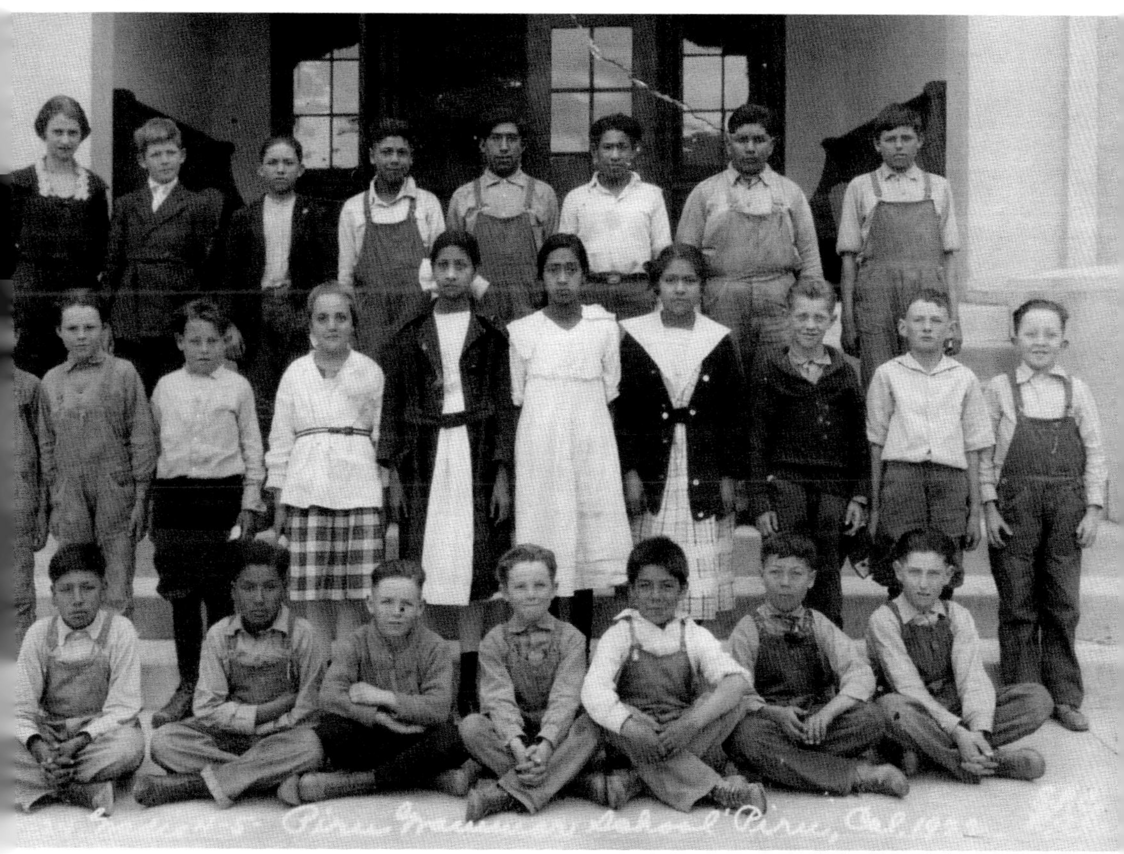

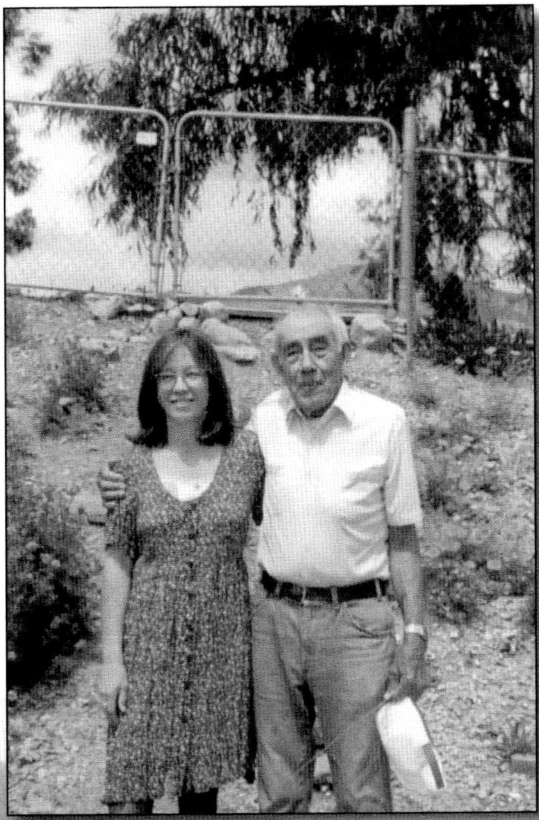

José Nuñez and Joanne Nuñez Fore
The Nuñez family is also counted among the first families of the historic Rancho Camulos Museum. José Nuñez married Nettie Ramirez in 1937. They had one daughter, Joanne Elaine. Pictured at right are Joanne and José, and José is pictured below. José and his family have lived in Piru for years. Joanne Nuñez Fore lives in the family home with her husband and children. She is currently employed as a teacher's assistant for the Fillmore Unified School District. (Both, courtesy of Joanne Nuñez Fore.)

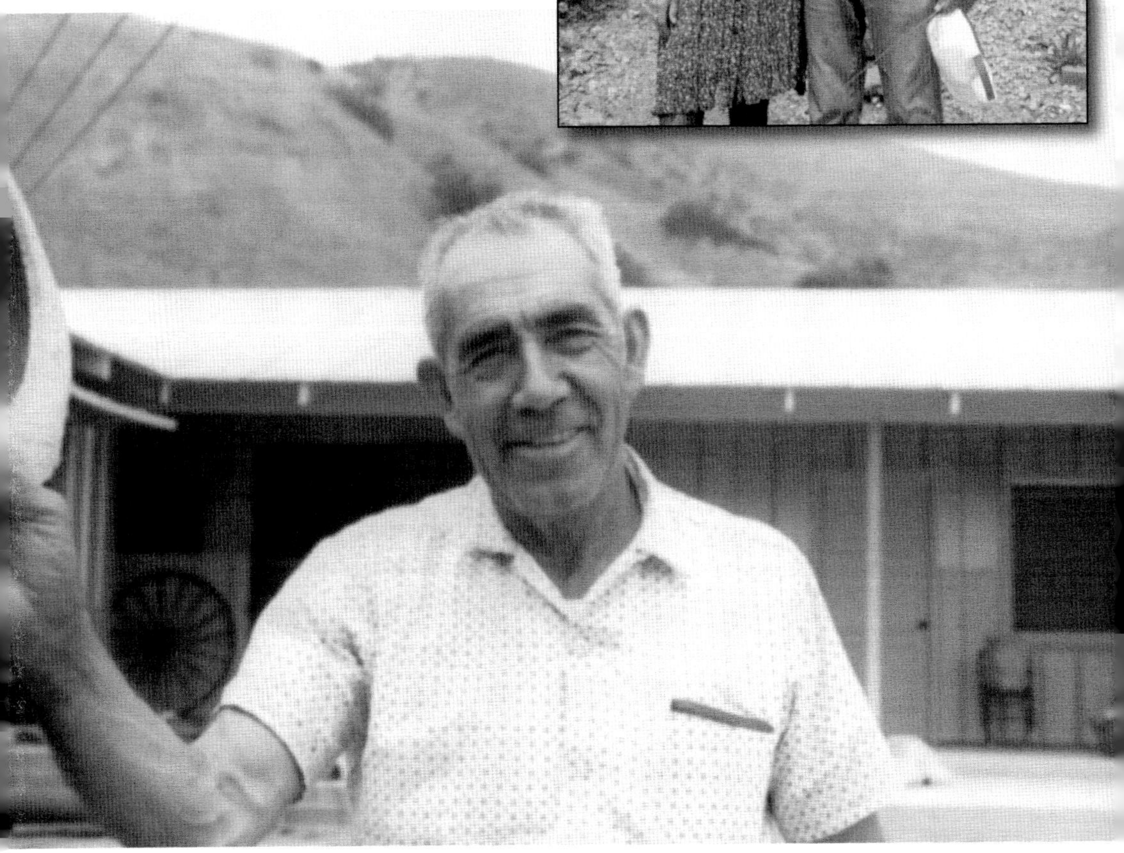

The Lechlers

The Lechler family managed the former Piru Hotel for many years. The hotel was made famous by Mary Pickford, D.W. Griffith, and others during the filming of *Ramona*. Later, it became the Mountain View Hotel and was managed by the Lechler family. It is currently the Round Rock Rest Home.

The San Salvadore Catholic Church in Piru was built between September 3, 1923, and April 4, 1924. It is said that one man, Juan Villa, laid each stone himself and would not allow anyone else to do the stonework. Mrs. William Lechler is credited with obtaining the donations that made construction possible; she promoted the church bazaars and also hired the workers and paid them. Donations came largely from friends who lived outside of the area. Mrs. Y.R. Del Valle, and Mrs. W.B. Cram of Rancho Camulos served on the building committee with Mrs. Lechler. The total cost of the building was $5,171.45. John Golonka hauled the stones; the floor was laid by William Lechler—gratis—and when it was completed, the church was free of debt. The sidewalk fronting the church was donated by Claude Baker and Joe Gottardi. (Joe lost his wife and five of his six children in the St. Francis Dam disaster) The earliest Catholic services in the Piru district were held in the Rancho Camulos chapel; they were later moved to the open air in the Lechlers' backyard and in the Lechler hotel building (Piru Hotel/Mountain View Hotel). For two years, the congregation met for worship at the old public school building, now known as the Hugh Warring warehouse. Henry Lechler (a third-generation descendant) and his wife, Margaret, are pictured inside their former Lechler Museum. The museum contents have been sold. (Courtesy of Michele McKinley family collection.)

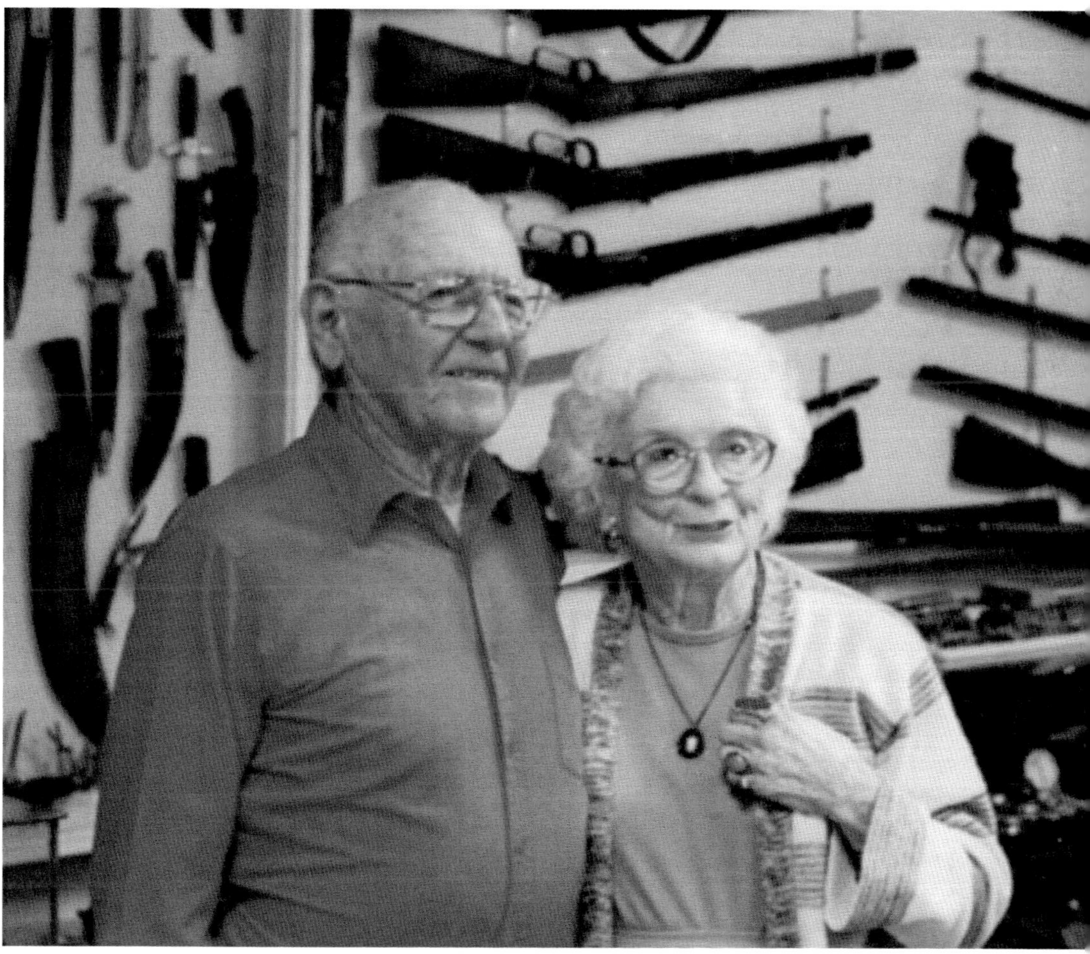

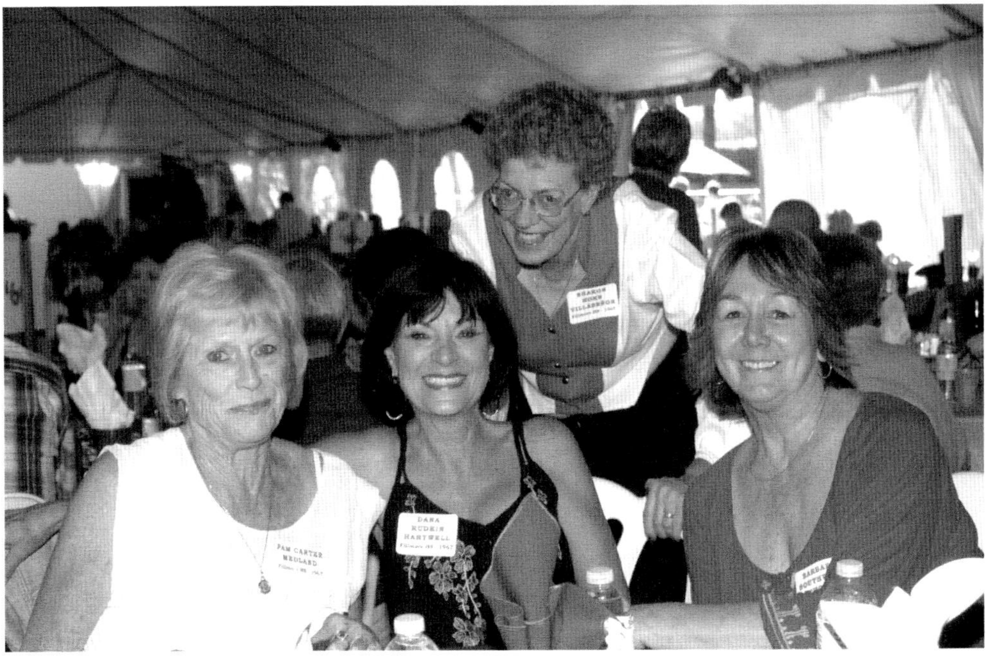

Fillmore Alumni
Pictured from left to right are Fillmore High School Alumni Association supporters Pam Carter Medland, Dana Rudkin Hartwell, Sharon Horn Villaseñor, and Barbara Southwick. (Courtesy of Bob Cox.)

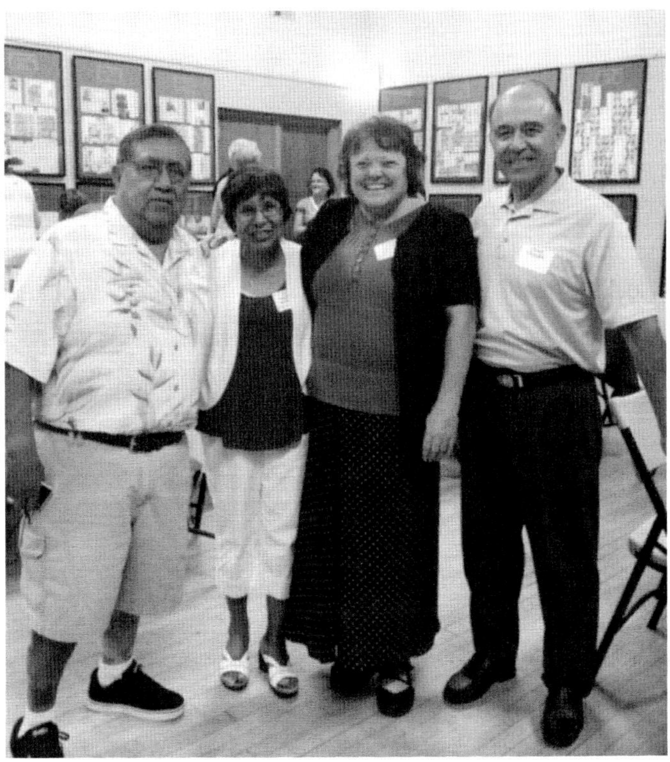

Jimmy and Lucy Sánchez
Arnulfo Sánchez purchased Sánchez Grocery in Piru and maintained and managed the market for the residents and the community. Arnulfo learned his trade when his father, Abundio Sánchez, had a market in Fillmore in the 1939s—Sánchez Mercantile. Arnulfo Sánchez and his wife, Susanna ("Susie"), managed the store for years. After his death, his youngest son, Jimmy, took over the store. Jimmy married Lucy Rangel, and together they maintain the market in Piru. Jimmy was responsible for bringing Hollywood to Piru; he encouraged the film industry to film in the area, and Piru has since become well known. (Courtesy of Bob Cox.)

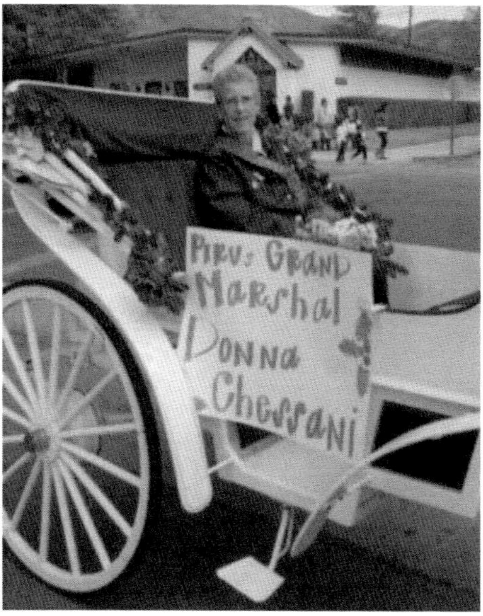

Donna Chessani as Piru Grand Marshal

Donna Chessani was honored as the grand marshal in the festival parade. Donna is an icon in the community of Piru, and she has always been there for the community activities, supporting fundraising efforts and she has giving very generously of her time. She and her family have resided in Piru for years, and they continue to be very active in the community. (Courtesy of Michele McKinley family collection.)

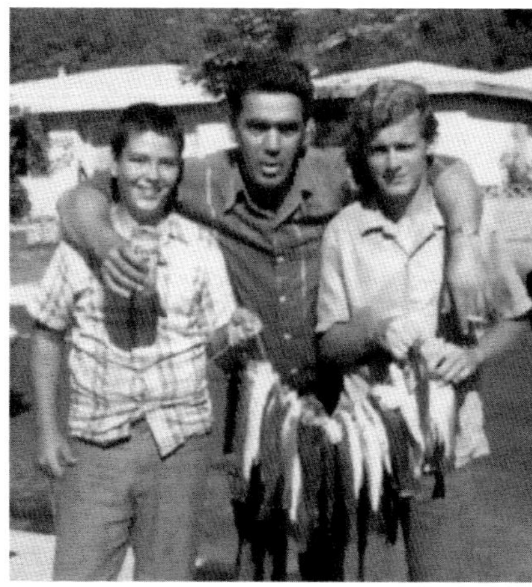

Obie, Don, and Roger Riddle in Piru

Don owned the welding shop in Fillmore, and he served his community very well. Don and his boys supported local sports programs and would all go out in force and assist in all the booster club activities. Pictured from left to right are Obie, Don, and Roger Riddle. (Courtesy of Michele McKinley family collection.)

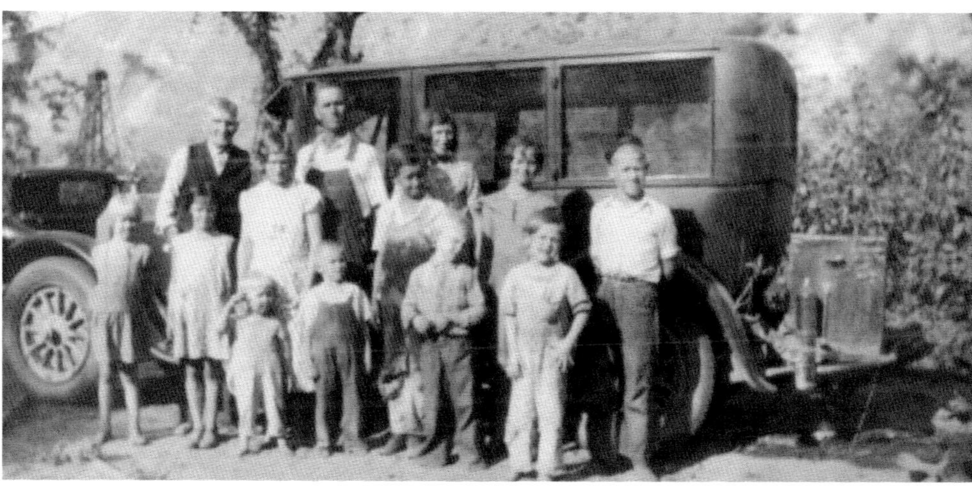

Everson Family

Many families continue the traditions of the Piru community. The Eversons resided there, and their children attended Piru and Fillmore schools. Other families from Piru include the Jimmy Ruiz family, Arnulfo and Susie Sánchez, the Jimmy Sánchez family, the King family, the Lechler family, and the Preciado family. Since David Cook cultivated the land and attempted to establish a larger community, others have resided in this quiet community. The Warring family was also instrumental in modernizing the town. (Courtesy of Michele McKinley family collection.)

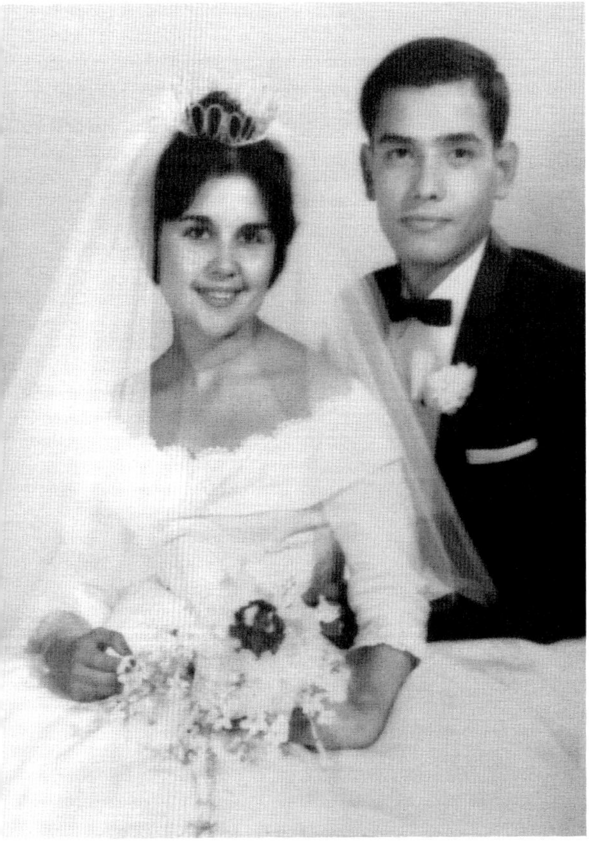

Ernest "Ernie" Morales and Becky Morales

Ernie was elected mayor of Fillmore and served on the city council for 16 years. Both Ernie and Becky have been active in the community, and they were always active in local fundraisers, clubs, and organizations. Ernie was on the Fillmore City Council during the tumultuous times of the English-only initiative as it divided the community. There were those who wanted to enforce a law that made it illegal to have voter materials written in any language other than English (in addition to various other restrictions). The initiative was rescinded by the city council of Fillmore. Both Ernie and Becky have given very generously to the community of Fillmore and Piru. Becky also served as the secretary for the Fillmore Historical Museum for many years. Their son Jeff Morales is a very successful documentary filmmaker and videographer. His work has been shown on the National Geographic Channel and the Discovery Channel. Ernie and Becky have three children and several grandchildren. (Courtesy of Ernie and Becky Morales.)

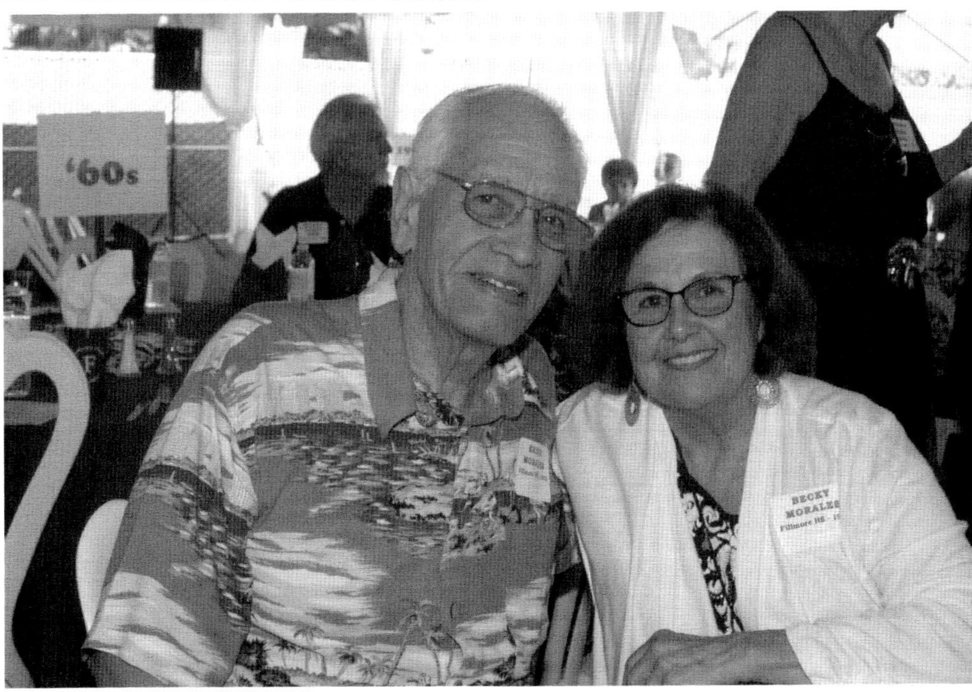

CHAPTER FOUR

Heroes from All Walks of Life

The 1928 St. Francis Dam Disaster was one of the most tragic engineering failures in American history, second only in California to the San Francisco earthquake of 1906 in terms of casualties. At least 500 victims lost their lives. The dam failed just three minutes before midnight, and a wall of water traveled down the Santa Clara River, decimating everything in its path. Where there had been no river, it made one. The people had little or no warning at all. Dedicated telephone operators were calling law enforcement so they could go and warn residents. Sirens were turned on to wake the communities of Fillmore and Santa Paula. Rancho Camulos and the Rubel family assisted the many in Piru. Miraculously, the water did not damage the rancho's adobe, for a row of trees on the edge of the property diverted the water. After it was all over, the community joined together to help collect the victims and clean them so they would be free of mud and therefore more identifiable, and they were claimed and buried. There were claims filed, and a three-person commission authorized monies paid to families for their losses. The communities mourned their dead and attempted to move on. After flooding hit the community of Fillmore in 1978, people again assisted their neighbors, and school even came to a halt for a week. Clean-up of all the mud and debris had to be done, and the city of Fillmore was again rebuilding homes. The earthquake of 1994 impacted Piru, Fillmore, and Bardsdale, devastating part of the business district on Central Avenue in Fillmore. In the face of adversity, families, friends, and strangers came together.

William Mulholland and the St. Francis Dam

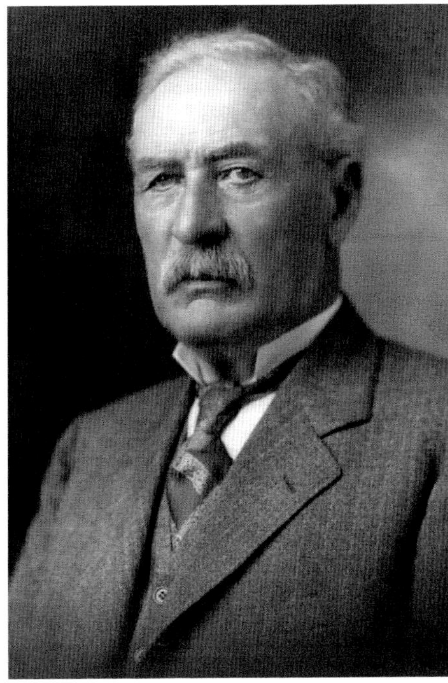

At 11:57 p.m. on the night of March 12, 1928, Ace Hopewell was riding his motorcycle up the San Francisquito Canyon road on his way to Powerhouse 1 of the Los Angeles Bureau of Power and Light. The dam had been completed two years earlier by Los Angeles water chief William Mulholland, and five days earlier it had been filled to capacity. Mulholland had been hired by the Sespe Land and Water Company in 1888 to lay out the water pipes for the city of Fillmore. He had completed the aqueduct project, which brought water from the Owens Valley to the Los Angeles area. He then directed the construction of a series of dams in Los Angeles. Ace Hopewell continued riding up the road when he heard a crashing sound coming from the dam area, which was behind him. He continued up the canyon to the powerhouse, where he learned that the huge dam had broken, spilling 12 billion gallons of water—a 180-foot-high wall of water. (Courtesy of Alan Pollack MD, Santa Clarita Valley Historical Society.)

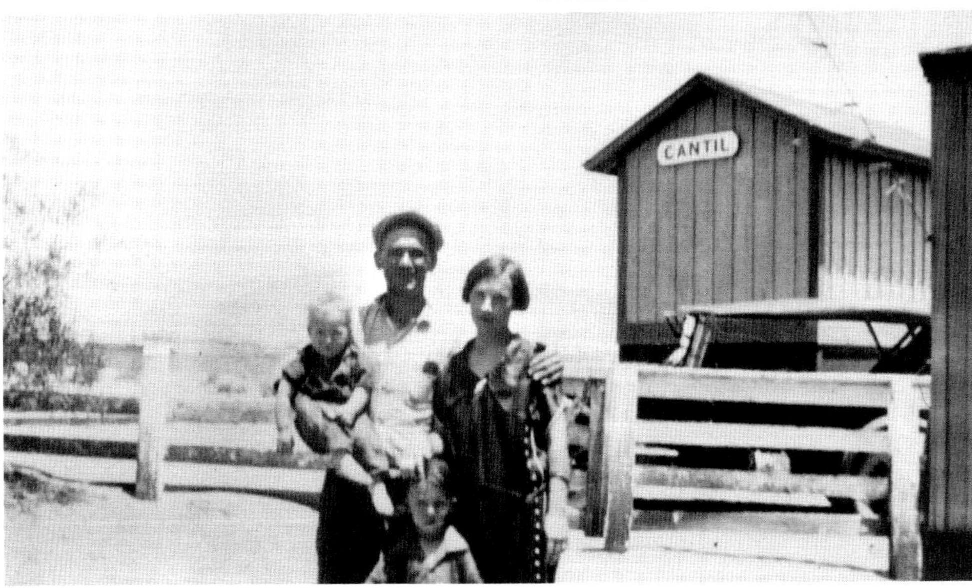

Tony Harnischfeger

Tony Harnischfeger, the dam keeper, had placed a frantic phone call to Mulholland earlier that day after he noticed muddy water leaking from the western abutment of the dam. The leakage indicated to Harnischfeger that the base of the dam might be eroding and could at least crack. Mulholland arrived about 10:30 a.m. that morning along with his assistant, Chief Harvey Van Norman, and together they inspected the dam. Mulholland concluded that the leakage appeared normal and returned to Los Angeles. After the structure ruptured, his partner's lifeless body was found at the base of the dam; Harnischfeger's body was never found. Harnischfeger is pictured with his girlfriend, their son, and her child. (Courtesy of Santa Clarita Valley Historical Society.)

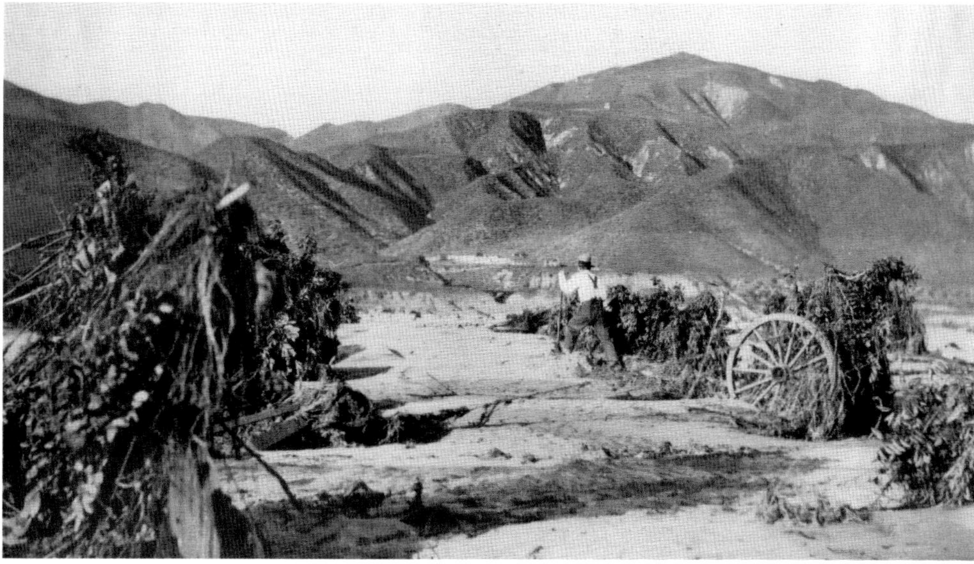

Joe Gottardi

The night of the disaster, Joe Gottardi and his family were asleep. Joe and one of his daughters were left holding onto a tree; the floodwaters washed away his wife and five of his six children. His family was finally found and laid to rest in the Piru Cemetery. To this day, the exact number of victims remains unknown. The initial death toll was approximately 500 people. Gottardi is pictured below searching for his wife and children. (Both, courtesy of Santa Clarita Valley Historical Society.)

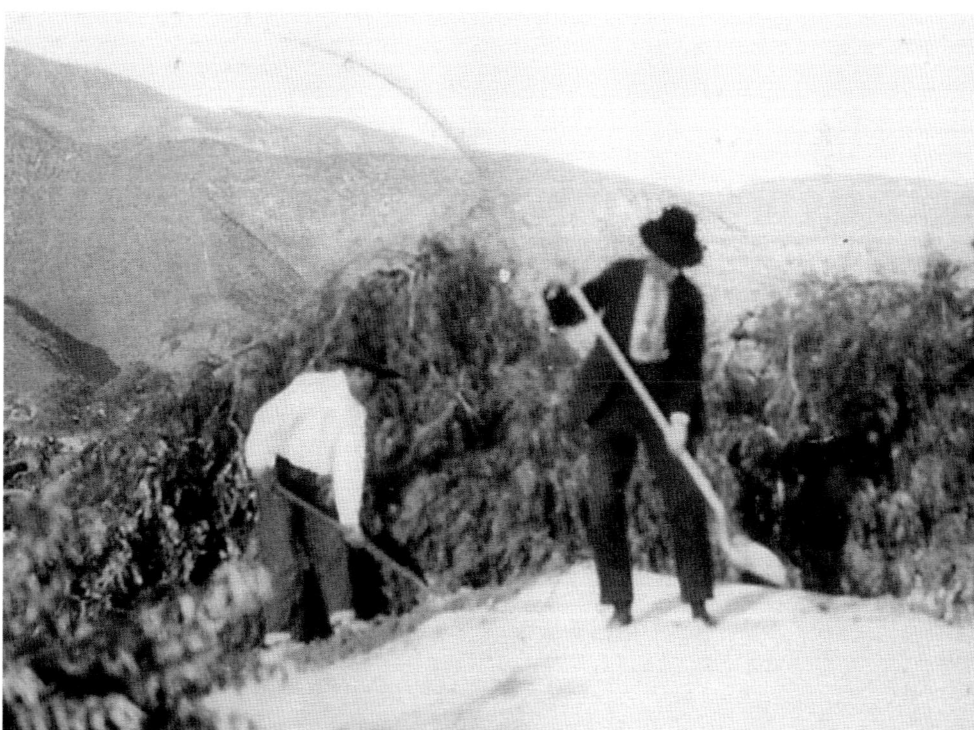

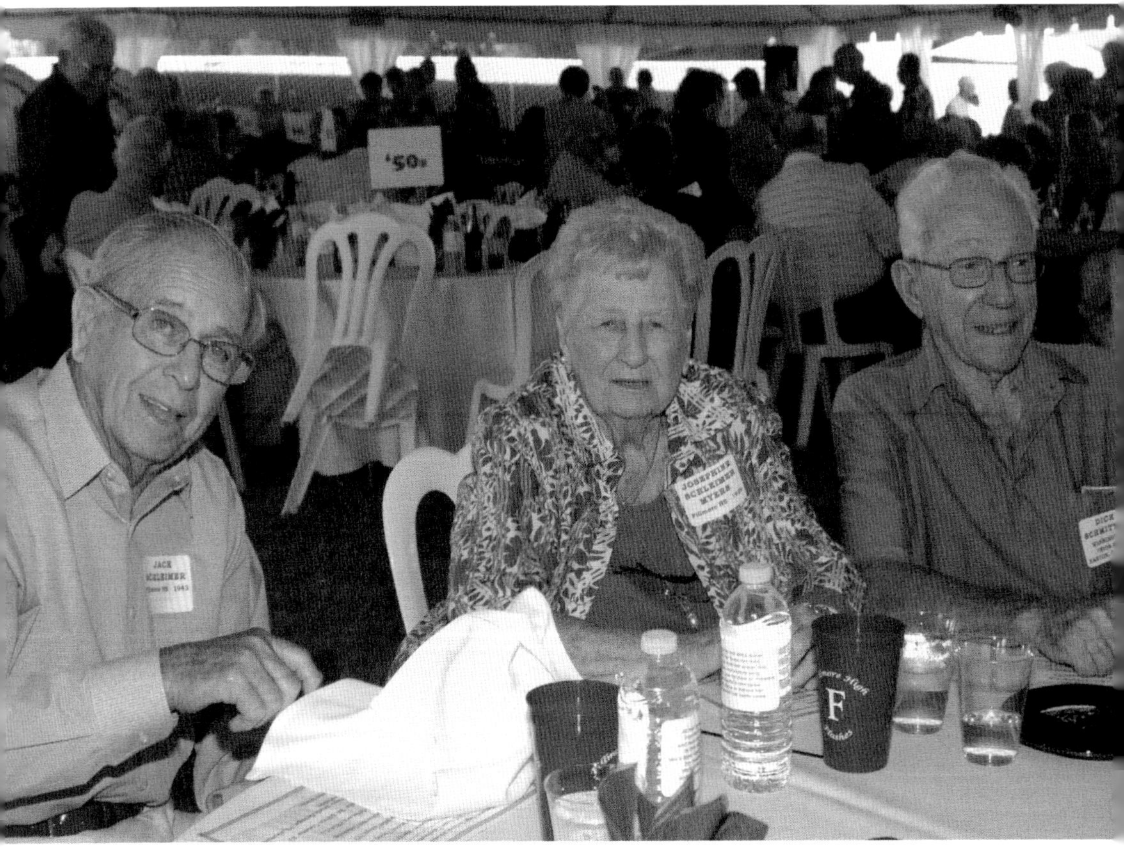

Jack Schleimer, Josephine Schleimer Myers, and Dick Schmittou

Josephine Schleimer (Myers) grew up in Bardsdale, and she and her brother Jack would ride their horses throughout the community and to school. Josephine graduated from the sixth grade with five other classmates, and they attended Fillmore Junior High together. Josephine shared, "I used to ride my old mare into town. I'd tie her up at Corral's Restaurant, then I'd walk into town to go to the movies. My dad would give me a quarter and I'd get into the movies and have money for candy and a drink." Of the St. Francis Dam disaster, Josephine says, "The night of the St. Francis Dam disaster, we were supposed to be at home in Bardsdale, but mom was going to have something done to the house, and at the last minute, she decided we would go to our relative's home in Los Angeles, so we weren't home when the dam broke. After the disaster happened, our friends and neighbors told us there were about 11 or 12 bodies in and around our yard which had been recovered. Some of these people were found hanging in the trees." The community of Bardsdale used Bardsdale School as a makeshift morgue. The town of Fillmore used Fillmore High School as a morgue as well.

The story is that some of the Boy Scouts assisted the volunteers in hosing down and washing the victims, cleaning them so they could be recognized and identified by their loved ones. (Photograph by Bob Cox.)

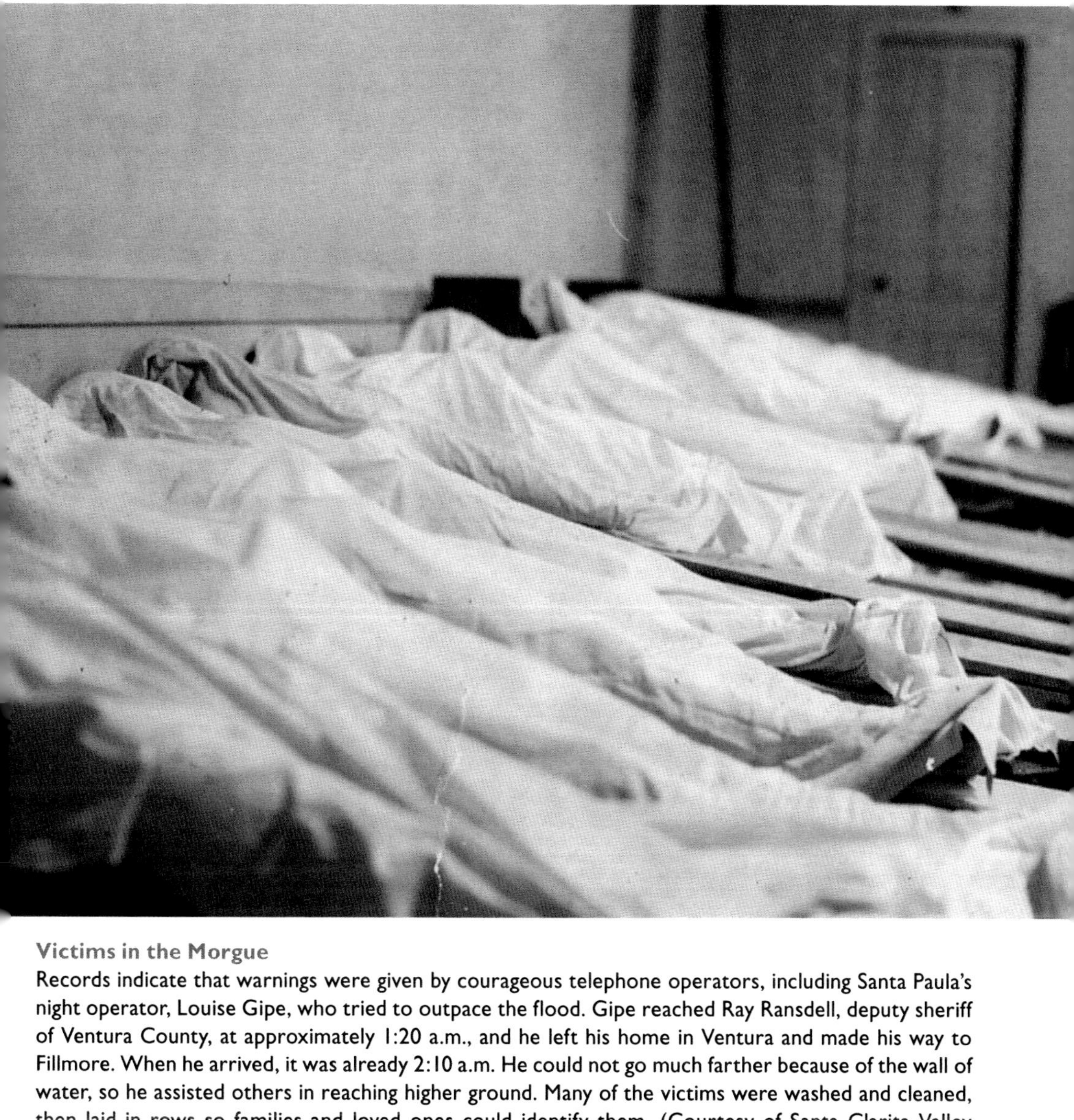

Victims in the Morgue

Records indicate that warnings were given by courageous telephone operators, including Santa Paula's night operator, Louise Gipe, who tried to outpace the flood. Gipe reached Ray Ransdell, deputy sheriff of Ventura County, at approximately 1:20 a.m., and he left his home in Ventura and made his way to Fillmore. When he arrived, it was already 2:10 a.m. He could not go much farther because of the wall of water, so he assisted others in reaching higher ground. Many of the victims were washed and cleaned, then laid in rows so families and loved ones could identify them. (Courtesy of Santa Clarita Valley Historical Society.)

'All the News 'All the Time
LARGEST HOME-DELIVERED CIRCULATION LARGEST ADVERTISING VOLUME

Los Angeles Times

In Three Parts — 44 Page
Equal Rights
Liberty [illegible] Law — True Industrial Freedom
Vol. XLVII. WEDNESDAY MORNING, MARCH 14, 1928. DAILY, FIVE CENTS SUNDAY, TEN CENTS

200 DEAD, 300 MISSING, $7,000,000 LOSS IN ST. FRANCIS DAM DISASTER

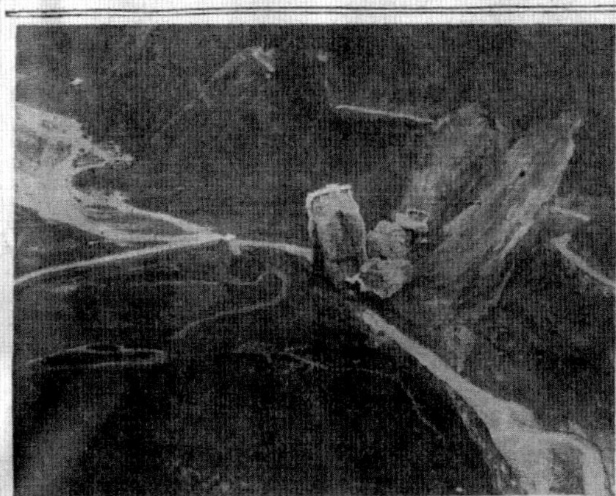

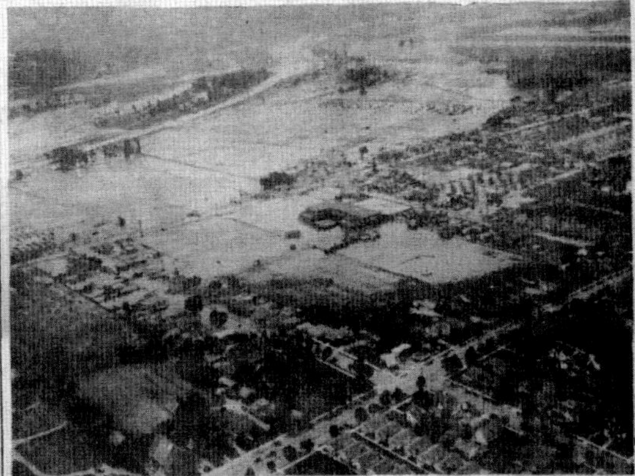

Plane Views Give Idea of Magnitude of Catastrophe

Left—View of the wrecked St. Francis Dam taken from the air at a point just below the dam. Right—Santa Paula, as seen from the air. Directly in the path of the raging torrents, portions of the city were inundated. [Photograp taken by Harry C. Anderson, Times staff photographer.]

THOUSANDS RUSH TO AID IN WORK OF RESCUE AND RELIEF

Red Cross Directs Gigantic Task of Succor in Devastated Area; Water Board Appropriates $25,000; Food and Shelter Needed Immediately

"TIMES" FLOOD RELIEF FUND

The Times will receive, acknowledge by publication and turn over to the proper authorities any contributions sent in care of this paper for the relief of the flood victims of the San Francisquito disaster. The Times announces a contribution of $1000 of its own to start this fund. The need for quick relief is very urgent and all able to do so are urged to subscribe at once and in as large sums as possible. All checks sent to The Times should be made payable to The Times Flood Relief Fund. Receipt is acknowledged of a check for $500 from Anita M. Baldwin. A telegram from Robert J. Foster at Louisville, Ky., states that $100 is being telegraphed by him to this paper for the fund.

Southern California mobilized yesterday on a wide-spreading front for the victims of the St. Francis Dam disaster. Shelter and food for homeless survivors are badly needed. Red Cross chapters of Los Angeles county, and of Ventura and Kern counties, responding quickly to the cry for help, last night had made much headway in the establishment of temporary housing for the hundreds whose homes had been destroyed and in the opening of kitchens for hungry survivors as well as for the hundreds of men employed in rescue work. The Salvation Army also was on hand aiding in the humanitarian work.

Men plowed through mud and debris as rescue work went on in the devastated area. Where once bloomed flowering trees and other vegetation, bodies of those trapped in the rushing wall of water lay exposed on slimy banks. Group here and there struggled through lanes blocked by clogging timbers, uprooted trees and mud-caked debris, pushing and pulling portable camp kitchens in an effort to get warm food to the sufferers, many of whom were stranded and shivering on small shoals in the middle of turbulent streams.

The work of the rescuers was disheartening. Many bodies were buried underneath tightly packed mud. Victims were trapped while they slept, clad only in night clothes. Hurled along on the [illegible]sting flood, their bodies were buffeted about making identification in many cases almost impossible. Dance halls, drug stores and almost every available place where rescue work could be conducted were commandeered. First-aid stations and morgues were established in all central points.

RED CROSS ON JOB

Before dawn the local committee of the Red Cross had established headquarters at Newhall where first aid and nursing service from the Los Angeles corps reported for duty. A hundred-bed hospital completely equipped to care for patients was loaded on trucks and reached the Newhall station early yesterday morning.

The Board of Water and Power Commissioners answered the call of the stricken people by appropriating $25,000 for relief work among the sufferers of the flood. The resolution was transmitted to the City Council and approved.

More than 300 members of the Los Angeles Police Department were dispatche by Chief Davis to the areas most seriously affected. All of these men were reported to have reached their destination before noon yesterday. Special details were rushed in fast cars to the stricken country about Saugus and Piru. Squads were deployed down the Santa Clara River co-operating with hundreds of county and State officials and other volunteers.

Members of the American Legion and details of police officers were rushed from Bakersfield to the Saugus district.

Linemen working on the restoration of wires between Saugus and Santa Barbara worked at a frenzied pace and completed their jobs early yesterday morning so that they could volunteer for relief work. More than 500 men left for different parts of the flooded sections to assist Red Cross nurses and doctors in rescue work.

Citizens of Oxnard and Fillmore reported late yesterday afternoon that immediate Red Cross aid is not needed in their districts

(Continued on Page 2, Column 1)

FLOOD AREA IN CONTROL

Army of Deputies Rule Region

Health Crews Working to Prevent Epidemic of Typhoid Fever

Ridge Route Traffic Turned Back at Burbank and North Hollywood

Every available man from the Los Angeles County Sheriff's office, from the County Health Department and from the motorcycle divisions of both Los Angeles and Kern counties and from the State Motor Patrol was dispatched to the scene of the flood during early morning hours yesterday and by nightfall the work of maintaining traffic control and of imposing the stringent sanitary measures deemed necessary was going smoothly but with energy.

Typhoid and contagions often present after flood disasters were being guarded against by the use of antityphoid serum and the enforcement of pure drinking water regulations.

The entire area around the Santa Clara Valley was under semimilitary control by deputy sheriffs, aided by volunteer citizens and members of the American Legion, and no one not included in the great

(Continued on Page 8, Column 3)

PARTIAL LIST OF PERSONS DEAD, INJURED AND MISSING IN FLOOD

The following is a partial and best obtainable list of identified dead, unidentified dead, missing and injured in the St. Francis dam break yesterday.

As well as the below listed persons the authorities are searching for hundreds of missing men, women and children in San Francisquito Canyon, Fillmore, Saugus region, Piru, Ventura, Santa Paula, Castaic, Oberg, Camulos and other sections.

According to figures from improvised morgues in the stricken area and from the Sheriff's office and police department more than 200 bodies of men, women and children have been recovered of which in the neighborhood of seventy-five have been identified.

The Dead

Identified dead at morgue at Newhall:

Earl Pike.
W. Y. Weisland.
Marlen Casper.
Mrs. Ruth Hoppe.
Mrs. Ray Rising.
Mrs. Nell Hansen.
Kenneth Coe.
John Parker.
Dick Pike.
C. J. Mathews, 2 years of age.
Mrs. H. E. Holt.
Sol J. Byrd.
Roland Errarehuo, 14 months.
Three children of Mrs. Ray Rising.
Thelma Mathews.
Vida Mathews.
Mrs. C. J. Mathews.
Eddie Price.
Griffith Hughes.
Rosario Ruiz.
Mrs. Rosie Errarehuo.
Will W. Nelson, Jr.
Mrs. Nora Coe.
Home Coe.
Eugene Frazier.
Mrs. Rita Kennedy.
May Mathis, 5.
Eugene Kennedy, infant.
Ethel Cochrane.
Francis Garcia.
Tootsie Garcia.
M. J. Garcia.
Joy Hughes.
Alberta Isaac.
Maxie Brosky.
George Mann.
Mrs. Louise Burns.
Margaret Ely.

IDENTIFIED DEAD IN MORGUE AT PIRU:

Edward Locke.

IDENTIFIED DEAD IN MORGUE AT FILLMORE:

Clinton Anderson, foreman, Edison Company.
Keith Andersen.
Ollive Gursber.
H. Patterson.
Nick Nendlock.
George Berzola.
Mrs. Ethel Boardman.
Mrs. .... Savala.
Mrs. .... Koffer.
Mrs. J. Carrillo.
Eight children of Mrs. J. Carrillo.
M. Miyachi, Japanese.
Mrs. .... Talley.
Two girls and two boys, children of Charles Rogers.
Oscar Doty.
John Kingsten.

Of the above dead, six were employed by the Edison company in a camp near Piru with 170 other men. Eighty of them have been accounted for.

Identified dead in morgue at Santa Paula.

Mrs. S. A. Whitehead.
L. G. Robertson.
Mattilda Samaniego.

Identified dead in morgue at Moorpark.

Elizabeth Torres.
Gordon Cummings.
Mrs. Gordon Cummings.
Bruce Lee.
Mrs. Ida Kelly.
Phillis Kelly, 7.
Delores Kelly, 4.
Mrs. D. Stevens.
Earl Cowden.
Mrs. G. R. Bordman.

Identified dead in morgue at Oxnard:

[illegible]eff Johnson.

UNIDENTIFIED DEAD:

Newhall, seven.
Fillmore, thirty.
Santa Paula, thirty-two.
Moorpark, nine.
Ventura, seven.

UNACCOUNTED FOR

In and around Santa Paula—One hundred and fifty.

KNOWN INJURED

Selma McCauley, Fillmore. She is in Santa Paula Hospital, not expected to recover from being battered by debris and due to exposure.

C. H. Hunick.
Bernard Ramos.
Miguel Ruiz.
Cecilia Fraser.
Mrs. Lena Fraser.
Charles D. Fraser.
L. R. Ruiz.
Lester Johnson.
Louis Heptins.
John Peiffer.
Curtis Randall.
Albert Davis.
Mrs. Mary Nichols.
Chester Smith.
Mrs. A. L. Garcia.
Benjamin Dernalecha.
Van Dernalcche.
Tenaso Ramos.
Mrs. F. Fraser.
L. M. Steenblock, Galt, Iowa.
Everett Goold, Victor, Colo.
L. F. Bennett, Fresno.
"Mase" Anderson, no address.
H. A. Whitaker, Los Angeles.
E. Gilbey, San Francisco.
William Davis, Los Angeles.
R. G. Barworth, Los Angeles.
Albert M. Hill, Tony, Wyo.
Samuel Ureran, Visalia, Cal.
Russell Roth, Bakersfield.
J. P. Toomey, Los Angeles.
J. R. Duke, no address.
G. E. Cameron, no address.
C. R. Kerr, Lindsay, Cal.
Peter Boustie, Los Angeles.
Herbert Anthony, Exeter, Cal. (broken right leg.)
Roy D. Purdy, Sawtelle, Cal.
R. A. Newell, Bakersfield, Cal.
Chris H. Kline, Tulare, Cal.
S. J. Hurd, Maryland.
G. F. Kanawayer, Fresno.
Oliver Crocker, Kansas City.
W. B. Smith, Picayune, Miss.

DEMOCRATS TO HEAR PALMER

William Fleet Palmer, formerly assistant United States Attorney, will be the speaker at the Democratic Luncheon Club tomorrow at the Alexandria. His subject will be "Issues and Leaders of the 1872 Democratic Convention."

The index to today's issue of "The Times" will be found on Page 5, this section.

SCORES MORE THOUGHT BURIED IN DEBRIS OF WILD WATER

Darkness Halts Rescue as Crews Sight Other Bodie Hundreds of Homes Crushed by Fatal Torrent and Many Bridges Washed Away

Approximately 200 persons dead, 300 others unaccounted for, and property damage estim at $7,000,000, according to the latest available figures, is the toll of the disaster following coll of the St. Francis Dam Monday night which released an avalanche of water upon the slee residents of San Francisquito Canyon and the Santa Clara Valley and left death and destru in its wake.

Of those listed among the missing it is believed by officials engaged in rescue work many will be found safe. Because of the confusion created by the establishment of mor at widely separated places it is believed that duplications in the compilation of the numbe unidentified dead has taken place.

That the death toll will continue to grow higher, however, was the conclusion of r crews who stopped work last night because of darkness and the inaccessibility of many ca and crevices were other bodies are believed to be lodged.

Many bodies, which could not be taken out last night, sighted by searchers and will be removed this morning.

FEAR MANY MORE ARE DEAD

Officials in charge of the rescue and body recovering last night estimated that probably fifty additional victi least will be found today.

Property damage throughout the area laid waste by the aster is estimated at $7,000,000, which is admittedly only a guess and it will be several days before an accurate surve be made.

The magnitude of the sweeping scope of death-dealing rent that plunged entire families and to their deaths and all their possessions away was emphasized in the estimated f on the number of dwellings destroyed.

Approximately 400 houses located in the San Franci Canyon in the sixteen-mile gorge between Piru and the site, were wiped out.

Not a standing timber was left as a marker to indicate once prosperous little farms that dotted the valley.

HOMES NOW MASS OF WRECKAGE

Three hundred houses at Santa Paula, in the southern tion of the town, were caught in the flood and swept into a of wrecked and tangled timbers as the wall of water from the dam down through the Santa Clara River bed. or forty houses were wrecked at Fillmore and fifteen at nine miles south of there.

Al bridges excepting the State highway bridge at Mo and the Saticoy bridge were wiped out.

The Los Angeles Bureau of Power and Light suffere heaviest single loss in the disaster in the St. Francis da power plant No. 2, located at the foot of the giant basin. city's loss will approximate $3,000,000.

The balance of the damage is in the homes and ranches San Francisquito Valley and the valley of the Santa Clara to which the downrushing flood was diverted near Castaic, i lic utility lines destroyed, highways and bridges washed o live stock drowned.

The loss in the Santa Clara Valley is estimated at than $3,000,000. A mile of paved highway between Pir Castaic is washed out. Two of the largest ranches in the trict, owned by T. M. Storke, publisher of the Santa B Daily News, and Gwyn Thurmond, were swept by water.

Immense pieces of the dam carried along by the fo the water, were found half a mile and more downstream, a ing to Lieut. Earl H. Robinson of the National Guard Aero who made an air survey of San Francisquito Canyon yest

Lieut. Robinson reported that the pumping stations and houses in the path of the flood seem to be wiped out.

The collapse of the dam still is a mystery to the eng of the Water Bureau who constructed it, and an investigati been launched to attempt to fix the cause of the tragedy.

William Mulholland, chief engineer of the Water Bure

(Continued on Page 2, Column 1)

ENGINEERS FIX BLAME

Dam Break Held Due to Fault

Mountain on West Side Grew Weak and Caused Flood, Mulholland Says

Others State Structure Was Last Word in Project of Gravity Type

The Board of Water and Power Commissioners yesterday started an investigation into the cause of the collapse of the St. Francis Dam and late in the afternoon Chief Engineer Mulholland and Assistant Chief Engineer Van Norman of the water department returned from an all-day visit to the dam and reported to the board. These engineers said the direct, immediate cause of the collapse was the giving way of the mountain on the west side of the canyon.

Due to causes unknown, possibly a fault in the mountain structure or to rains, the mountain on the west side of the dam had become weakened. The west side of the dam was the first to go, and it caused the anchorage of the dam on that side to give way. This was not a part of the dam proper, but a 1500-foot dike or secondary dam which acted as an abutment or anchorage for the main central arch of the dam, which still stands. As the west-side dike gave way, water poured through into the canyon.

On his return from his trip to the scene of the disaster, Chief Engineer Mulholland of the Municipal Water Department issued the following statement:

"I would not venture at this time to express a positive opinion as to the cause of the St. Francis Dam disaster.

"Mr. Van Norman and I arrived

(Continued on Page 6, Column 4)

Charles Rogers (OPPOSITE PAGE)
Charles Rogers lost his four children and his own mother in the disaster. His wife was expecting their fifth child, so she was away. After the disaster, Mrs. Charles Rogers gave birth to K.B. Rogers, and she and Charles began a new family. Charles's father's name is listed among the missing and dead on the cover of the *Los Angeles Times*. K.B. lived in Fillmore and he owned the Fillmore Billiard Parlor, known as the "Pool Hall" to the locals. He retired and he enjoys taking part in community activities. (Courtesy of Santa Clarita Valley Historical Society.)

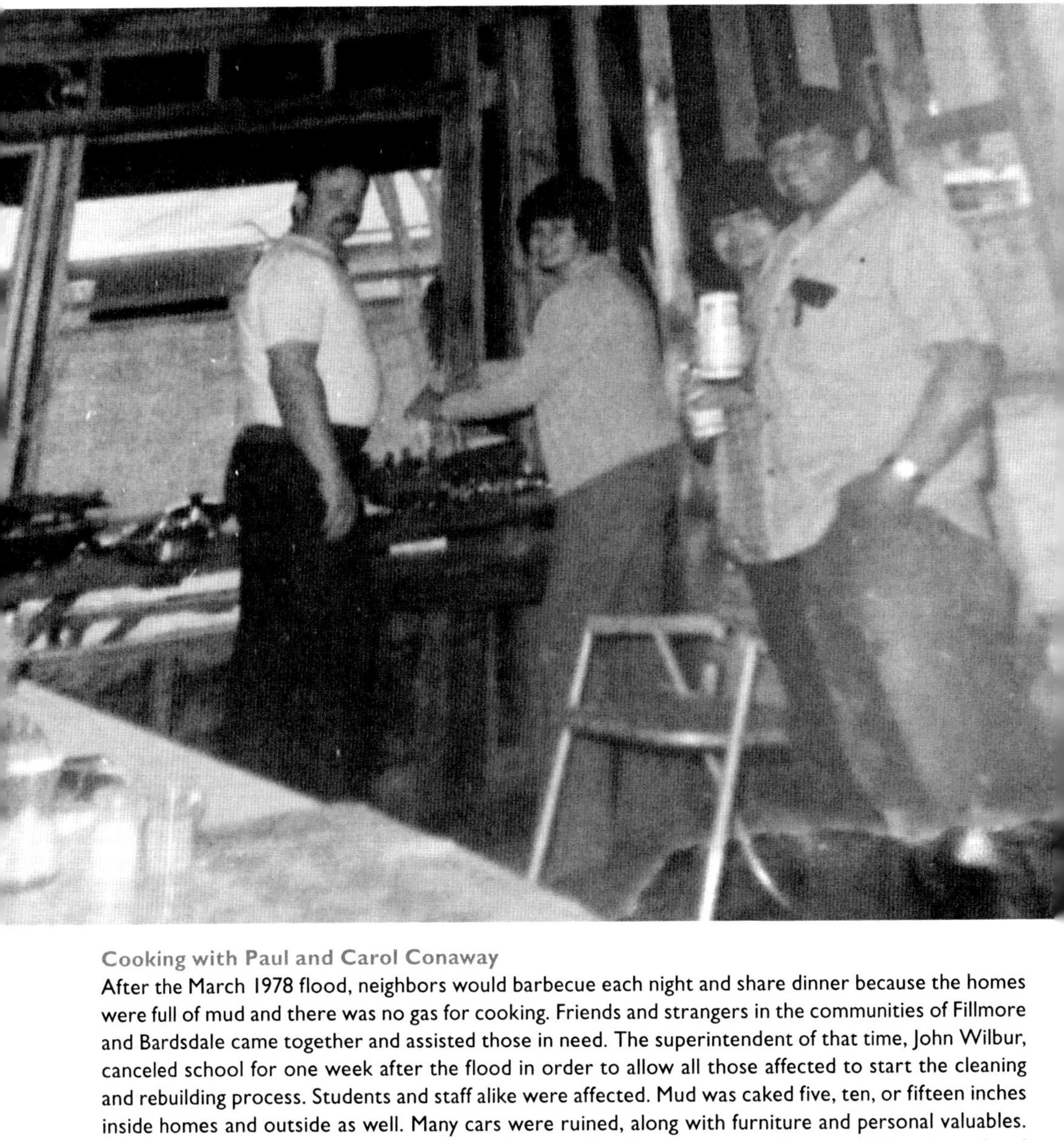

Cooking with Paul and Carol Conaway

After the March 1978 flood, neighbors would barbecue each night and share dinner because the homes were full of mud and there was no gas for cooking. Friends and strangers in the communities of Fillmore and Bardsdale came together and assisted those in need. The superintendent of that time, John Wilbur, canceled school for one week after the flood in order to allow all those affected to start the cleaning and rebuilding process. Students and staff alike were affected. Mud was caked five, ten, or fifteen inches inside homes and outside as well. Many cars were ruined, along with furniture and personal valuables. Friends often picked up boxes of personal photograph collections to see if any could be cleaned and salvaged. Mementos and baby pictures were lost, as were many pets. It was finally revealed that debris from the Sespe Creek area had gotten caught in a railroad trestle and diverted the water toward the homes in the area. Ellis VanNoy and his crane service—VanNoy Crane Company—assisted the city of Fillmore as well. (Courtesy of M. Ybarra family collection.)

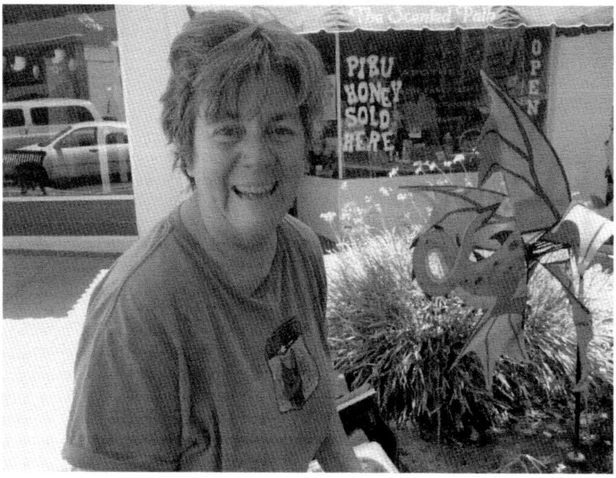

Janine Rees and the Scented Path
Janine Rees and her husband own the Scented Path in Fillmore, and Janine's sister Wendy assists her at times. Janine assists the community in many ways. Janine and Wendy are both daughters of Ralph and Patricia Rees. (Author's collection.)

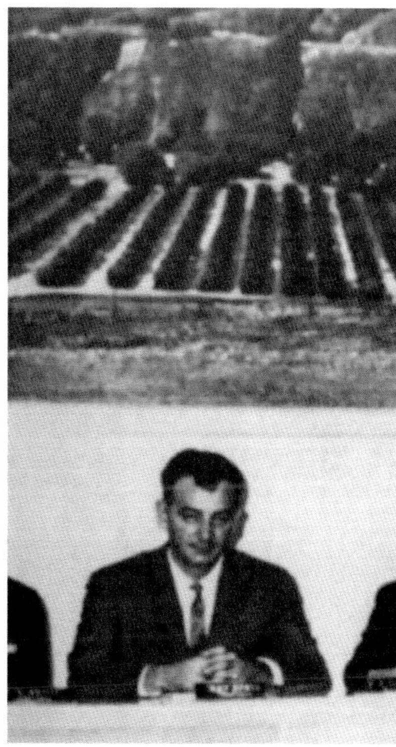

Ray Stull
Ray Stull was on the Fillmore City Council in the early 1960s and was also the manager of the Western Auto store on Central Avenue. His wife, Marguerite ("Marge") was a dispatcher for the Fillmore Police Department. Together, they participated in many civic affairs and had two children: Jan and Tom Stull. (Courtesy of Jan Stull Pavletich family collection.)

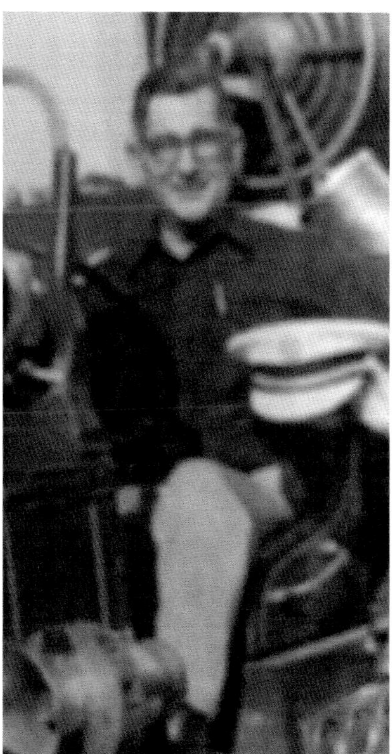

Oscar de Fever
Oscar de Fever was the fire captain for the City of Fillmore, and his "76" gasoline station was in the center of town where the volunteer firemen would gather. When the fire alarm sounded, the volunteer firemen would rush from their locations and jump on the fire truck and go to fight the fire. (Courtesy of Katie de Fever family collection.)

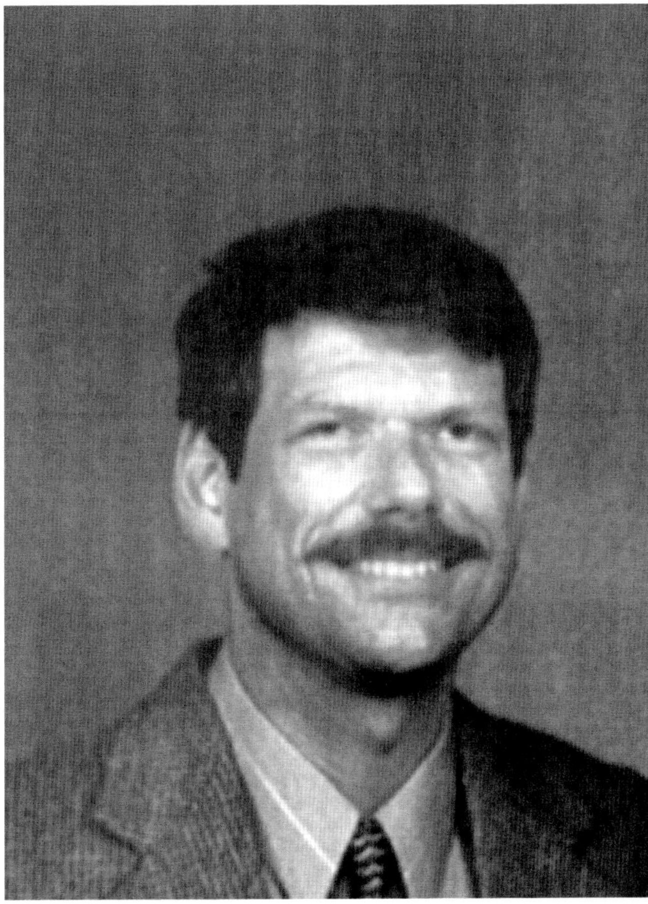

Philip Hardison
After graduating from Fillmore High School, Philip Hardison, the son of Russell and Betty Hardison, attended Cal Poly at San Luis Obispo and earned his degree in architecture. Within hours of the earthquake in 1994, Philip was summoned to assess the damage at Rancho Camulos. He invited his older brother Tom Hardison to go along. Upon arrival, they witnessed firsthand the rescue of Ed Berger, whose bedroom wall had collapsed as a result of the earthquake. Berger suffered complications and never returned to Rancho Camulos. It was Philip's 400 photographs that enabled the Newhalls to rebuild the Piru Mansion after the devastating fire in 1981. Philip Hardison passed away after a long illness in 1995. (Courtesy of Hardison family collection, contributed by Tom Hardison.)

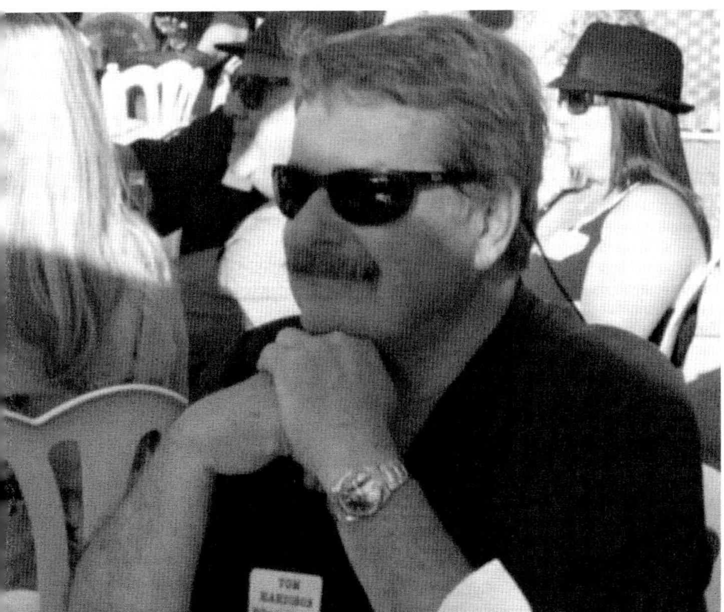

Tom Hardison
Thomas Edward "Tom" Hardison is the son of Russell and Betty Hardison, and he grew up on his family's Sespe area citrus ranch and dairy. He attended Saint Sebastian's School in Santa Paula, Fillmore High School, and the University of Santa Clara. Tom worked with several cooperative citrus-packing associations in Ventura County and Southern Arizona to coordinate their marketing efforts with Sunkist and other marketing organizations. He shared with his brother Philip an avid interest in local history and historical architecture. His sister Geraldine is an educator. (Courtesy of Bob Cox and Tom Hardison.)

CHAPTER FIVE

Authors, Politicians, Sports Figures, and Civic Leaders

There are numerous legendary locals from the community of Fillmore who had an impact through business, civic duties, or volunteer activities. Frank Munoz was the first Hispanic mayor of Fillmore. Many of these notables went about their way helping others or organizing community fundraisers and activities. They came from all walks of life—professionals and nonprofessionals—and worked together. They coached little league or volunteered with the Boy Scouts and Gene Wren's Troop No. 406. Others sewed costumes for high school plays or volunteered as gardeners for the elderly or for their church.

Many have given and continue to give selflessly. Bob Cox takes the photographs at the Fillmore High School alumni dinners each year. Dr. William French and Dr. Donald Musgrave served the community tirelessly for many years, as did Dr. Charles Nelson, the town's veterinarian. Kathi Briggs and Martha Gentry assist the Fillmore Historical Museum with their exhibits, as do many others. Don Burroughs played for the Los Angeles Rams after playing for Fillmore High School and Ventura College, and Kevin Gross graduated from Fillmore High School and played professional baseball as a pitcher for several teams, including the Los Angeles Dodgers. Rick Stewart, a graduate of Fillmore High School, played professional baseball as well. Mary Ann McFadden is a poet who has written several award-winning poetry books, including *Eye of the Blackbird*, and she grew up in Fillmore. Gene Wren volunteered numerous hours for Boy Scouts Troop 406, and his wife, Marie Wren, who owned and managed an insurance business in Fillmore, assisted him with the demands of scouting. Ernie and Becky Morales donated their time to help in community events and fundraisers. Father Ken of the Episcopal Church made a positive impact on the lives of local youths, as did many others.

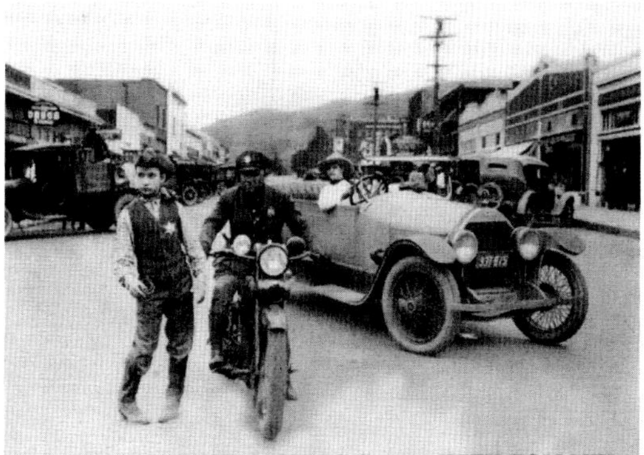

EARL HUME IN THE MOVIES C. 1920 WITH TOM MIX

Chief Hume

Chief Hume was the longest-serving police chief in the United States for a few years, until his retirement. He had his photograph taken with Tom Mix, as seen above, and he and his small police force kept law and order in the community of Fillmore. Everyone knew "the Chief," and he knew everyone else. Keeping law enforcement was a full-time career for him, and he still found the time to keep all the young people on the straight and narrow. If a young adult had a problem, he would telephone the parents and assist them in dealing with it. Sometimes, this meant high school students would be seen washing police cars after school.

Before the cafeteria was built at Sespe School, all children took a lunch. They would eat at the picnic tables under the trees, then rush off to play sports with their friends. Chief Hume's dog Pierre, a gentle and large French poodle, would come on campus to visit the children. He never barked, nor did he frighten the children. (Courtesy of Harold Michel family collection.)

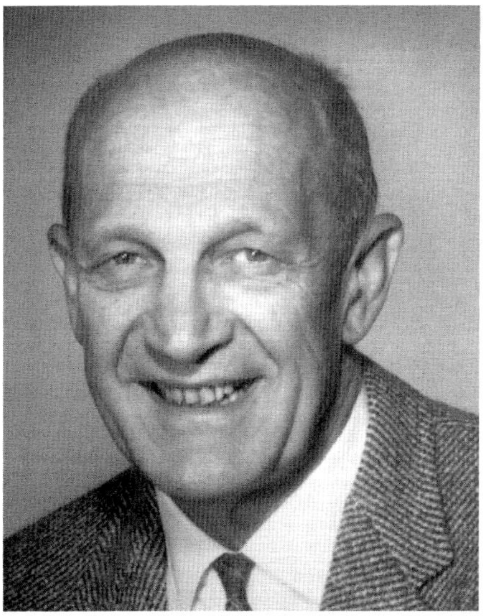

Fred Bryce

Very active in community affairs, Fred Bryce also supported educational activities. He could be seen attending school events with his daughter Shanna. Mrs. Bryce worked for Sunkist Growers, and both remained avid supporters of the business community. Fred served on the city council and was also mayor of Fillmore. Shanna is now a pharmacist, and she returns to Fillmore to support fundraising activities and assist the Fillmore High School alumni association. (Courtesy of Bob Cox family collection.)

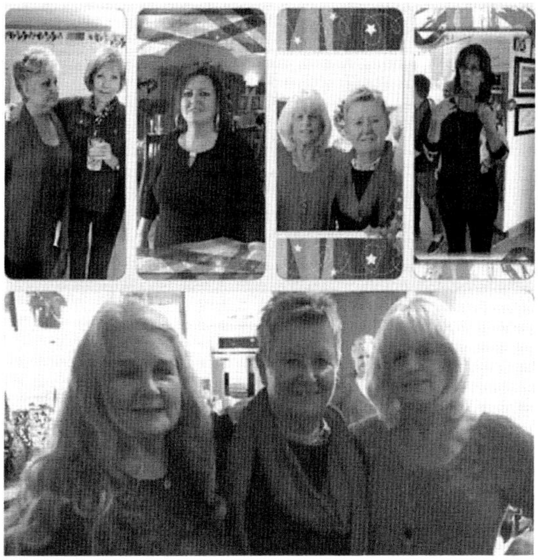

Christmas Lunch

The Fillmore girls still get together and reminisce about growing up in Fillmore. They share births, weddings, marriages, and even divorces. Another pastime is sharing their animal stories, as several are active in animal rescue and assist at the Humane Society of Ventura County. From left to right are (top) Kris Jaynes Hyatt, Jan Beekman Lewis, Jeanie Goforth Allred, Connie Guinn Young, Elizabeth Michel Kemp, and Melissa Mozley Coleman; (bottom) Linda Starnes Faris, Elizabeth Michel Kemp, and Connie Guinn Young. (Author's collection.)

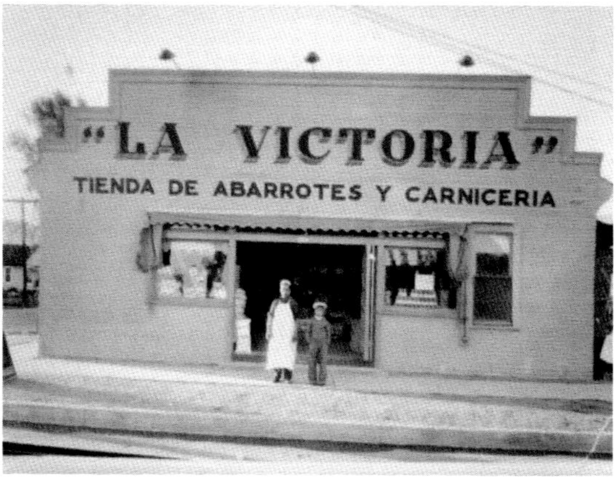

Cipriano Garcia and La Victoria Market
La Victoria Market still stands on the corner of Main Street and Saratoga Street and has been in business for years. It was purchased by Cipriano Garcia, and his family has managed and maintained it. (Courtesy of Kathy Corley Recicar collection.)

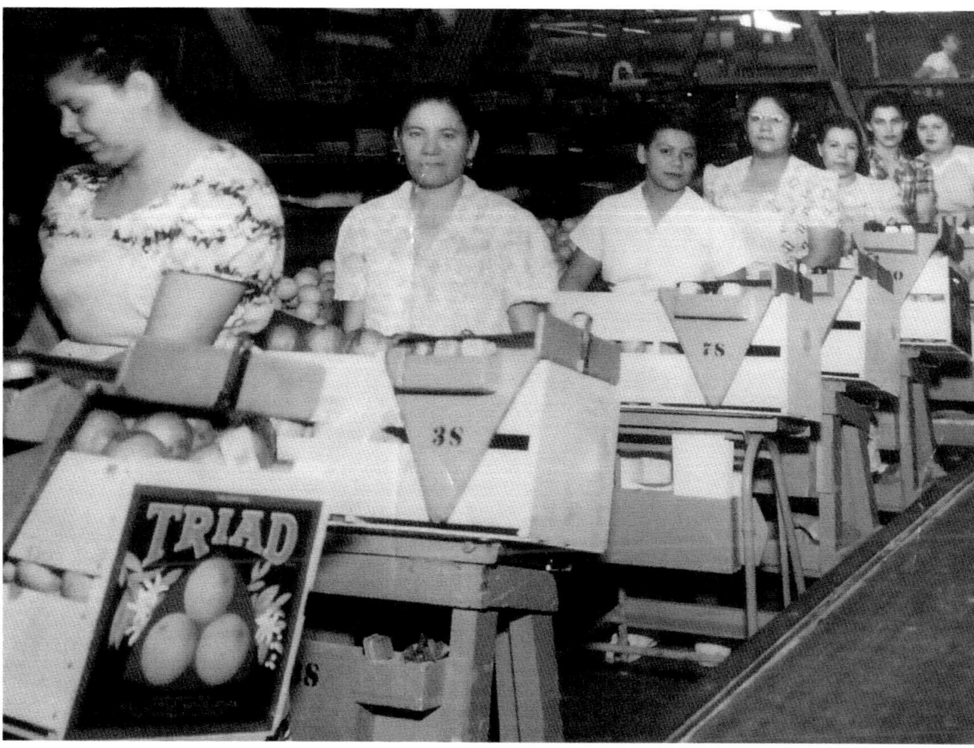

Ladies Working in the Packing House
These ladies are shown working in the packinghouse in Piru, California. From front to back are Alvedi Alverdi, Nickie Lopez, Jessie Ponce, Mrs. Ponce, Maria Alcocer, Mrs. Ortega, and Lucille Ortega. Piru and Fillmore people remember when there were prisoners of war from Germany working at Rancho Sespe picking fruit. Becky Morales remembers seeing them picking the fruit and that they could not speak English.

The POWs from Germany were brought in from the Saticoy area, where they were housed as part of a prisoner of war camp. Many of the boxes of citrus fruit yielded 75–80¢ per box for the ranchers, and the fruit picker/laborer was paid 2¢ per box. Many laborers depended on the company store for purchasing dry goods and cans of food, among other things, and they were allowed to charge what they needed each month, and their bills were paid from their monthly wages. (Courtesy of Lucy Rangel family collection.)

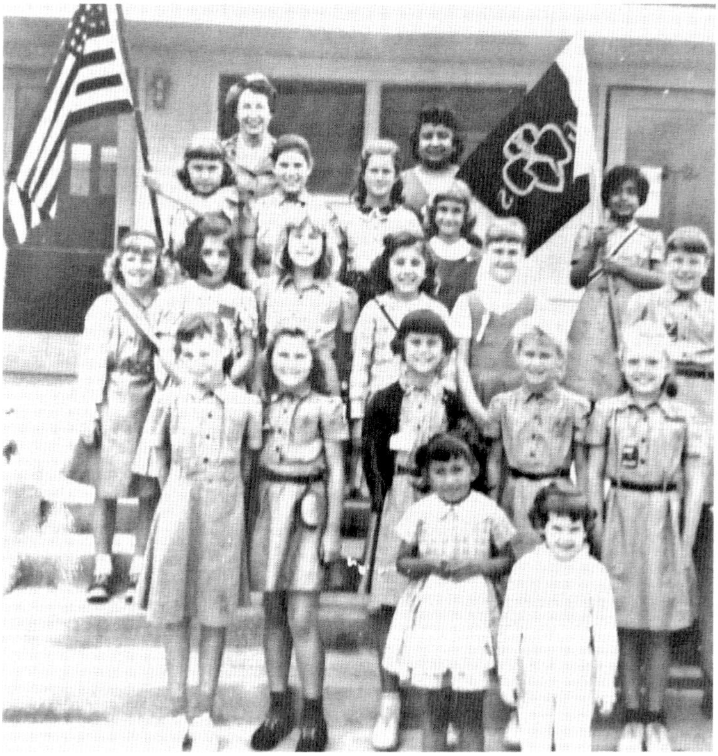

Loretta Crawford

Loretta Crawford came to Fillmore from Oklahoma with her husband, "Bud" Crawford, and they purchased a local furniture store. Crawford's Furniture remained in business for over 15 years. They had two daughters, Valerie and Debbie, and both girls attended Fillmore schools. They became an important part of the community as they supported the chamber of commerce and all of the local festivities and events. Loretta and Bud enjoyed square dancing, and Loretta would be a caller for many of the dances.

Loretta Crawford was the Brownie and Girl Scout leader for many years in Fillmore. Besides having fun at their meetings, the girls in Troop 21 participated in community service projects. October and November were the months the girls prepared for their holiday gift giving. Each year, they made candy-filled gifts for a ward of ladies at Camarillo State Mental Hospital. They also went on campouts together and learned how to cook for a large group and how to work together as a team. Giving and sharing was a big part of their experience—and to this day, many of the girls remember selling Girl Scout cookies and have daughters of their own that are selling them now.

Many of the girls went on to college, and a few entered the teaching profession. Others opened their own business, and still others became nurses.

The girls remained in Brownie Troop 21 until they become Girl Scouts, and Loretta Crawford moved on with the girls and she led them as the troop leader for another five years. Christy Morris owns her own speech and language clinic in San Francisco and is now a grandmother. Linda Starnes Faris attended college and worked in the banking industry. Kristine Jaynes Hyatt still remembers when Brownie Troop 21 took the Christmas goodies to the ladies in the ward at Camarillo State Mental Hospital. In addition to Loretta Crawford, Mrs. Ybarra volunteered her time as well for Troop 21.

Pictured from left to right are (first row) Barbara Ybarra and Debbie Crawford; (second row) Cindy Sweeney, Kristine Jaynes, Debbie Schmidt, Linda Starnes, and Marilyn Headley; (third row) Jan Beall, Wanda Sanders, Gerry Hinckley, Linda Sanders, Christy Morris, and Cheryl Cochran; (fourth row) Susan Hertz, Valerie Crawford, Laurie Legan, Patsy Costa, and Evie Ybarra; (fifth row) Mrs. Loretta Crawford and Mrs. Ybarra. (Courtesy of Linda Starnes Faris family collection.)

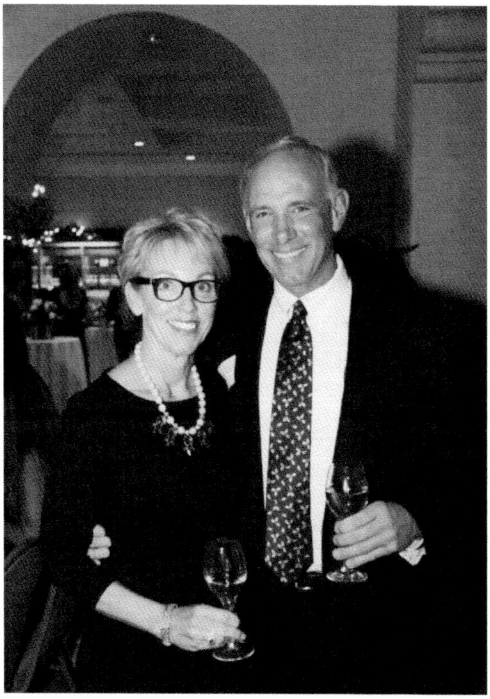

Steve and Shelley Barnard

Steve and Shelley Barnard own Mission Produce. Steve graduated from Fillmore High School and is part of the Barnard ranch family in the community. He and Shelley have developed their knowledge of ranching and marketing in the global marketplace with their successful company. (Courtesy of Steve Barnard collection.)

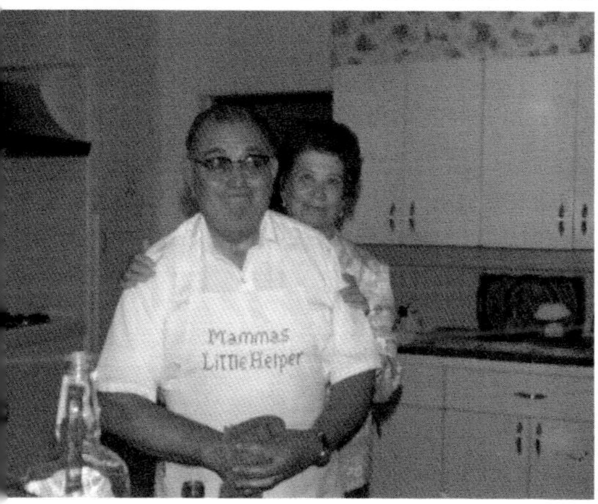

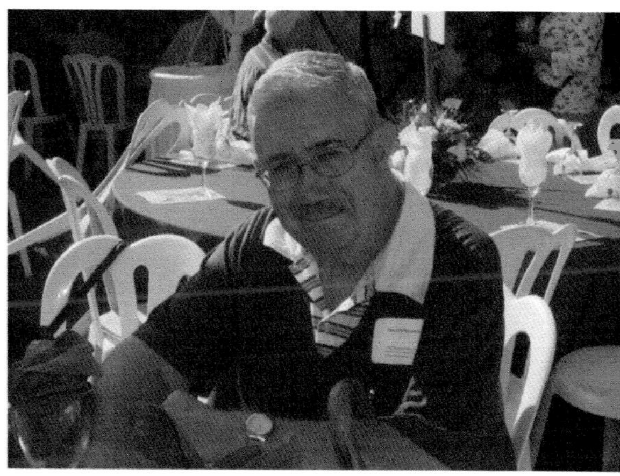

Herky, Enriqueta, and David Villasenor

In 1942, after the arrival of the braceros, Herky Villasenor (pictured in the photograph at left, wearing apron) and his father were approached by the Citrus Association growers while working in their Mexican restaurant and they were asked to prepare and serve meals for the braceros in Fillmore and Piru. They soon closed their restaurant and began a partnership with the citrus industry. Their day began at 2:00 a.m., and they served the workers their meals in the camp's dining hall. Soon, the family began managing the camps not only in Fillmore and Piru, but also in Rancho Sespe, Santa Paula, Somis, Tapo, and Moorpark. Today, the family is only managing the camp in Fillmore. They purchased this camp from the F and P Growers in 1979, and it is located west of the association offices on Sespe Avenue. Today, Herky's son Albert runs the business, serving as many as 150 workers who reside at the camp. Herky's son David Villasenor (pictured right) and his wife, Sharon Horn Villasenor, continue the family tradition of contributing to the community and participating in community events. (Courtesy of Sharon Horn Villasenor family collection.)

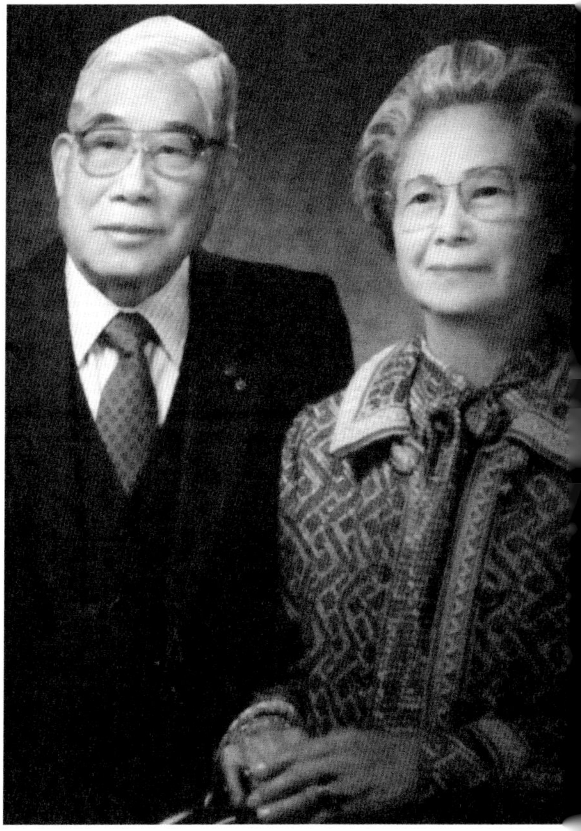

Manuel and Anna Inadomi and Family

When brothers John and Manuel Inadomi arrived in Ventura County, they both started working for the Limoneira Company in Santa Paula, picking fruits such as oranges and lemons. They saved their money and worked together to purchase a grocery store that came up for sale in Fillmore on Main Street. They made a few improvements and opened for business as the Inadomi Market; later, they added department store items and called changed their name to Inadomi Market and Department Store. Their initial market opened at about 1933. Anna Inadomi and Manuel had four children. George was the oldest of the four. (Courtesy of George and Jeanette Inadomi family collection.)

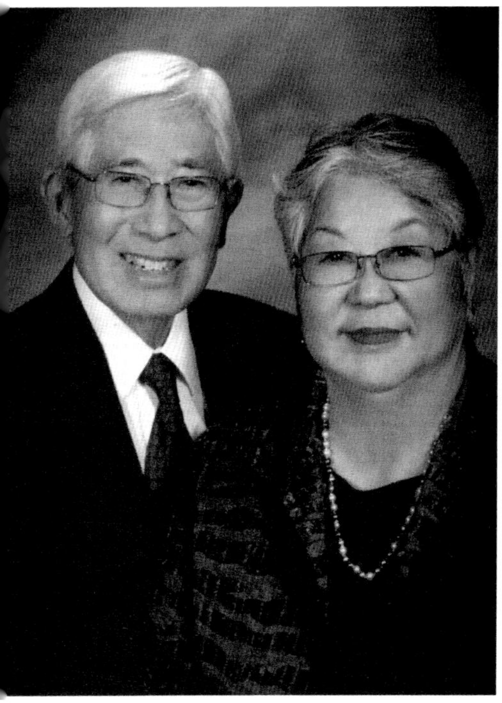

George and Jeanette Inadomi

George Inadomi was present in the family home when the FBI came to pick up his father. It was the early morning of March 19, 1942, that the FBI arrested Manuel K. Inadomi on a presidential warrant as an "enemy alien" and took him from his Oxnard home. Manuel had moved to Oxnard by that time, and he and his family were sound asleep. According to the *Oxnard Courier* of March 19, 1942, Manuel "was lodged in the county jail and charged with being an 'enemy alien.' He was ordered held for the Department of Immigration which is handling all enemy alien cases. He is being held without bail." The newspaper wrote of him in the past tense, "Inadomi for years, owner and operator of the Inadomi Market and allied businesses, was one of the most prominent Japanese residents of Oxnard. He belonged to various civic and social organizations and was a large property owner." The Inadomi families were moved to detention camps in southern California, then to Gila Bend, Arizona. Someone had reported George as a spy to the federal government, and he was wrongly accused of spying for the Japanese along the Pacific coast. (Courtesy of George and Jeanette Inadomi family collection.)

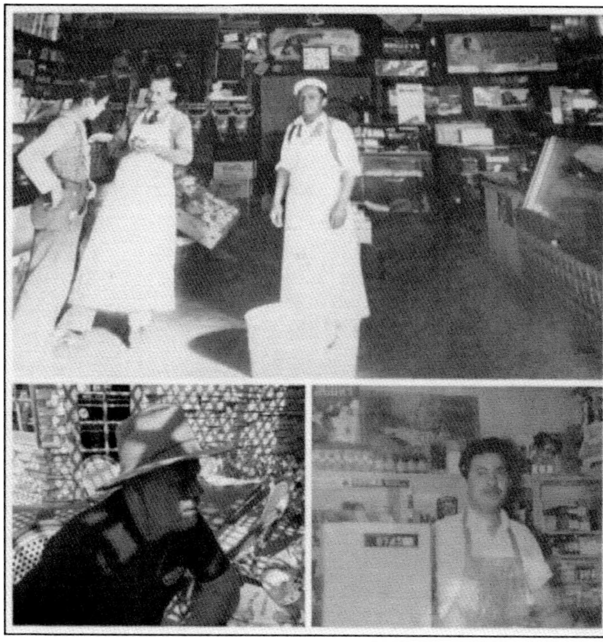

The Inadomi Story and Richard Gonzalez

The Inadomi family owned Jonson's Market on Main Street. John Inadomi remained in Fillmore with his family, while his brother Manuel, also his partner, moved his family to Oxnard to open another store. On a cold February day, assigned military soldiers knocked on the door to the John Inadomi home, escorted them out of the house, and led them to the train station nearby. Richard Gonzalez Sr. recalls seeing them being led away: "It was cold and I saw them walking out of the house. They had on coats and they were carrying a suitcase. They just took them . . . They left everything." Richard had his own store by that time, but he merged them for a few years. The John Inadomi family ended up at the Gila Bend, Arizona internment camp during the war, and the George Inadomi family was taken to Colorado. When the war was over, the Inadomi family returned for a short time so their son could graduate from Fillmore High School and so they could settle their affairs and move. They relocated to the Los Angeles area, where they opened Jonson's Market in Torrance, California. Richard Gonzalez Jr. is pictured in the bottom left panel (wearing hat), and Richard Gonzales Sr. is pictured in the bottom right panel (behind the counter) when he took over the store. (Courtesy of Richard Gonzalez Sr. family collection.)

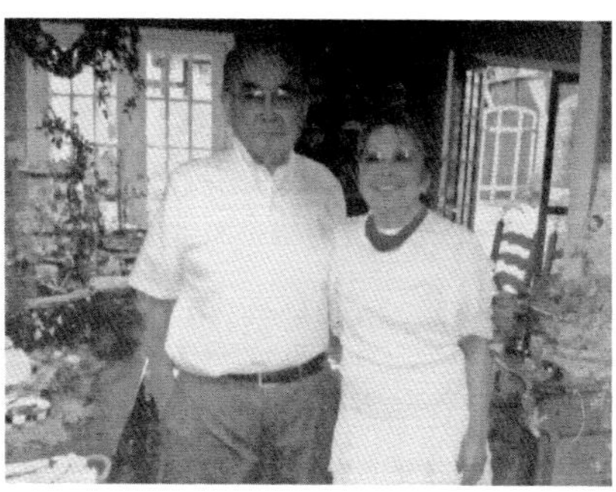

Robert and Iris Teragawa

Iris Inadomi became a successful dress designer. Iris is Manuel and Anna's daughter, and she was very young when the family was taken to the internment camp. Those events did not prevent her from pursuing her passion for designing. The Inadomi family is an inspiration to all who know their story. (Courtesy of Inadomi family collection.)

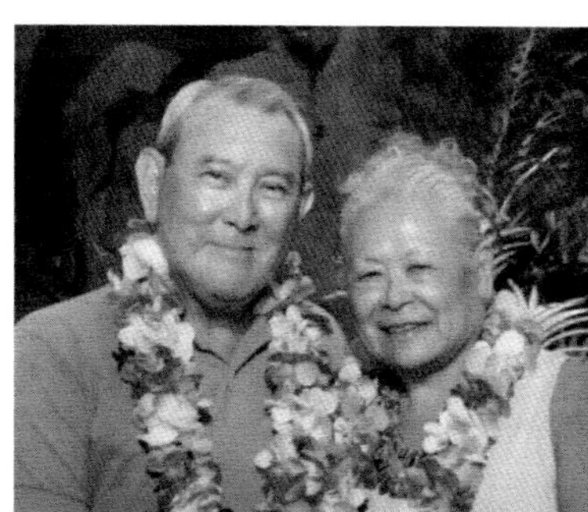

Honorable A. Wallace Tashima and Kiyoyo Tashima

Kiyoyo was a successful opera singer and now enjoys retirement with her husband. They travel throughout the world. The Inadomi family reunion is held each year, and the members of the family have all become successful. They worked hard and strived for success in spite of the disastrous roadblocks imposed by President Roosevelt's executive order. (Courtesy of Inadomi family collection.)

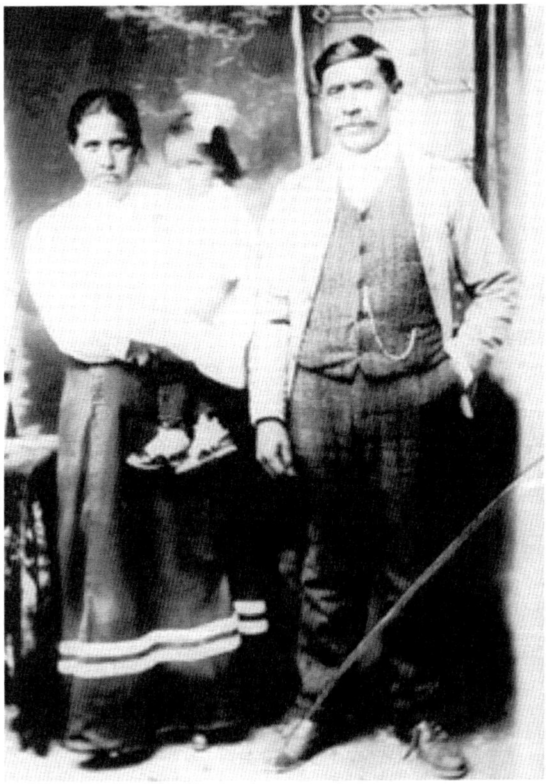

Abundio and Concepción Sánchez

Abundio and Concepción "Concha" Sánchez made their way to California to seek a better life for their family. Silao, Guanajuato, is where they were born. Life was difficult there for the growing Sánchez family, which included Carlos (1895), Dolores (1900), Soledad (1902), Guadalupe (1903), and Arnulfo (1905). Abundio and Concha left Mexico with their children and, after working in the citrus fields picking fruit, moved to Fillmore. Abundio and son Carlos, with the help of Manuel Rivas, built their first house. Carlos also helped his father build their store, Sánchez Brothers Mexican Mercantile. Abundio and Concepción Sánchez were among the first immigrants to own and operate a business in the community of Fillmore.

Later, Jose and Jessie Gonzalez bought the store, and it was named La Mexicana Market, then Richard's Market. The Sánchez Brothers Mexican Mercantile remained in business from 1921 until approximately 1933. The family gave credit to its customers for staples, and this eventually put them out of business because the people could not afford to pay their bills.

As for Abundio and Concha, after they sold the market to Jose and Jessie Gonzalez, Concepción and their children—Carlos, Dolores, Soledad, Guadalupe, Arnulfo, Maria (1906 or 1907), and Refugio (1908)—made tortillas and tamales out of their home and sold them to the neighbors. They went door to door and were successful at this business endeavor. They made the tortillas and packaged them; then, the boys would go and sell them. They earned enough money to put food on the table and to help pay monthly expenses. The large tortilla press they used is now on display at the Smithsonian Institution. One of Abundio's sons, Arnulfo, purchased his own store in Piru, California, in the 1950s, and it has remained in the family. His son Jimmy, along with his wife, Lucy, manage the market. A photograph of Concha Sánchez's children, taken in 1919, is on display at the National Museum of American History and includes Refugio, Soledad, Guadalupe, Arnulfo, and Maria.

Their building no longer stands on the corner of Main and Mountain View Streets. It was deemed unsafe after a recent earthquake. (Courtesy of M. Ramirez family collection.)

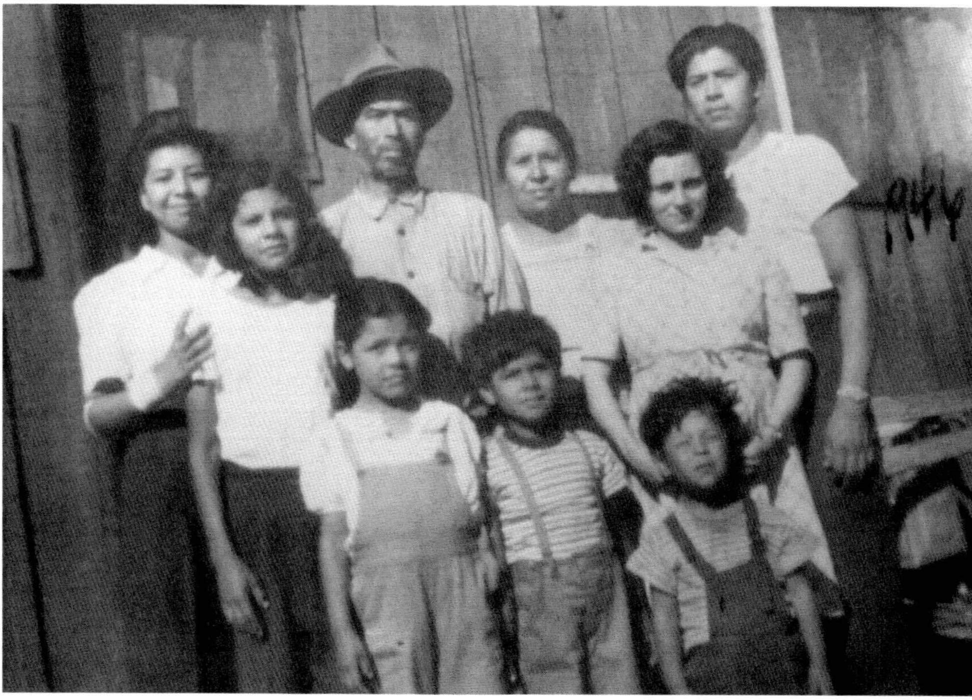

Soledad and Aurelio Ybarra

Soledad Sánchez married Aurelio Ybarra, and they lived on Saratoga Street after saving their money. Aurelio was a farm laborer, and he worked on the Limoneira Ranch in Santa Paula before moving to Fillmore. When the family lived on the Limoneira Ranch, their children attended Olivelands School, and their son Marcelino "Woody" Ybarra had Mary Galvin as his kindergarten teacher. Three decades later, Mary Galvin had Woody and Minnie's daughter Barbara in her last kindergarten class. Mary Galvin retired in Fillmore after more than 35 years of teaching. Her brother John Galvin served as the city attorney for Fillmore for many years.

Pictured in 1946, counterclockwise from far left, are Margaret, Mary Helen, Mary, Louis, Eddie, Paulette, Fidencio, Soledad, and Aurelio (in hat). (Courtesy of M. Ramirez family collection.)

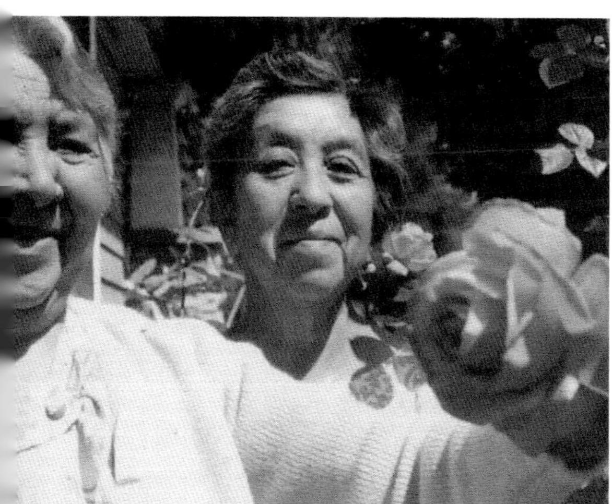

Fillmore Festival Flower Show

It is a tradition in Fillmore to enter the best roses from one's garden into the Fillmore Flower Show. There are numerous awards and prizes in recognition of one's best displays. Soledad and Felipa entered their flowers every year and won prizes and awards. (Courtesy of Diane Galvan family collection.)

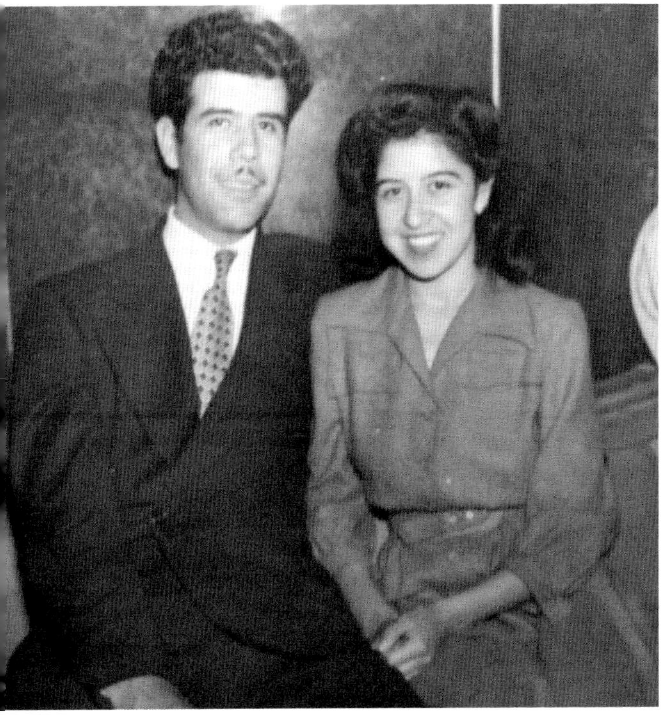

Isabel Ramirez Galvan and Joe Galvan

Isabel and Joe Galvan were a positive element in the community of Fillmore. Joe worked hard and learned English when he arrived in the United States in the late 1930s. He worked as part of the bracero program and found his way to Fillmore, California. When he met Isabel, it was love at first sight. Soon after, they married and had two children, Diane and Albert. Joe was very active in the Lions Club and other civic organizations. Isabel worked as an English-as-a-second-language teacher's assistant and also was very active in the community. She was part of the Business and Professional Women's Club and the Ebell Club. The couple donated much of their time to these organizations and to their church, St. Francis of Assisi Catholic Church. (Courtesy of Diane Galvan family collection.)

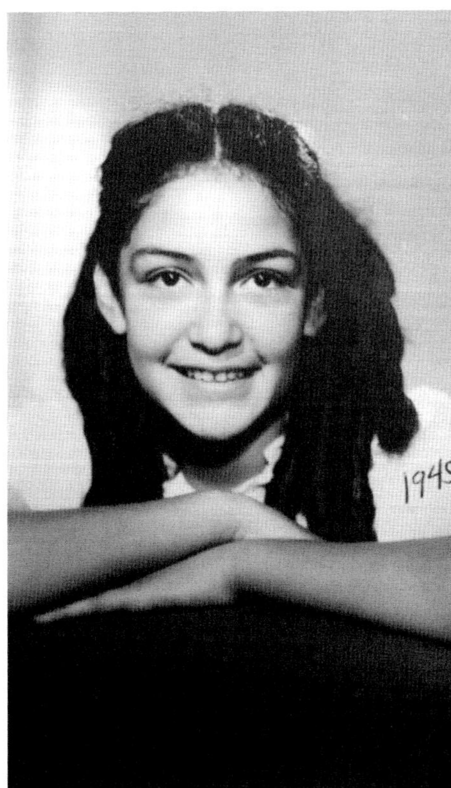

Mary Ellen Ramirez Alvarez

Mary Ellen Ramirez (Isabel's sister) married Charles "Charlie" Alvarez, and they settled in Fillmore. The couple had two children, Kathy and Steven. There is a story Myrna Taylor shares about Mary Ellen and Isabel. A few days after the 1994 Sespe flood of the Los Serenos tract, Walt and Myrna Taylor, like everyone else who lived in the area, were salvaging their belongings. Mary Ellen and Isabel arrived and they were helping them dig their family photographs out of the mud. They took all of the boxes of photographs home and saved as many as they could for the Taylors. Now, Myrna is grateful because she has these photographs to share with her children and grandchildren. (Courtesy of Diane Galvan family collection.)

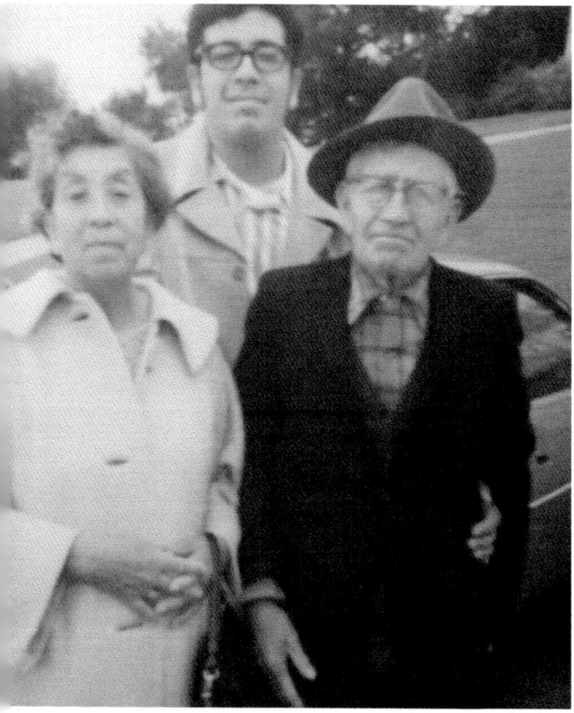

Felipa Ybarra Ramirez, the Late Albert Galvan, and Alberto Ramirez
Diane and Albert Galvan were very close and were always each other's good friend. Diane built a career in the medical field as a phlebotomist, and Albert pursued a professional career as well. They spent much of their time at their grandparents' home in the 1950s and 1960s. Albert Galvan and Jeff Fairbanks, born within hours of each other, became best friends in junior high and high school. After college, they maintained their friendship, and each married. As their families grew, they still made time to visit one another. Albert became ill and passed away; within hours, Jeff lost his life in a tragic car accident—he was returning from watching his son's basketball game near Sacramento. Again, fate stepped in and took them within a few hours of one another. (Courtesy of Diane Galvan.)

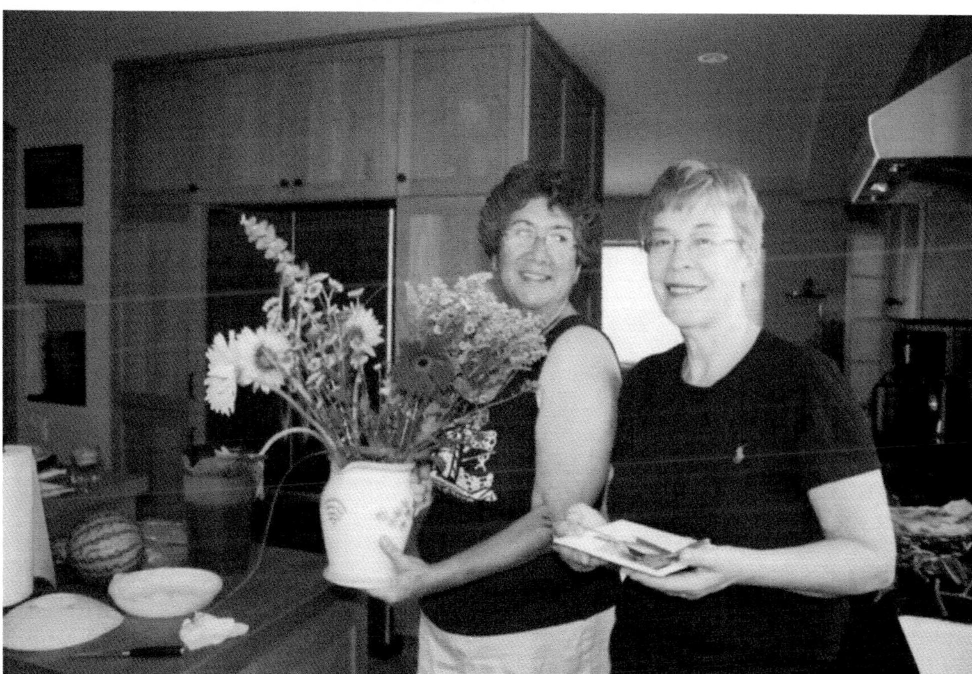

Diane Galvan and Cathy French
Diane and Cathy have been good friends since they were young girls. Here, they are visiting one another and enjoying cooking dinner together for their husbands and families. Cathy's father was Dr. William French, one of the town's physicians. (Courtesy of Susan French-Arnold family collection.)

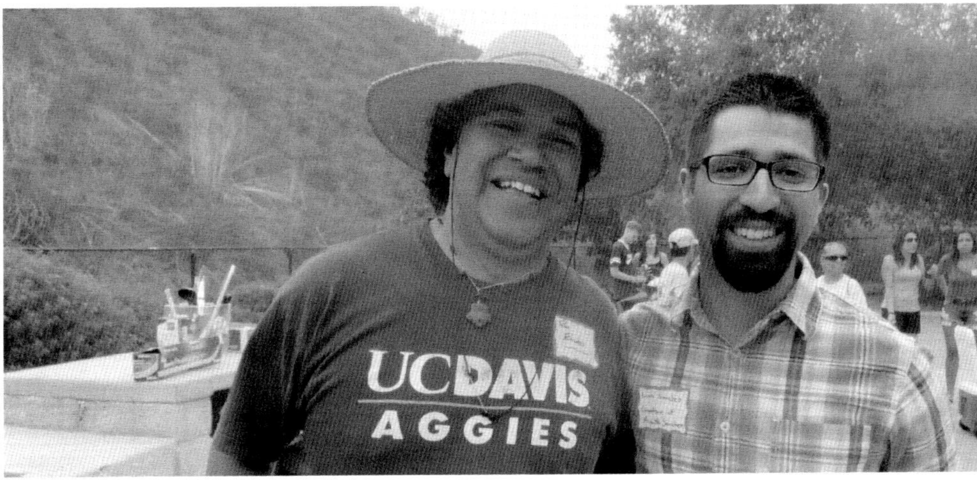

Dr. Richard Ramirez and Dr. Luis Sánchez
Dr. Richard Ramirez (left) attended schools in Fillmore and Ventura, then graduated from the University of California, Davis. He pursued his doctorate in education and today is the director and counselor of transfer studies at American River College. He is married to Debra, and they live in the Sacramento area. Dr. Ramirez is the son of Tommy Ramirez and Mary Ann Ramirez.

Dr. Luis Sánchez (right) is the son of Luis Angel Sánchez and Lori Sánchez and the grandson of Arnulfo Sánchez. He is an assistant professor of sociology at California State University Channel Islands (CSUCI). As a student, Luis was selected as the university's homecoming king, becoming the first-ever Latino to receive that recognition. In addition, he teaches courses at the school in social statistics, research methods, and demography (population studies). (Author's collection.)

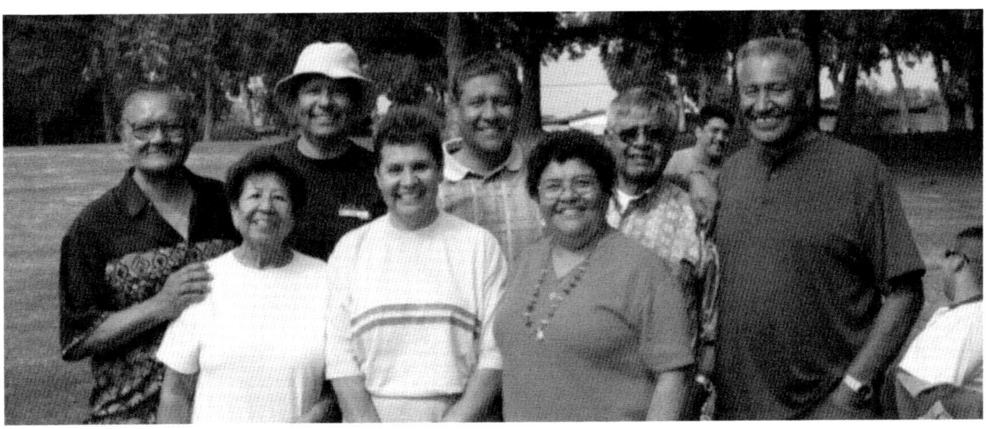

Ybarra Descendants at Family Reunion
Pictured here are more descendants from the Ybarra family. Ed Ybarra is the youngest child of Aurelio and Soledad Sánchez Ybarra. He and his brother Louis played little league in Fillmore and were active in sports throughout high school. Mary Helen Monahan Ybarra pursued a career in graphic design and computer-assisted drafting as well. Lupe Ybarra and Mary Ann Ramirez Ybarra also continued their educations after graduation from Fillmore High School. They enjoy getting together and reminiscing about growing up in Fillmore. All have children, and they are in various parts of the country pursuing their professional careers. Pictured from left to right are (first row) Margaret, Mary Helen, and Mary; (second row) Lupe, Louis ("Kito"), Eddie, Woody, and Tony Ybarra. Vincent Ramirez, Mary's son, is in the background. (Courtesy of Laura Monahan Dickinson.)

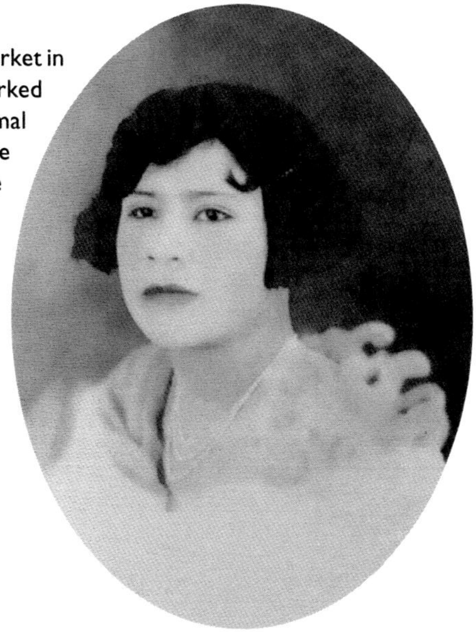

Jessie Gonzalez

Richard Gonzalez Jr. owned and managed La Mexicana Market in the 1980s and 1990s. Richard recalls how his parents worked hard to keep the market open and functioning at optimal levels. After his father passed away, his mother, Jessie Gonzalez, managed the store, and Irene Sánchez, Charlie Sánchez's youngest daughter, assisted her. (Courtesy of Richard Gonzalez family collection.)

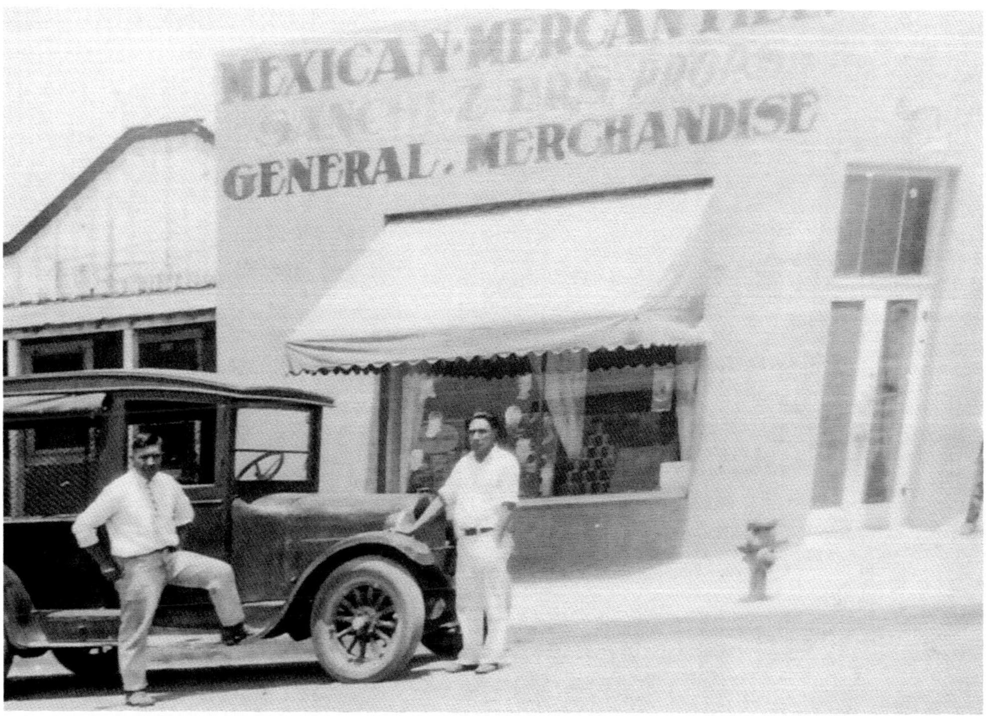

Richard Gonzalez Sr. Shares His Story

The Fillmore Theater was the scene of much activity for moviegoers and film aficionados of all ages. As Richard Gonzalez and Lupe Ybarra both recall, in the days of the 1920s, 1930s, and early 1940s, the theater was segregated. Mexican people sat on the right side, while the Anglo people filled up the rest of the theater. Only Anglos were allowed to sit in the Lodges Area. Richard and Lupe also remember that, in those days, Mexicans could not go downtown after sunset. After the war, things changed in Fillmore, and segregation practices stopped. (Courtesy of Richard Gonzalez family collection.)

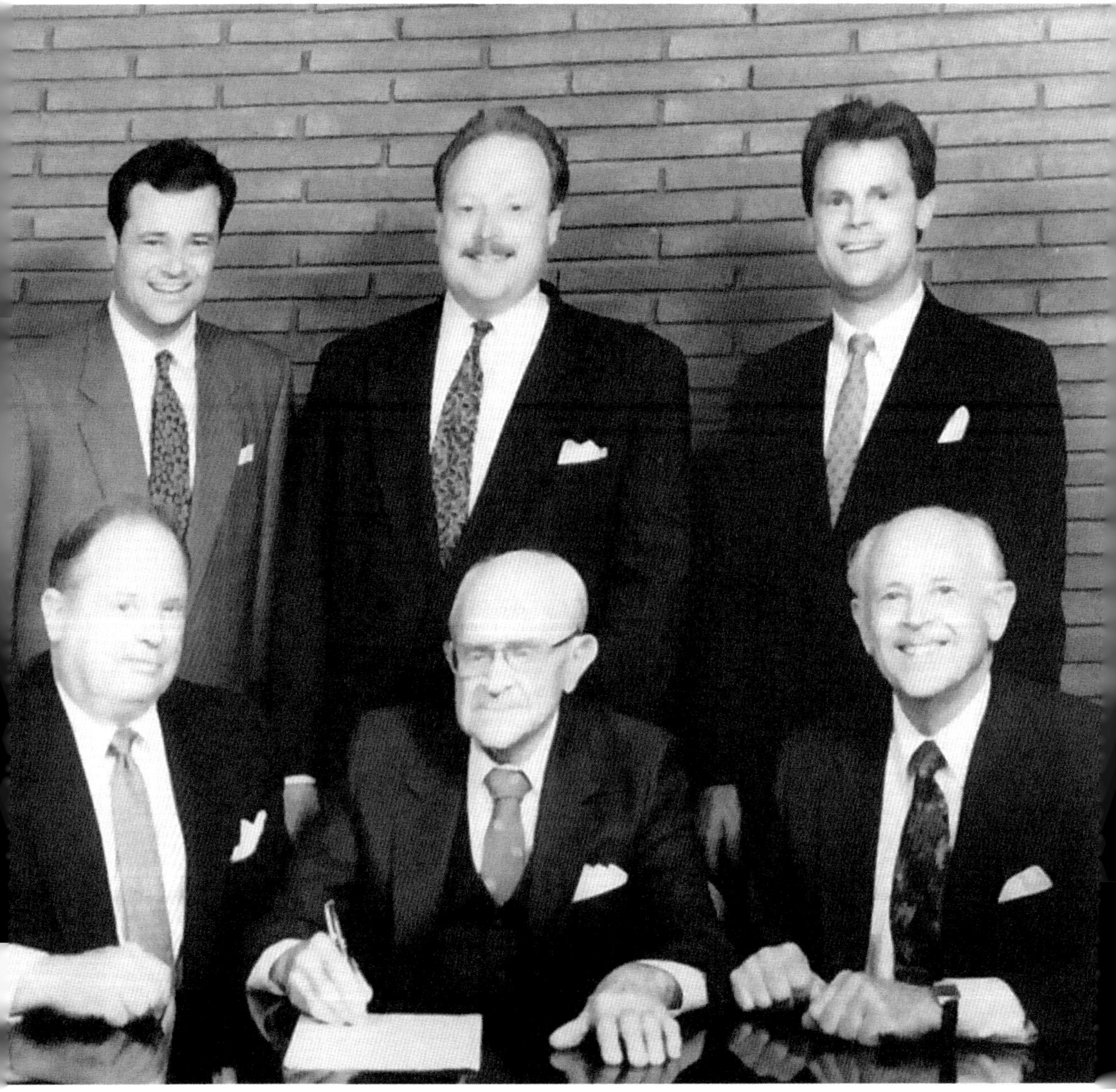

William L. Morris and Sons in Business for Over 100 Years

William L. Morris Chevrolet has been in business in Fillmore since 1914. Many community members purchased their first (and then second and third) cars from William Morris. The community patronizes the dealership because they have been honest and helpful to members of the community. William L. Morris Jr. and Chapman "Chappy" Morris managed the dealership, which is now run by their sons. The dealership celebrated its 100th year in business as part of Fillmore's Centennial celebration. Pictured in front from left to right are Chapman "Chappy" Morris, William L. Morris Sr., and William L. Morris Jr. (Courtesy of William L. Morris family collection.)

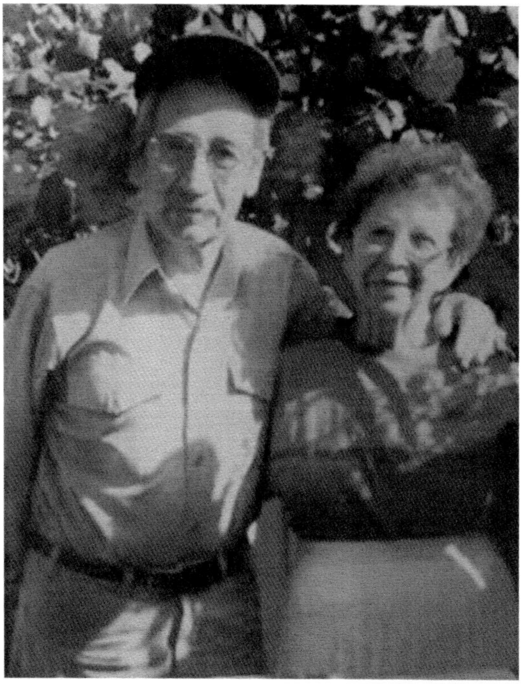

Angel and Esperanza (Hope) Carrera
Angel and Esperanza Carrera had two children, Olivia and Angel Jr. Both attended Fillmore schools. Angel and Esperanza both worked for the William Shiells and William L. Morris families, respectively. Esperanza, or "Hope," as she was called by her friends, saved Chappy Morris's life when he was an infant by rushing into his room when the house was on fire. She snatched him out of his crib and carried him outside. The Morris family was forever grateful to her for her bravery. Angel tended the gardens in the Shiellses' home and killed all the snakes near the house. He was given his own parcel of land by the Shiells family where he could grow citrus trees. (Courtesy of Olivia Carrera Lopez family collection.)

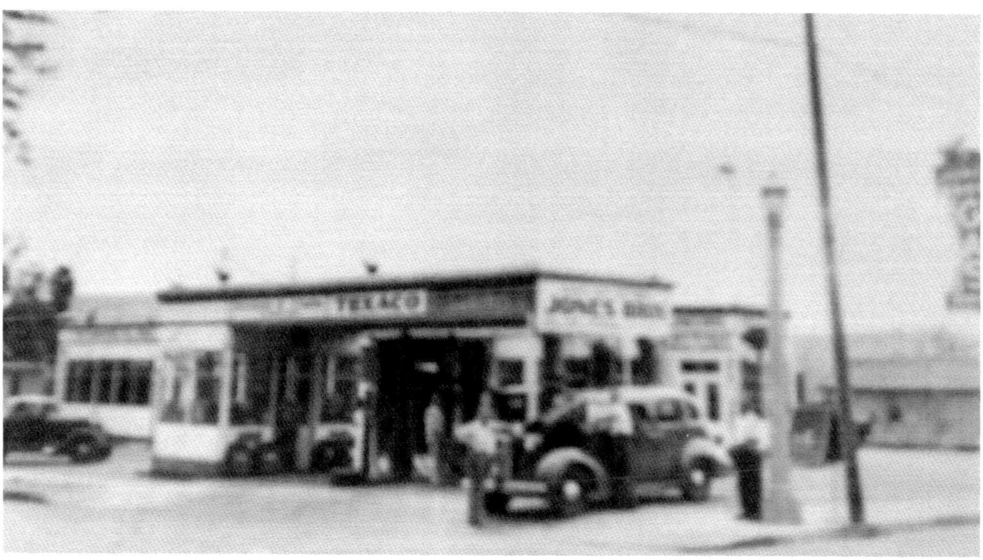

Otto Jones and the Texaco Station
Otto Jones opened his business as Jones Brothers, then changed it to Jones Brothers and Sons. He and his wife owned the Texaco gas station in town. During the wee hours of morning after the St. Francis Dam disaster, Otto decided he had to open his gas station because people needed to drive places and get around during after the disaster. He and his expectant wife were safe, so he went downtown and opened the station for customers. Mrs. Jones went with him to help fill the cars with gas. She felt well enough to go because their first child was not due for a few more months. Laurabelle and Stanley Jones, Otto's children, grew up in Fillmore and were part of the family business. (Courtesy of Linda Starnes Faris family collection.)

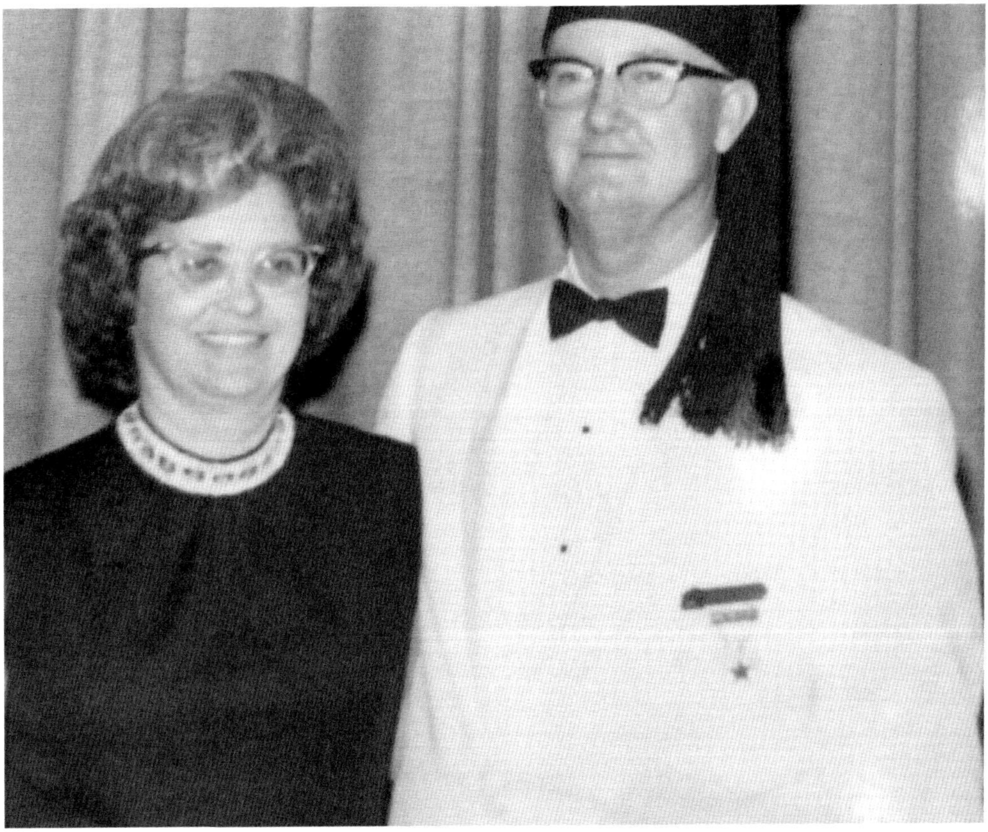

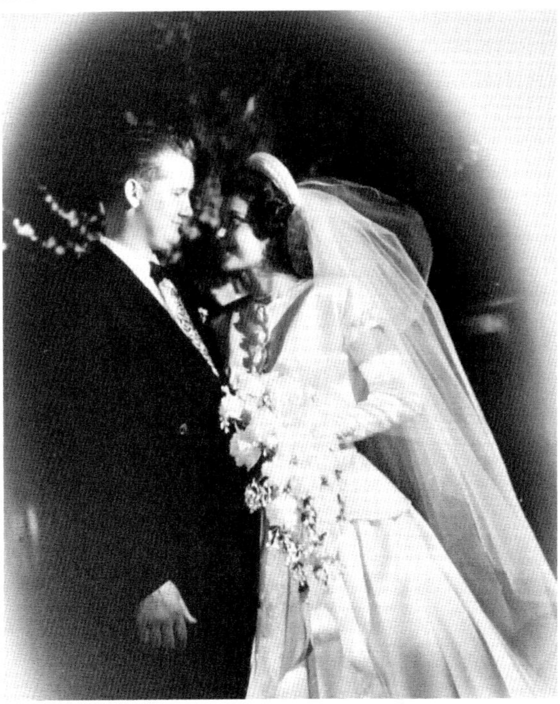

Jack Starnes and Family

Jack Starnes married Laurabelle, and they had two daughters, Linda and Kathy. After graduating from Woodbury College, he and Laurabelle settled in Fillmore, and their daughters attended Fillmore schools. Jack delivered milk for the Sanitary Dairy for about 10 years, then he worked in the family business as part of Jones Bros. and Sons. Jack was active in the Masons, and his daughters were crowned Queen of Jobs Daughters two years apart. The Starneses were very active in the community, and Jack served in various organizations, such as the Lions Club and the Fillmore Chamber of Commerce. (Courtesy of Linda Starnes Faris family collection).

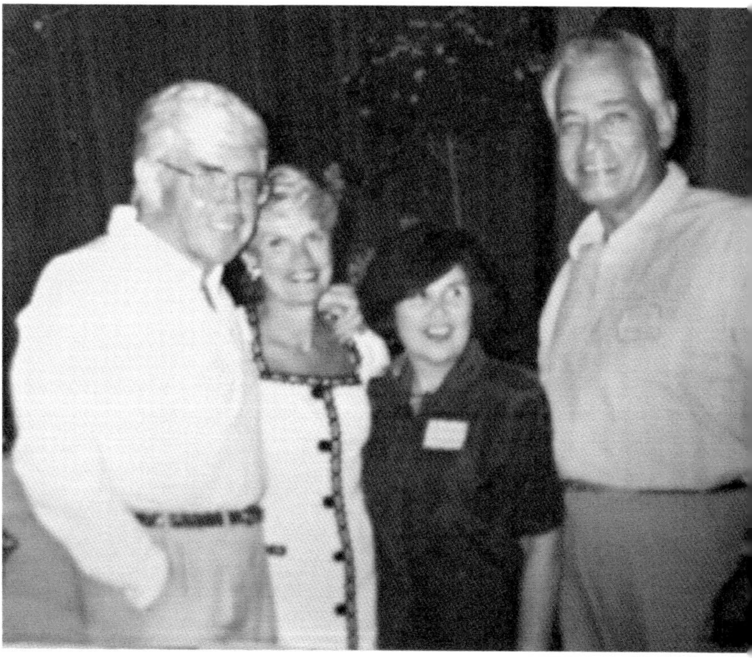

Jack Kemp, Joanna Kemp, Becky Morales, and Ernie Morales

Former secretary of housing and urban development Jack Kemp was visiting his in-laws, Joanne's parents, and he attended a campaign fundraiser with Becky and Ernie Morales. Joanne's father, Donovan Main, was a former superintendent of the Fillmore Unified School District for over 10 years. Ernie Morales and Becky were both active in the Sespe Players, a theater group, and they volunteered their time to many organizations. Ernie is a former mayor of Fillmore. (Courtesy of Ernie and Becky Morales family collection.)

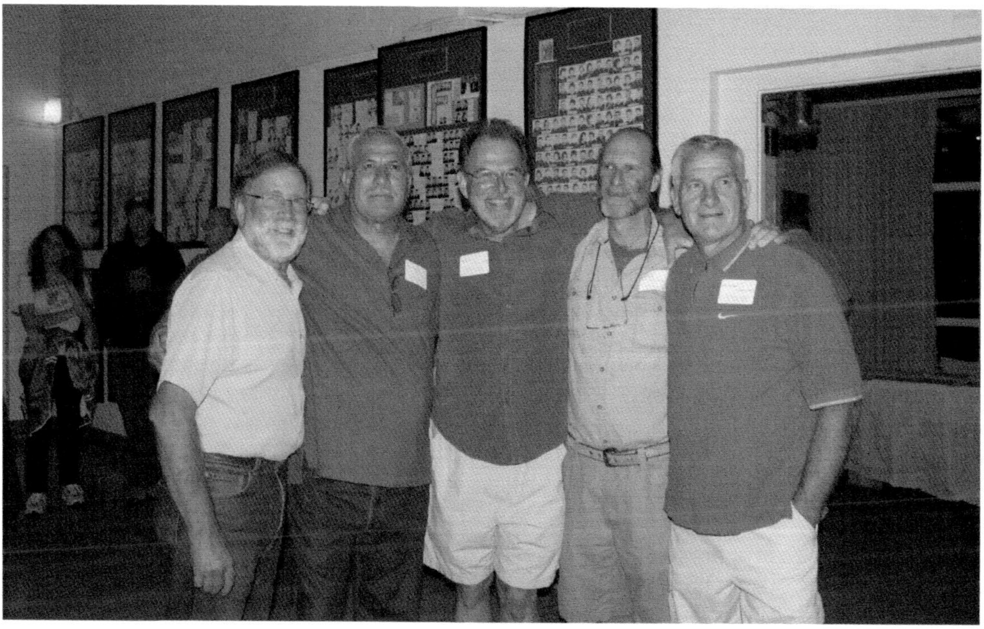

Tom Wilson and Other Fillmore Locals

From left to right, this image shows Ed Epperheimer, Manuel Romero, Ray Hoover, Tom Wilson, and John Romero. Tom Wilson's father, John Wilson, purchased and managed the Ford dealership on the corner of Central Avenue and Highway 126. He was also a rancher of citrus fruits. He instilled a work ethic in his children, all of whom became successful in their own right. Jean Robertson Wilson and John Wilson were the proud parents of Mary Ann McFadden, Bruce and Dorothy Wilson (Leland), Carolyn and Tom Wilson. Bruce Wilson preceded his brother and sister in death, but he is not forgotten. (Courtesy of Bob Cox.)

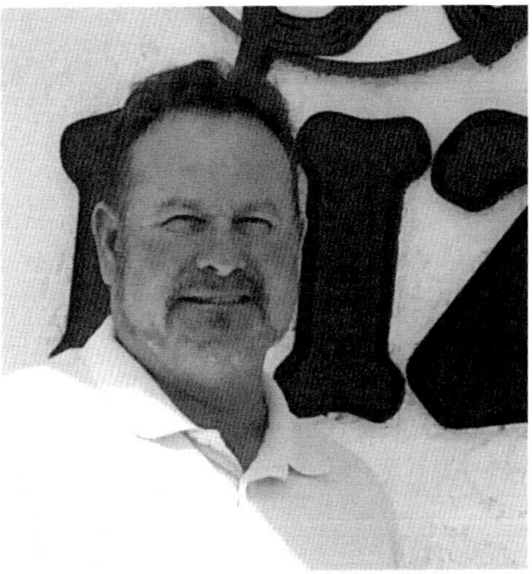

Tom Dann

Tom is the son of Carol and Jerry Dann. Jerry Dann was a principal in Fillmore schools for a number of years, and his wife, Carol, would manage the household and attend to the needs of their children. Tom grew up in Fillmore and Ventura and now owns five Valentino's Pizza Restaurants. (Author's collection.)

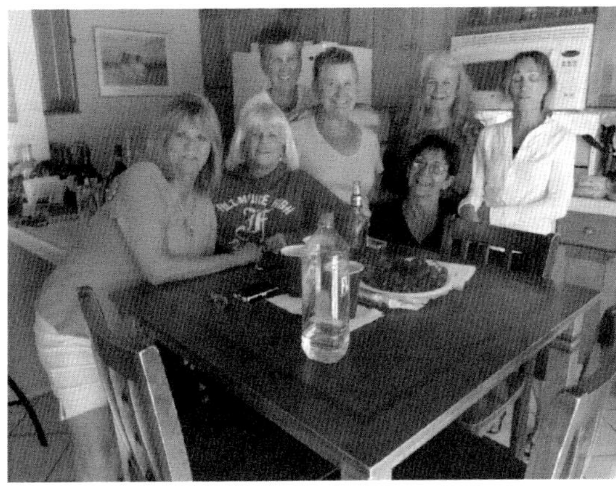

Fillmore Notables Planning the Next Get-Together at the Beach

These women continue the tradition of supporting local projects. Pictured from left to right are Melodie Smith Ramsey, Connie Guinn Young, Shanna Bryce, Elizabeth Michel, Linda Starnes Faris, Terri Amrhine Johnson, and Carolyn Wilson McCabe. (Author's collection.)

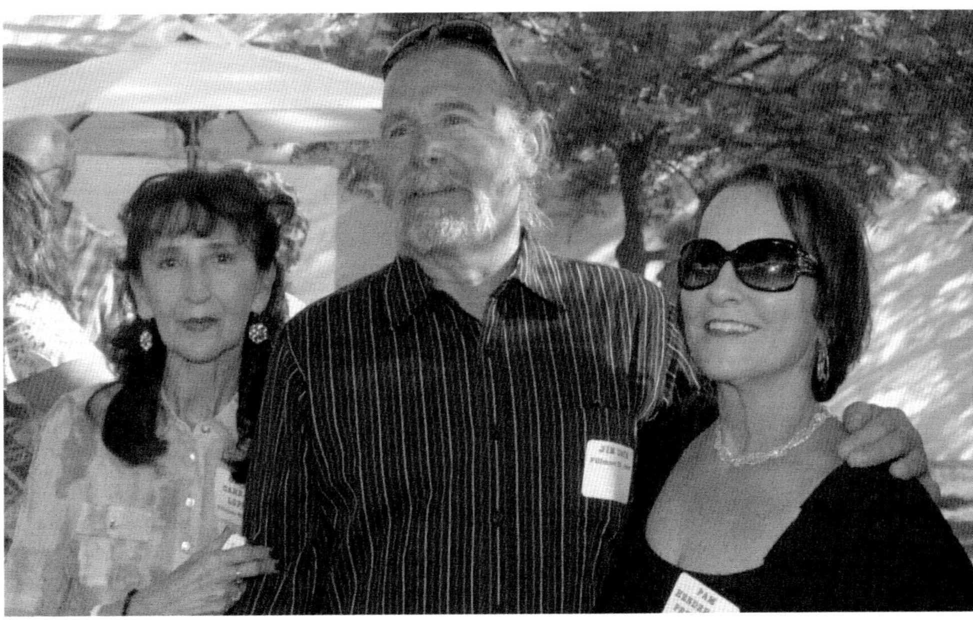

Olivia Carrera, Jim Data, and Pam Henderson Preciado

Olivia Carrera, Jim Data, and Pam Henderson Preciado are pictured at the Fillmore High School reunion. Olivia is the daughter of Angel and Hope Carrera and is working on her family history. Jim supports many community causes, and his parents are longtime residents of Fillmore. Pam assists the Fillmore High School Alumni Association. (Courtesy of Bob Cox.)

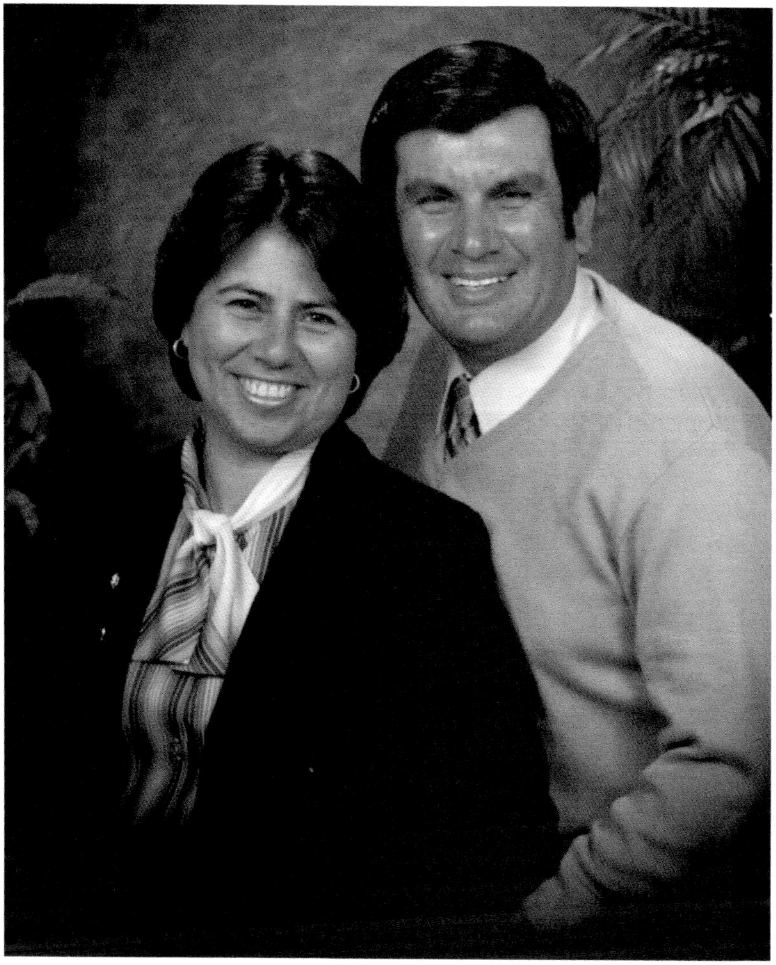

Jimmy and Lucy Rangel
Jimmy Rangel is a fallen firefighter. Lucy Rangel is a well-known figure in the community of Fillmore because she has always championed children's causes and has fostered parent-school relations. Her many years as an educator and parent have placed her in a position to do so. She is a descendant of one of the first families of Rancho Camulos and is currently serving on the Fillmore Unified School District governing board. One of the many causes she champions is that of raising awareness for organ donors. She was married to James "Jim" Rangel, who was a firefighter for 21 years, until his death in 1993. James Rangel is listed on the state and county monuments that honor fallen firefighters. He passed away June 10, 1993, while awaiting a lung transplant.

Together, they had five children. Kristen is teaching kindergarten in Fillmore and graduated from California State University, Northridge. Eric graduated from Humbolt State with a degree in fisheries and now manages a home-based business with his wife, Lisa, with whom he has two sons, Luke and Josh. Third child Jason graduated from California State University, Los Angeles, with a degree in fire administration and is currently the captain of Ventura County Fire Station 27 in Fillmore. Jason and his wife, Melody, have two children, Jacob and Makena. Fourth Rangel child Amy is working as a medical administrator and has one son, James Joseph, who was named after her father. Lastly, Maria Rangel graduated from the University of Nevada, Las Vegas, with a degree in hotel administration. After working in the hotel industry for 16 years, she is now pursuing a career in marketing in Los Angeles. (Courtesy of Lucy Rangel family collection.)

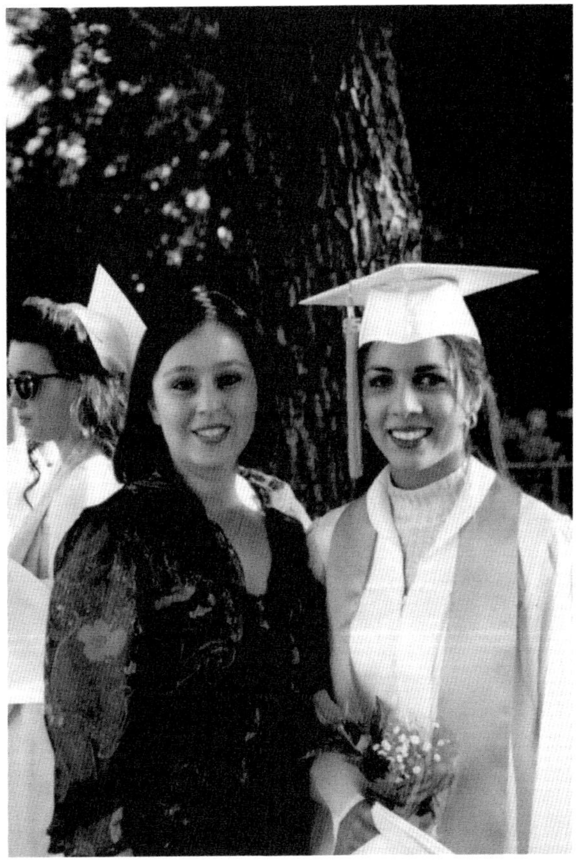

Kristen Rangel and Maria Rangel
Maria (right) went on to compete in various beauty pageants, inspired to highlight the importance of organ donation as her platform. She was crowned Miss Channel Islands and was among 15 finalists in the Miss California USA Pageant. She also was crowned Miss Thousand Oaks, USA, and Miss Jaycee State Fair Queen for Nevada, among many other titles. Kristen (left) has enjoyed teaching in Fillmore, and she is an outstanding and effective at her job. (Courtesy of Lucy Rangel family collection.)

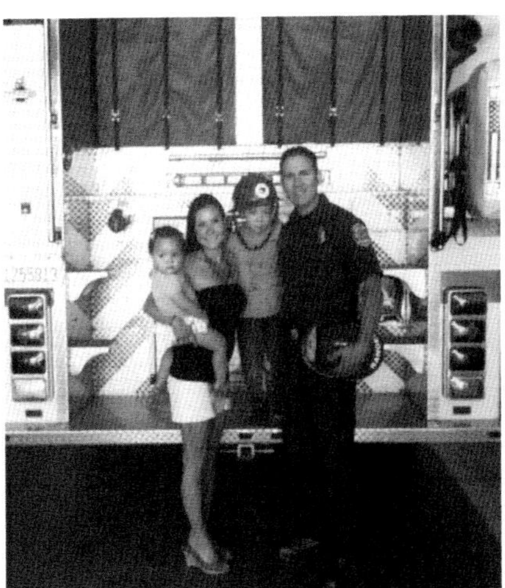

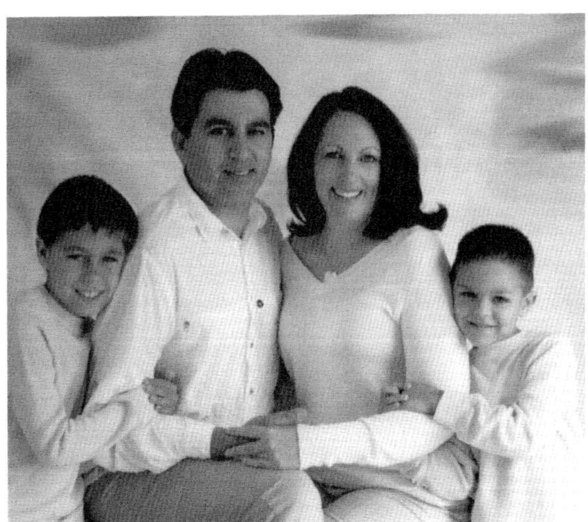

Capt. Jason Rangel and Eric Rangel
Shown at left are Capt. Jason Rangel and his family. Jason has followed in his late father's footsteps, and he serves the Fillmore unincorporated areas. Eric Rangel is pictured above with his wife and children as well. He manages a home-based business. Both attended college and are pursuing their dreams. (Courtesy of Lucy Rangel family collection.)

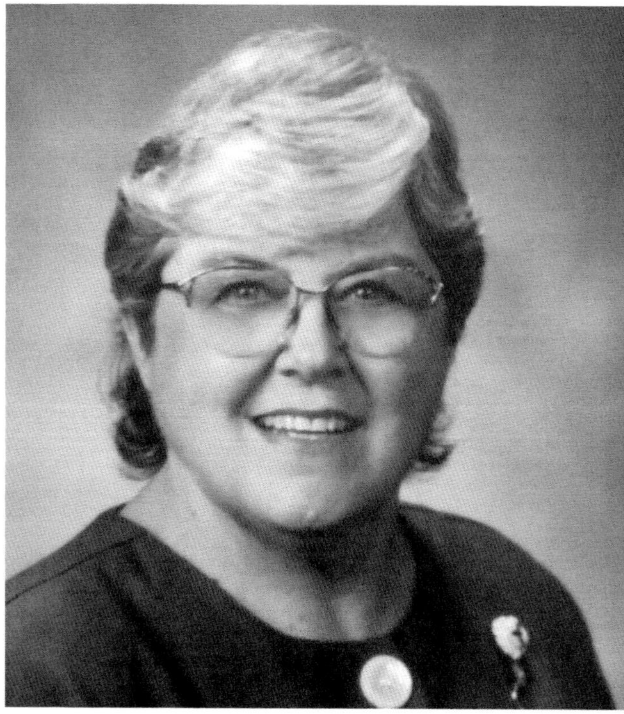

Wren Family

Marie Wren (pictured at right, and fourth from left in the photograph below) was an insurance broker. Gene and Marie had three children, Steven, Kathy, and Jessica. Marie was a businesswoman in her own right from the early 1970s, and Gene Wren was an active scoutmaster for Boy Scout Troop 406. The Boy Scouts had their own scout house at the end of Sespe Avenue, and they would hold their special meetings there and not disturb the neighborhood. Both Marie and Gene gave selflessly to the Boy Scouts for numerous activities and campouts. Pictured below are Jessica, Gene, Steve, Kathy, and Marie. (Courtesy of Marie Wren family collection.)

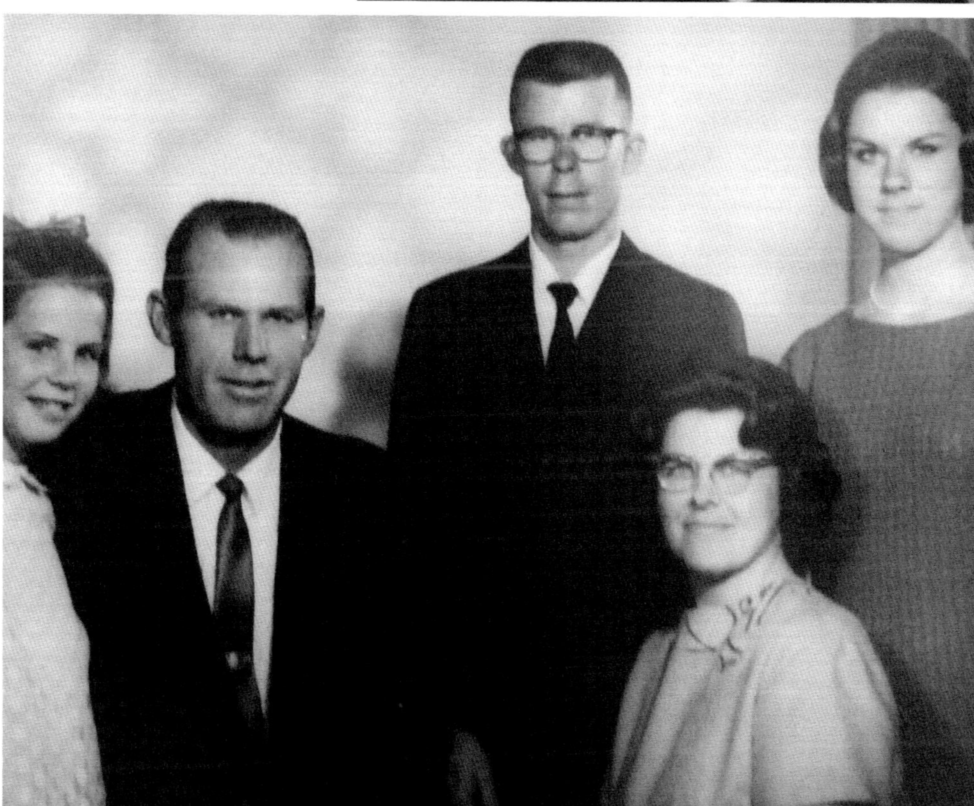

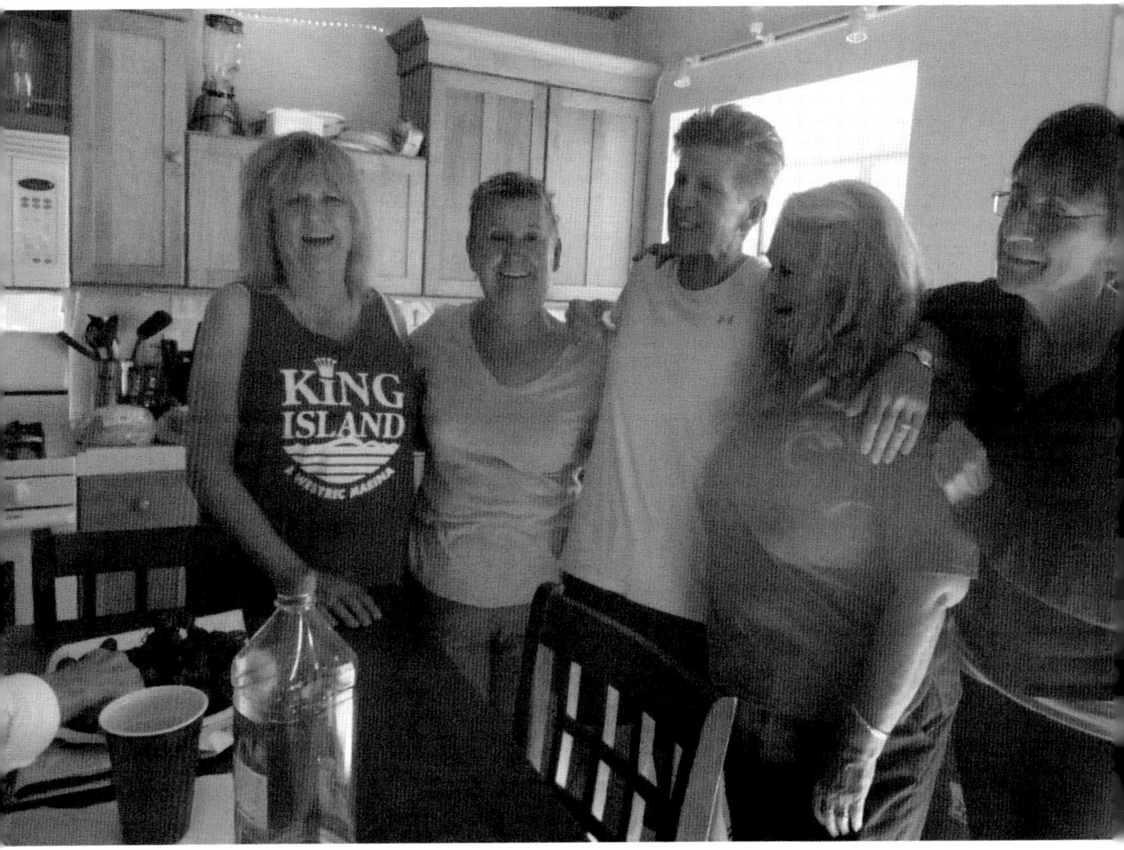

Melodie Smith Ramsey shares her Aunt Nellie's Story
Pictured from left to right are Melodie Smith Ramsey, Elizabeth Michel Kemp, Shanna Bryce, Linda Starnes Faris, and Terri Amrhine Johnson.

Nellie M. Davis, born in 1887, assisted many women when the doctor was not available. She delivered many babies who grew up to become productive citizens of the community. Known as "Mom Davis" of Fillmore, she was Ventura County's 1962 "Mother of the Year" and was honored for having raised five children, all graduates of Fillmore High School. She also operated a maternity home for many years in Fillmore. She was a registered nurse, and in 1962 she estimated that 40 of the 70 persons she brought into the world were still living in Fillmore. Her daughter was Laura Smith Davis, and her sons were Gerald, Burt, and Perry. In 1962, she was still driving around town running errands for the elderly.

Melodie is the daughter of Clair and Laura Smith of Fillmore, and she spent one of her summers on the East Coast with the nondenominational Scripture Union Beach Missions, spreading her message about religion. Melodie plays the guitar, and she attended Whittier College, where she majored in drama. She acquired the skills to run a business from her father, Clair Smith, and her mother, Laura Smith, who owned and managed Smith's Apparel for many years. Melodie's grandparents came to California from Colorado, and her grandfather Carl Smith managed the JC Penney department store in Los Angeles. They moved to Fillmore, and he bought his own store, Smith's Apparel, in 1928. After he passed away in 1950, her grandmother, Bessie Smith, took over. Within a few years, Bessie married Earl Hite, and together they managed the store.

Charles Earl Hite, Melodie's step-grandfather, was honored with the military's third highest honor, the Silver Star, for saving many comrades during World War I. The Department of the Navy thought he was dead for 41 years, and they gave him this honor when they learned he had survived. He was at St. Etienne, France, on October 18, 1919, when he saved his many comrades. (Author's collection.)

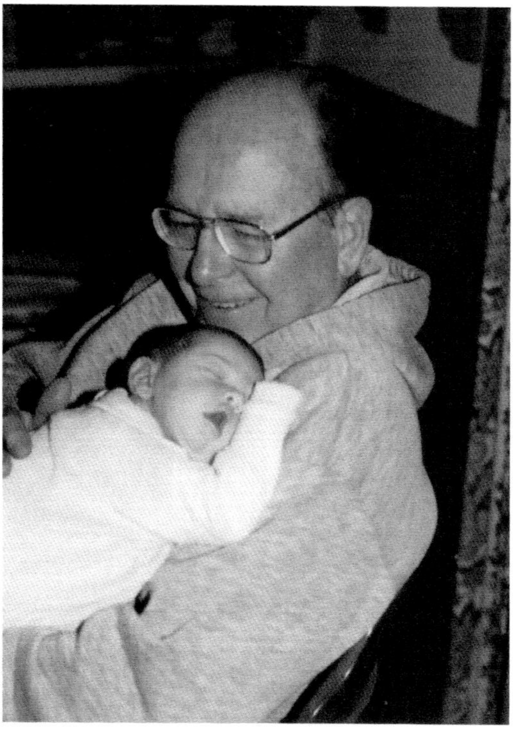

Dr. William French
Dr. William French had a quiet manner about him. He was a family man and very patient. His wife earned her pilot's license and was a nurse by profession. She assisted William in his family-practice office in Fillmore. They had three daughters, Penelope, Cathy, and Susan. (Courtesy of Susan French-Arnold family collection.)

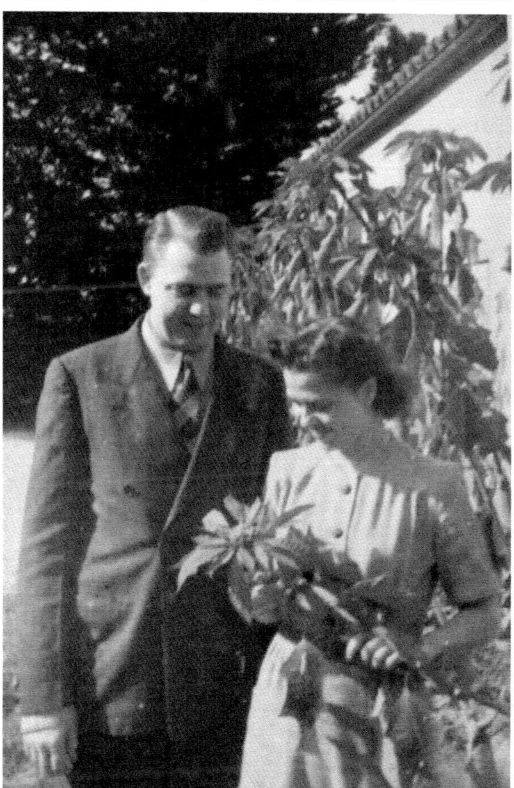

Dr. Don Musgrave and Mrs. Musgrave
Dr. Musgrave was another family-practice physician remembered by so many Fillmore residents. Both he and Dr. French would make house calls in an emergency. Dr. Musgrave and his wife had three children, Ann, Joy, and John. (Courtesy of Joy Musgrave Asenas family collection.)

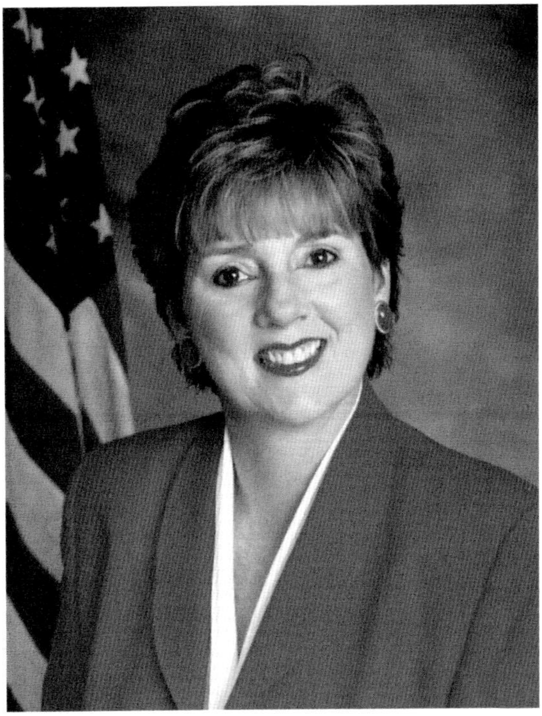

Supervisor Kathy Long

Supervisor Kathy Long attended the centennial celebration. She is a member of the Ventura County Board of Supervisors and represents Fillmore, Bardsdale, and Piru. She is one of eight women supervisors thus far in Ventura County's 142-year history. She has partnered with Fillmore city officials to provide quality services "by expanding seven-day bus service for the Santa Clara River Valley." Additionally, she assisted in developing the Heritage Valley Tourism Bureau. (Courtesy of Supervisor Kathy Long's Office.)

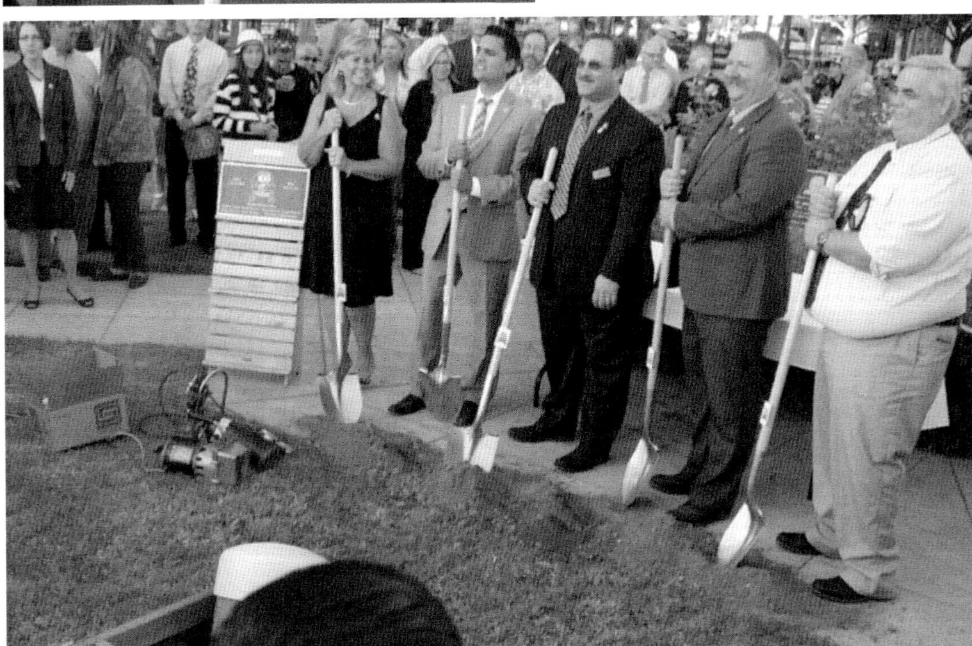

Fillmore City Council

Mayor Minjares is addressing the crowd prior to the burial of the 100-year time capsule. The 100-year celebration took place on July 10, 2014, exactly 100 years after Fillmore was incorporated as a city. From left to right are Diane McCall, Manuel Minjares, Mayor Douglas Tucker, Rick Neal, and Steve Conaway. Carrie Broggie is not pictured. (Courtesy of the *Fillmore Gazette* and publisher Martin Farrell.)

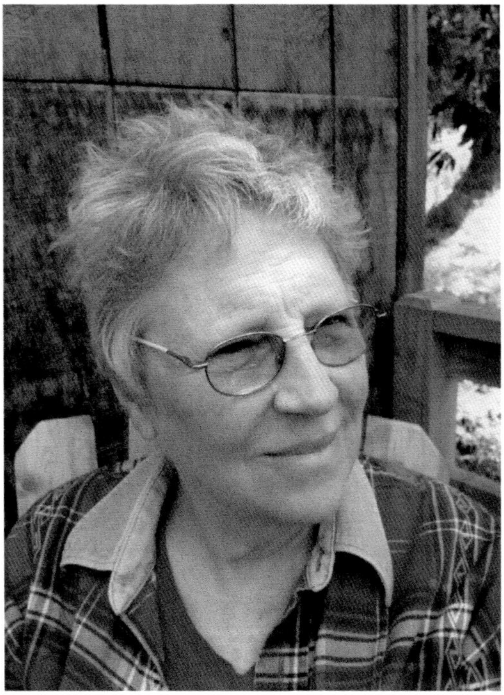

Mary Ann McFadden
Mary Ann is the daughter of Jean Robertson Wilson and also the sister of university chancellor Dorothy Leland.

A poet, she recently returned to the United States after 15 years living in Mexico. McFadden's first book, *Eye of the Blackbird*, won the Four Way Books Intro Prize and was published by Alice James Books in November 2014. McFadden taught at Brooklyn College, CUNY, and ran workshops at the New York City Libraries and at the Biblioteca in San Miguel del Allende, Mexico. In 2010, she was awarded a MacDowell Fellowship. She currently lives in Riverside, California. (Courtesy of Mary Ann McFadden.)

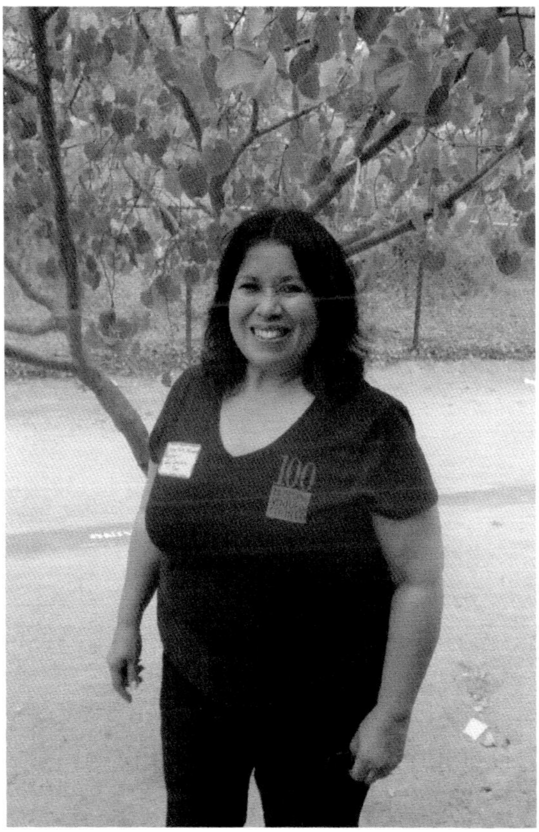

Anna Rios Bermudez
Anna Bermudez is the curator of collections at the Ventura County Museum of History and Art in Ventura, California. She attended Catholic schools in Ventura County and, after receiving her college degree, married and had three children. She and husband Mario have always been supportive of cultural and historical projects that benefit the community. (Author's collection.)

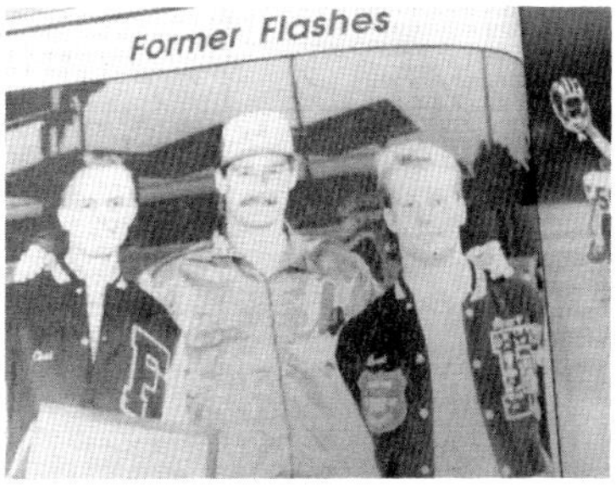

Kevin Gross and Rick Stewart

Kevin Gross (center) played professional baseball for the Los Angeles Dodgers and other teams. Rick Stewart (left) played for the St. Louis Cardinals. Another athlete, Don Burroughs (not pictured) played professional football for the Los Angeles Rams in the 1950s. (Courtesy of the *Fillmore Gazette* and publisher Martin Farrell.)

Gabriel "Booty" Sánchez

Gabriel "Booty" Sánchez was a custodian in the Fillmore schools and was a young father and husband. One summer, he was working with Woody Ybarra and a few others as they cleaned San Cayetano classrooms. Booty went home for lunch and did not return. He became ill and passed away. The community has honored Booty by naming a baseball/softball field after him—the Booty Sánchez Field—and his memory still lives on in Fillmore. His family was recently recognized when Booty was admitted into the Hall of Fame. Booty enjoyed baseball, and he helped organize the first softball teams for girls in the community before his death. Pictured from left to right are Dora Sánchez (mom), Debbie Sánchez and her sons. (Courtesy of the *Fillmore Gazette* and publisher Martin Farrell.)

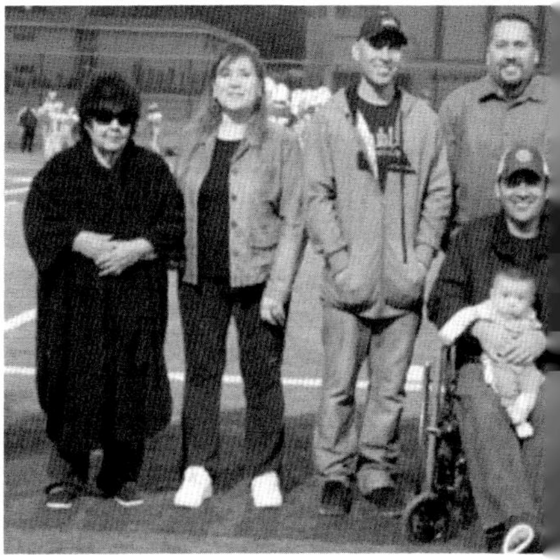

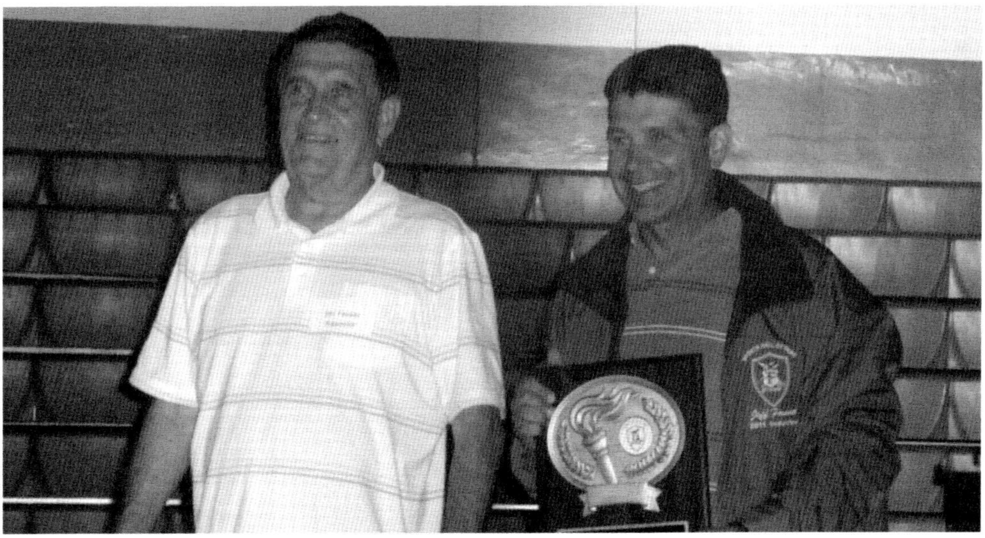

Jim Fauver

Jim and Carmen Fauver moved to Fillmore from Gary, Indiana, in 1964. Superintendent Don Main hired Jim to teach science and to coach the Fillmore Flashes basketball team. Coach Jim Fauver was a very positive force in the Fillmore High School sports program. In addition to teaching science, he also taught driver training, which required a good deal of patience. He had all the qualities to help his students become successful and safe drivers. Carmen worked as the school secretary at San Cayetano School after their children were older. (Courtesy of the *Fillmore Gazette* and publisher Martin Farrell.)

CHAPTER SIX

In the Schoolhouse

The school experience rests on the classroom teacher. Fillmore's schools fostered positive home-school relations, and the lines of communication were always open. Ralph Rees and his printing classes printed the school newspapers, bulletins, announcements, newsletters, and much more. Dick Mosbarger and his Future Farmers of America (FFA) program encouraged students to go into ranching and livestock production. During the 1950s, 1960s, and 1970s, many parent meetings with school officials were not translated, and the Spanish-speaking parents could not understand what was being discussed. It was during the 1970s and 1980s that Minnie Ybarra organized many meetings at Rancho Sespe for the Spanish-speaking parents and school personnel. Minnie Ybarra and her daughter Barbara Leija would translate these meetings for the families. The all-English amendment passed the Fillmore City Council, but after receiving negative publicity and fracturing the community, it was rescinded. John Wilbur, superintendent in the 1970s, worked with the universities to bring in Spanish-speaking teachers. Lucy Rangel was already teaching at Sespe School, but other Latinos were almost nonexistent. The first group of intern teachers was assigned at the elementary schools of San Cayetano and Sespe School. These groundbreaking new teachers were Rosa Romero, Manuela Aguayo, Robert Romero, and Epimenio Torres, who taught at Fillmore Junior High. A year later, Ofelia Romero Motlagh joined the group, as did Barbara Ybarra Leija. There was a blending of cultures; children were taught in English, and if they could not understand, the teacher could translate. Education was rigorous, as evidenced by many who continued to the university level and advanced in their professional careers. It was at San Cayetano School that Woody Ybarra became legendary in his later years. Everyone still remembers Woody the custodian. He assisted all teachers and students alike. The author recalls the pleasure of teaching at San Cayetano School and working with her father. If a child needed special attention, Woody could always be counted on. Dorothy Leland Wilson received her doctorate from Purdue University and is now the chancellor at the University of California, Merced. Dorothy was president of the Science Club when Bill Brisby was the advisor, and they brought in some of the most renowned scientists as part of the speakers' program: Dr. Edward Teller (father of the hydrogen bomb) and Dr. Charles Francis Richter, to name a few. Dr. Richter created the Richter magnitude scale.

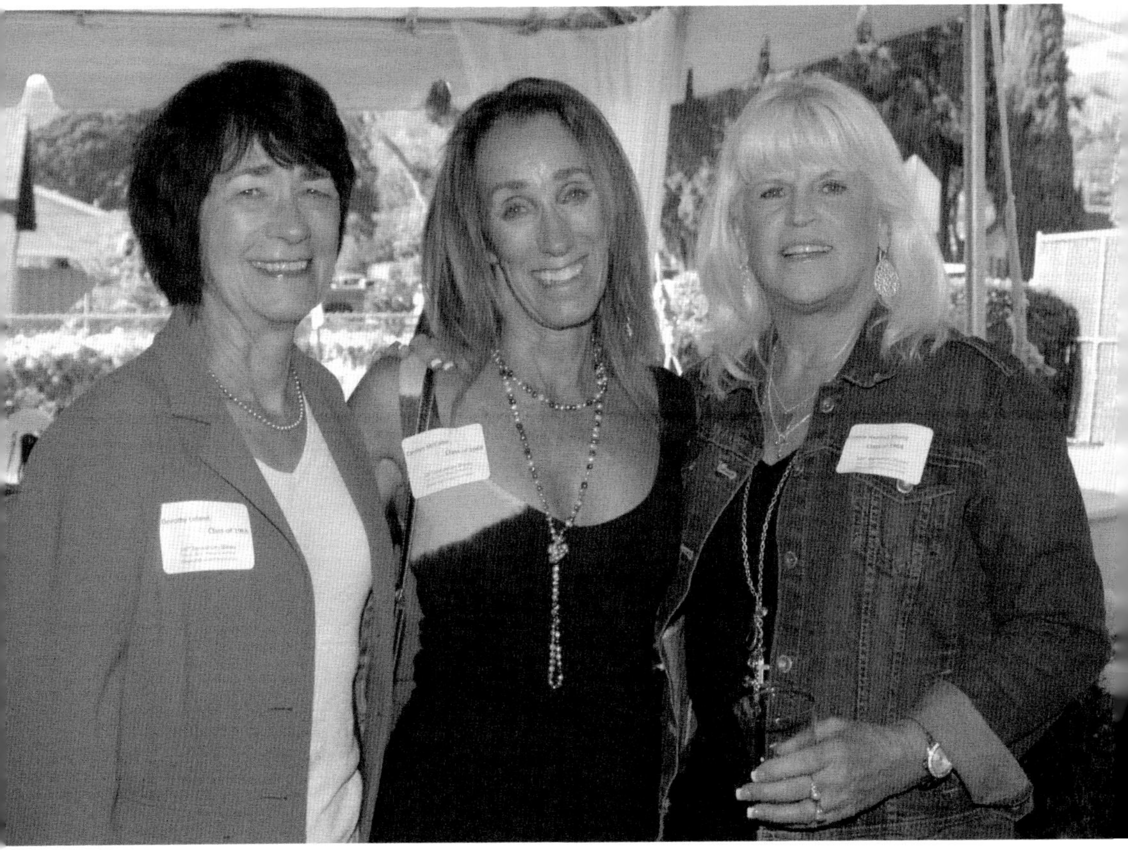

Dr. Dorothy Leland

Dorothy Leland is the third chancellor of the University of California (UC), Merced. An accomplished institution builder and educator, Leland was appointed by the University of California Board of Regents to lead the next major phase of development for the newest UC campus, which opened in 2005. Leland has excelled in higher education for over 30 years, having held senior administrative positions at leading public research universities (Purdue University and Florida Atlantic University). She is the recipient of numerous awards and honors for her leadership and contributions to higher education and communities. She holds a bachelor of arts in English, a master of arts in American studies, and a doctoral degree in philosophy from Purdue University. In 1963, Dr. Leland was president of the Science Club and was responsible for organizing the science fair. Under the direction of famed science teacher William Brisby, Dr. Leland organized the fair and brought Dr. Edward Teller to speak at the awards presentation. Dr. Teller presented all the winners with their awards and medals. Pictured from left to right are Dr. Dorothy Wilson Leland, Carolyn Wilson McCabe, and Connie Guinn Young. (Courtesy of Bob Cox and the Office of the Chancellor, University of California, Merced, and Dr. Dorothy Leland.)

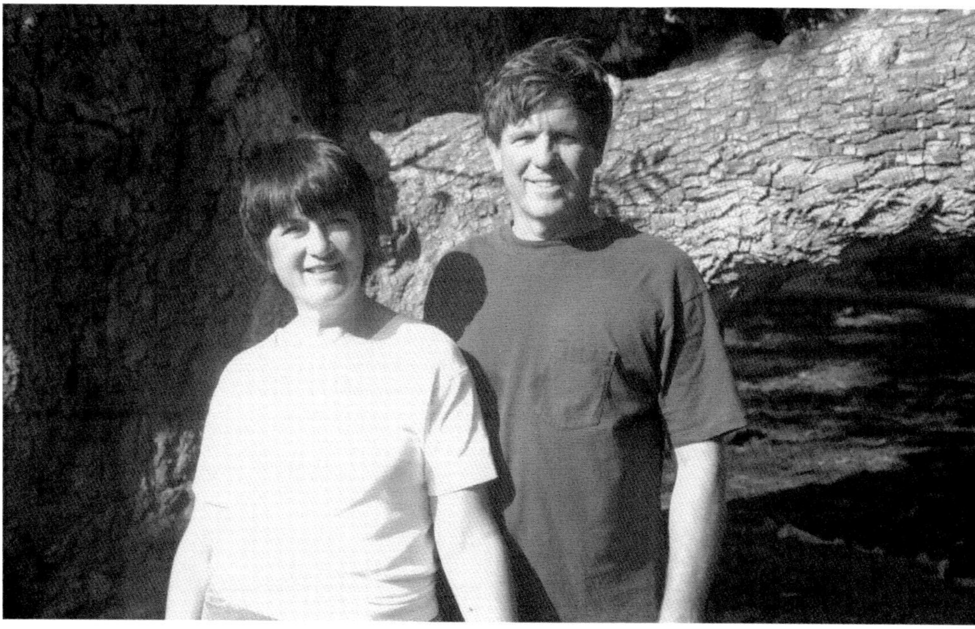

Bob and Diana Cox Find Time to Assist Rancho Camulos Museum as Docents
Diana Nichols Cox is the daughter of Wesley Nichols and Mrs. Nichols. Wesley was the city manager for the City of Fillmore for over 15 years. Bob Cox is the renowned photographer of many events and is the grandson of Ray and Stella Deardorff Fremlin. Both Diana and Bob volunteer in the community and are docents for Rancho Camulos Museum. Marie Wren and many others volunteer their time and energy assisting with all the special projects Rancho Camulos Museum sponsors. (Courtesy of Bob Cox family collection.)

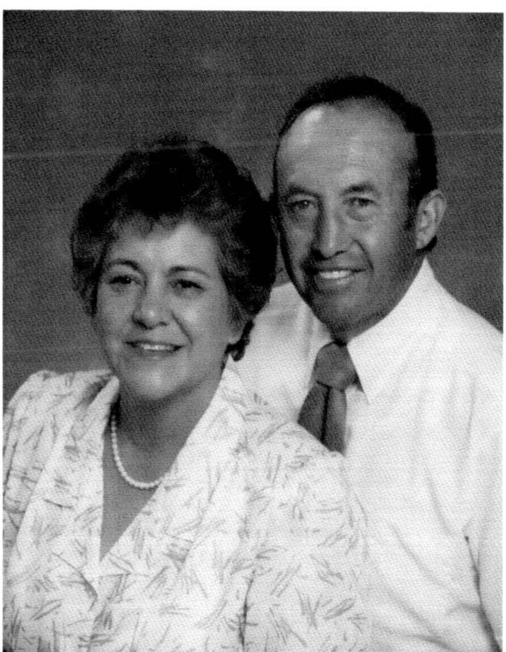

Viola Riesgo Garnica and Louie Garnica
It is a well-known fact that people of color attended Mountain View School and Anglos attended Sespe School, located on Sespe Avenue. When Viola was ready to start kindergarten, she wanted to go to school with her friends at Sespe School. Not wanting to be left out, she went to Sespe School and enrolled herself into kindergarten there so she could be with her friends. She was independent and feisty. After she married Louis Garnica, they had their children and remained in Fillmore, where they lead productive lives. (Courtesy of Louis Garnica family collection.)

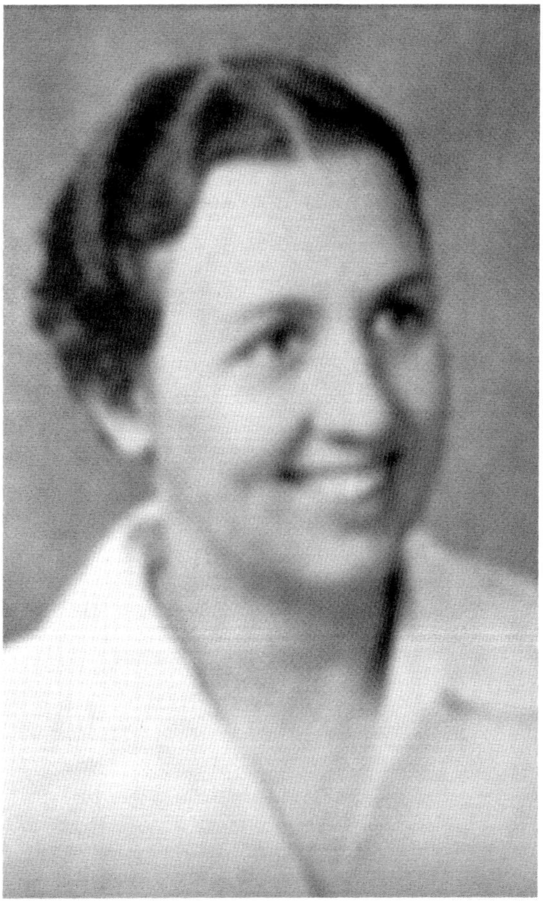

Vera Fremlin and Harry Bigger

Vera Fremlin was a favorite schoolteacher for so many young students in Fillmore Junior High. She had previously taught at high school level. She remained in Fillmore as an educator until her retirement. Harry Bigger (pictured below in the second row, far left) was a famed coach and teacher at Fillmore High School. He coached Woody Ybarra while Woody was a star pitcher on the school's baseball team. In the 1940s, players of Mexican or Latino descent could not seek an opportunity to play professional baseball. According to Harry Bigger, Woody would otherwise have definitely been recruited to play in the major leagues. (Left, courtesy of Kathy Corley Recicar collection; below, courtesy of Ernie Morales family collection.)

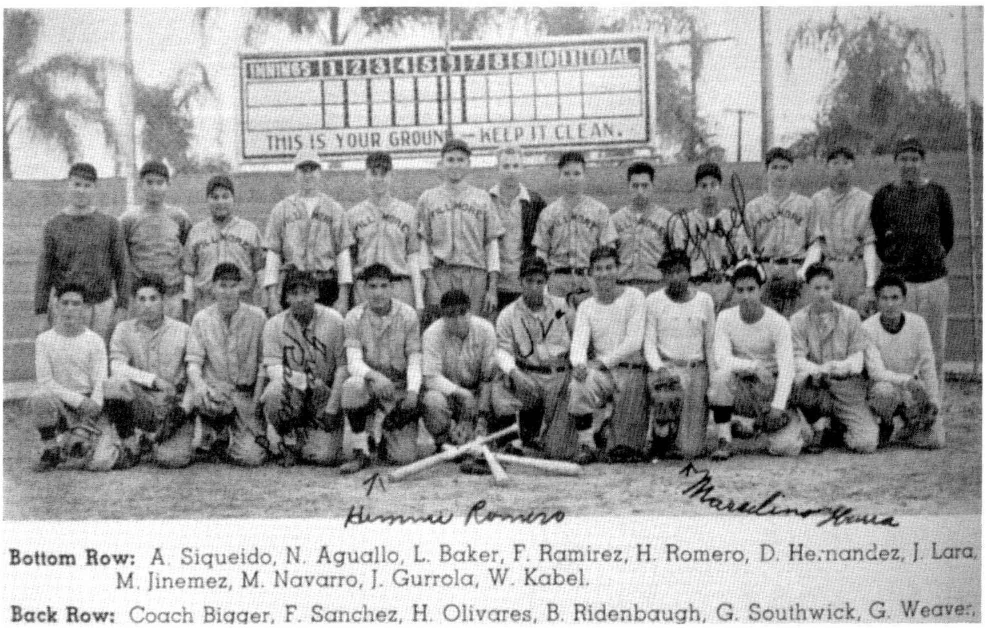

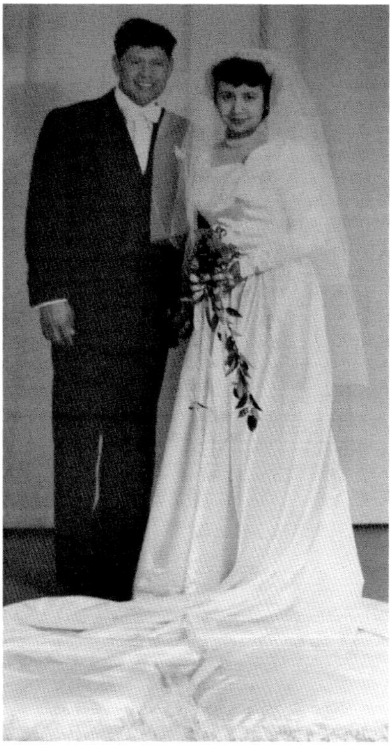

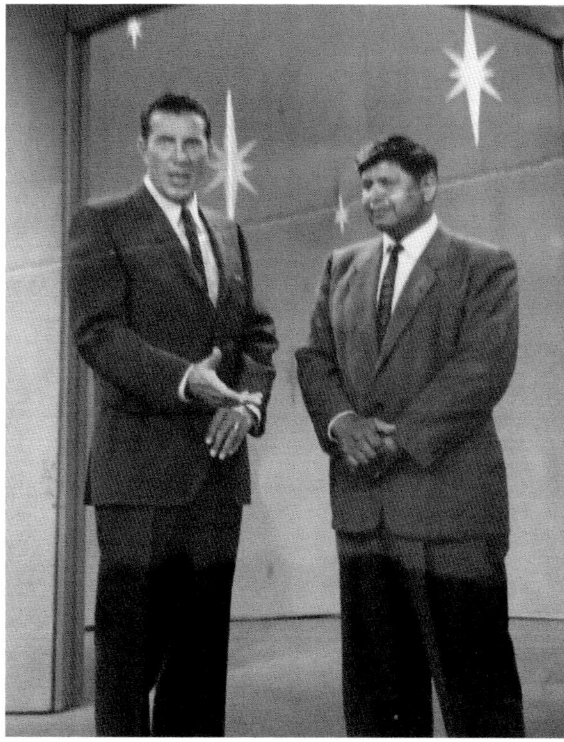

Woody the Custodian

Woody and Minnie Ybarra are pictured at left on their wedding day. At right, Woody is pictured with Bill Leydon, the host of *It Could Be You*. In the 1960s, Glen Philips invited Woody to a baseball game in Los Angeles to see the Yankees play the Los Angeles Dodgers. Glen Philips was a teacher to Woody's sisters and brothers when they attended the junior high school, and he knew the family and understood how much Woody loved the Yankees. Later that night, after Woody returned home, he shared how he had met Mickey Mantle and shaken his hand. Glen had seats right next to the dugout, and the group approached Mickey Mantle and introduced themselves. Woody shared that story with his friends.

Woody would take care of the cafeteria at San Cayetano School, keeping it sanitary and clean. He would raise the flag in the courtyard in the mornings before school started, then he would take the flag down at the end of the day. He was always there to help, and he and fellow custodian Chester Kruse enjoyed their work. Woody would get called to clean a classroom after a child had become ill, and every week he delivered the school supplies each teacher had ordered. He had a kind word for all, and his extraordinary sense of humor was legendary. He had a positive attitude that made others realize that what may have seemed important two minutes before was really not. One day, a teacher approached him about a young boy in her class. The student did not have good shoes, and he needed a few clothes. He had been wearing some hand-me-downs that were too large for him. Woody took the young boy into town and bought him shoes and several pairs of socks. He told his wife, Minnie, and she got the correct sizes for the boy. Together, they were able to help this boy with new jeans, shirts, underwear, and a jacket and sweater. (Both, author's collection.)

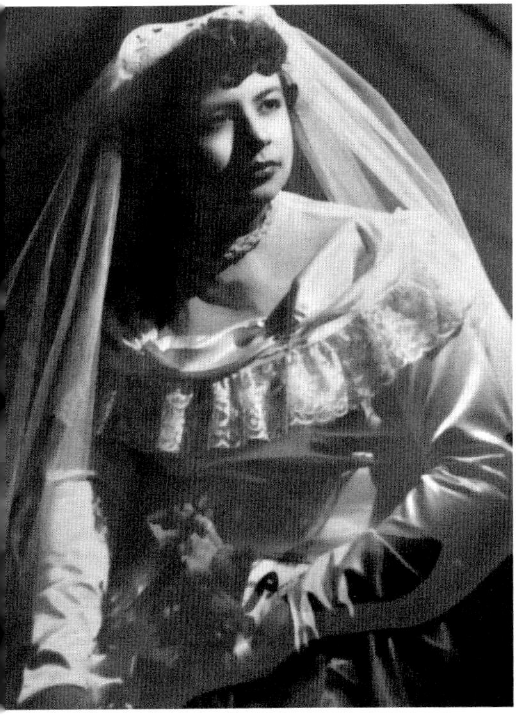

Minnie Ybarra and Barbara Ybarra Leija's Story
Minnie would take her daughter Barbara to parent meetings at Rancho Sespe, and both would translate the meeting into Spanish as school personnel presented information.

Barbara Leija was the first Hispanic to receive the DAR award while a student at Fillmore High School. She attended college and graduated with her degree and teaching credential. After having taught at Moorpark School District, she transferred and taught at Sespe School in Fillmore.

Minnie Ybarra, Woody's wife, worked for the school district as a secretary and an assistant for the migrant program. She would help translate materials into Spanish for the families to better communicate with the schools. Minnie organized and held meetings for parents at Rancho Sespe, and the school principal, the school nurse, and others would attend with her in order to disseminate information for parents. She did this for many years until her retirement. The California State Office of Migrant Education honored her and recognized her efforts, including her story in their review journal. (Courtesy of M. Ybarra family collection.)

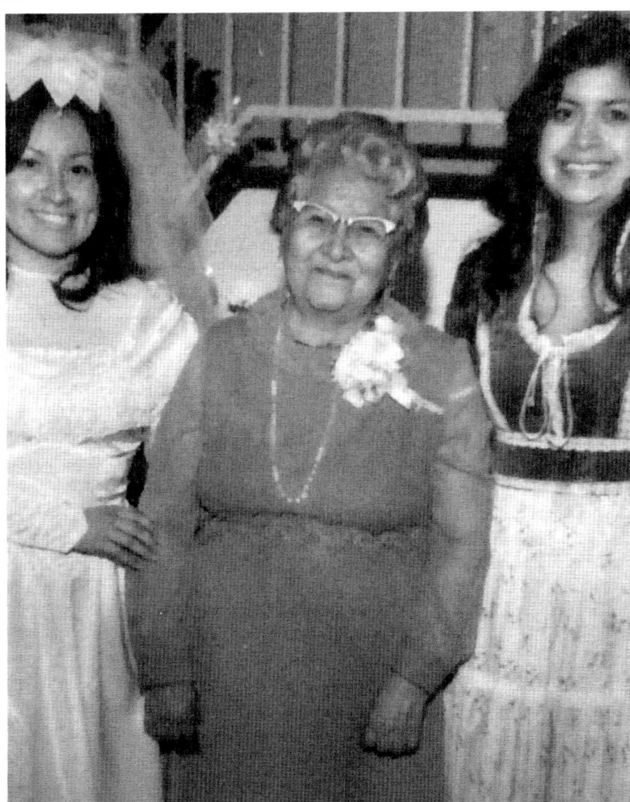

Barbara Ybarra's Wedding Day
Barbara Ybarra is pictured on her wedding day with her grandmother Soledad Ybarra and her sister Evie Ybarra. Evie and Barbara both taught school in Fillmore. (Courtesy of M. Ybarra family collection.)

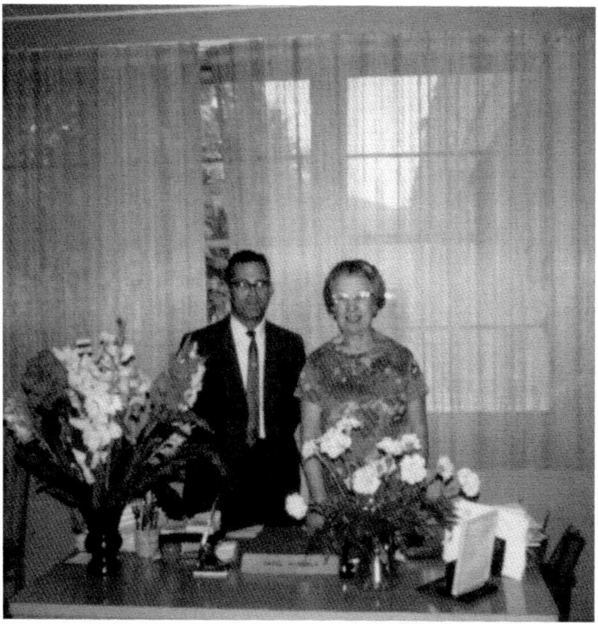

Hazel Hiberly and Don MacBrine
When longtime schoolteacher and principal Hazel Hiberly retired, Don MacBrine became principal of San Cayetano School. (Courtesy of W. Ybarra family collection.)

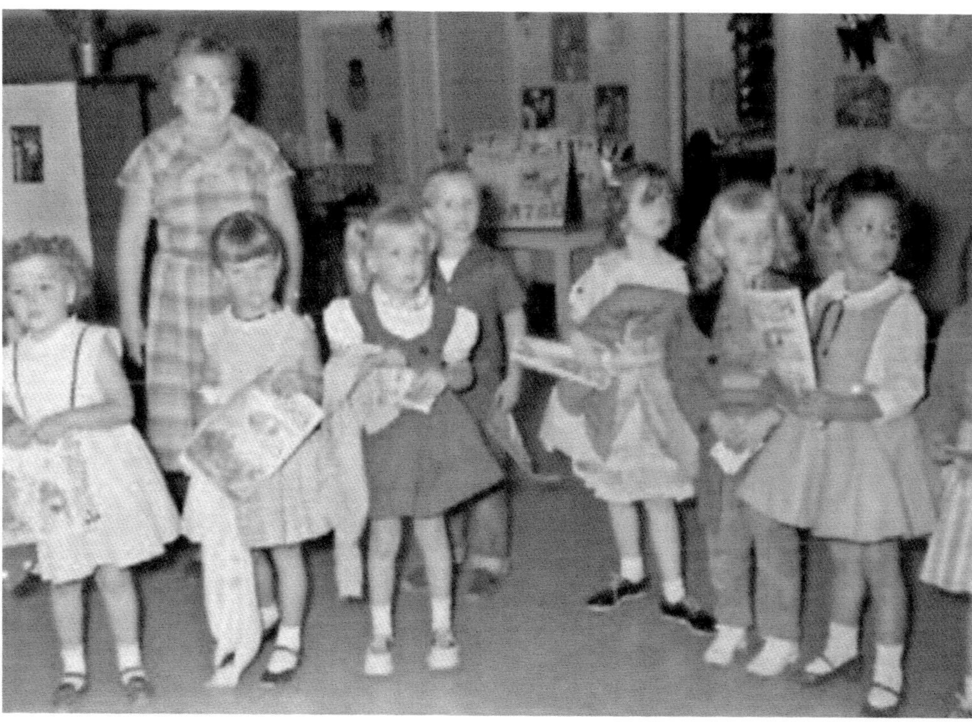

Mary Galvin
Mary was sister to former city attorney John Galvin. She was a kindergarten teacher for many years, having taught at the Olivelands School at the Limoneira Ranch in Santa Paula before coming to Fillmore. Woody Ybarra was in her kindergarten class in the 1930s; later, Woody's daughter Barbara was also in her kindergarten class. The following year, Mary Galvin retired. (Courtesy of Kathy Corley Recicar family collection.)

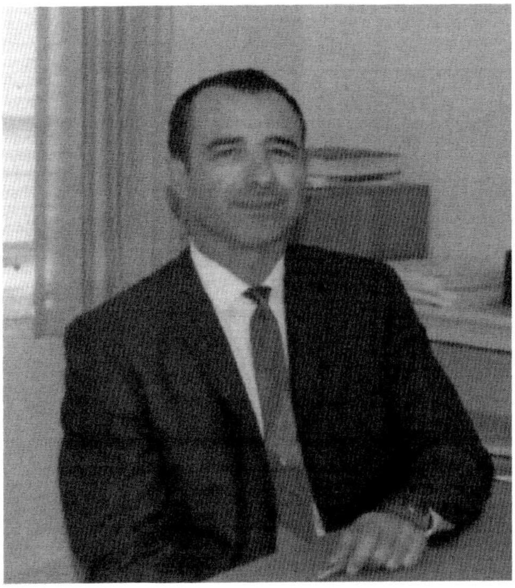

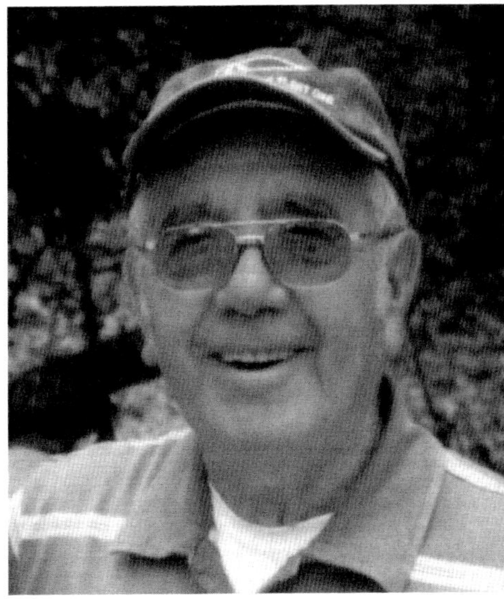

Walt and Myrna Taylor

Walt Taylor was a principal at Sespe and San Cayetano School. He implemented the noontime sports activities, and all the classes were involved. They would have competitions, which motivated all the students. A lover of the sea, he enlisted in the Merchant Marine and sailed throughout his life. Myrna Taylor was the librarian at San Cayetano School. When classes went to check out books, they had to be quiet and maintain their discipline and listen. Myrna would read to the students, then they could check out books. She was kind, and there was always a relaxed atmosphere in the library. Below left, Walt Taylor is pictured as a Merchant Marine. Below right, Walt and Myrna Taylor are seated. (Courtesy of Myrna Taylor family collection.)

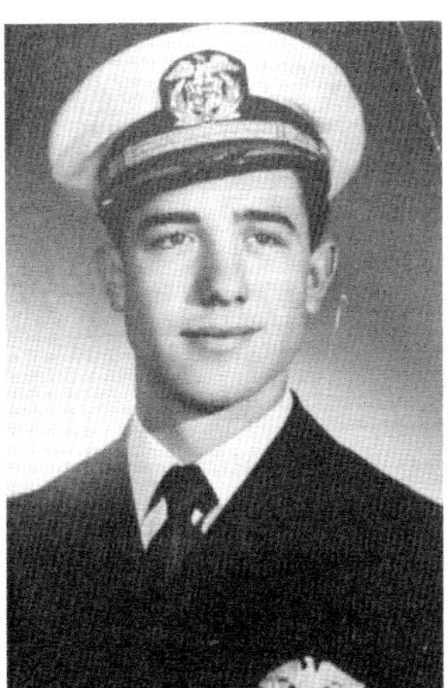

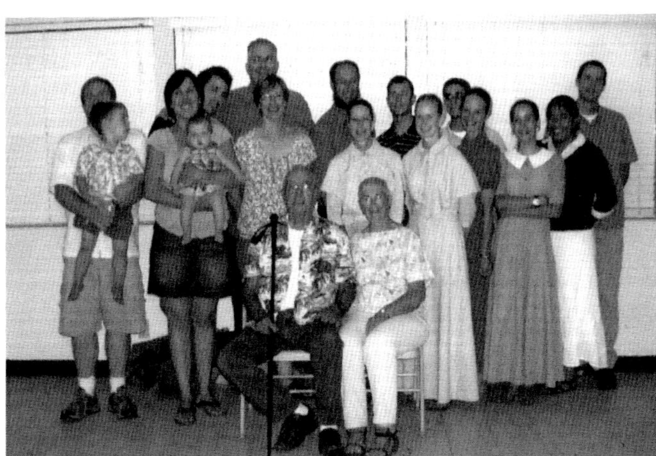

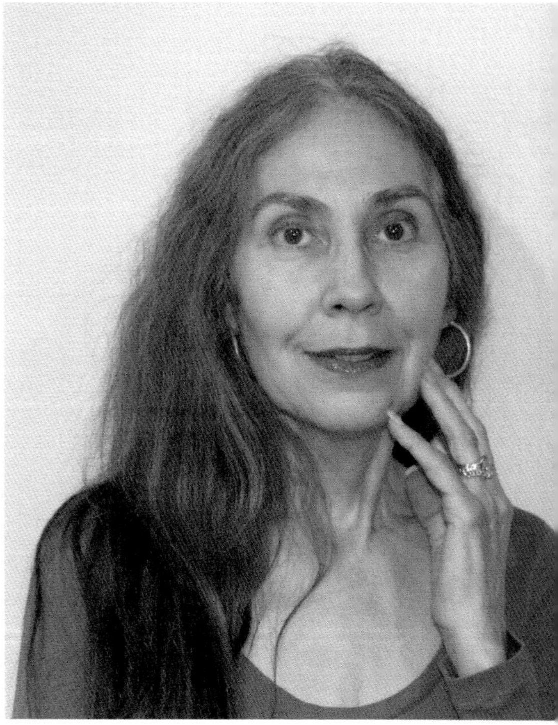

Dr. Ofelia Romero-Motlagh and Rosa Romero Supina

Dr. Ofelia Romero-Motlagh (pictured) and Rosa Romero Supina were part of a loving family in Fillmore. There were 17 children born to their parents, and each grew up and either attended college or went into business. Ofelia started her career teaching second grade at San Cayetano School. Dr. Ofelia Romero-Motlagh earned her doctorate from the University of California, Los Angeles, and she taught at California State University, Northridge, and Moorpark College. She taught women's studies and was a counselor to students. Ofelia is married, and she finds time for her academic projects. Rosa (Rosie) Romero Supina started teaching in Fillmore as part of the intern teaching program. She instructed first grade and taught numerous children how to read. Rosie taught first-, second-, and third-grade students at San Cayetano School. Her ability to speak Spanish assisted her in teaching students who had limited English skills, to acquire English. Their brother Frank Romero was a principal for a number of years. (Courtesy of Dr. Ofelia Romero-Motlagh.)

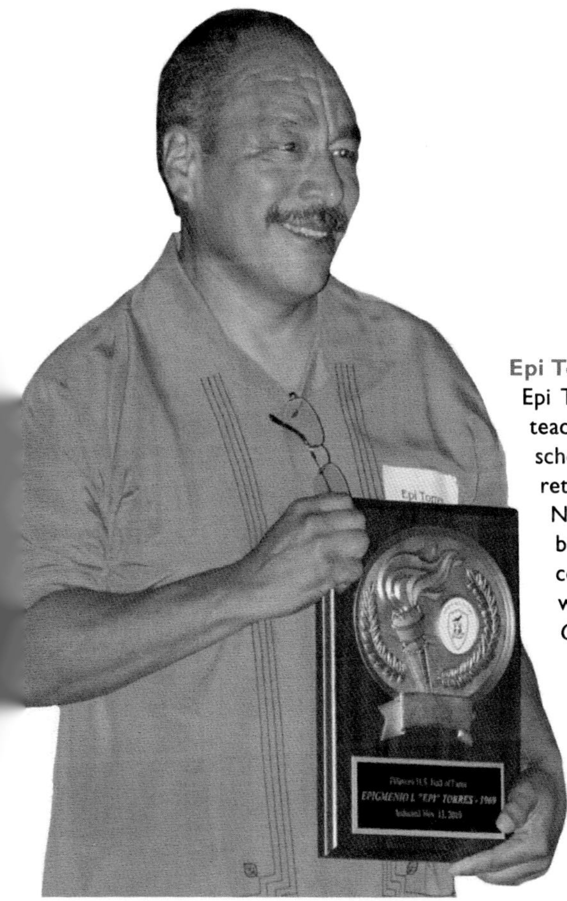

Epi Torres

Epi Torres started his teaching career as an intern teacher in the 1970s, and he related so well to middle school students that he remained in Fillmore until retirement. He also coached and was a club advisor. Not only could he speak English and Spanish, but he also promoted positive home-school communication with all parents, including those who spoke Spanish. (Courtesy of the *Fillmore Gazette* and publisher Martin Farrell.)

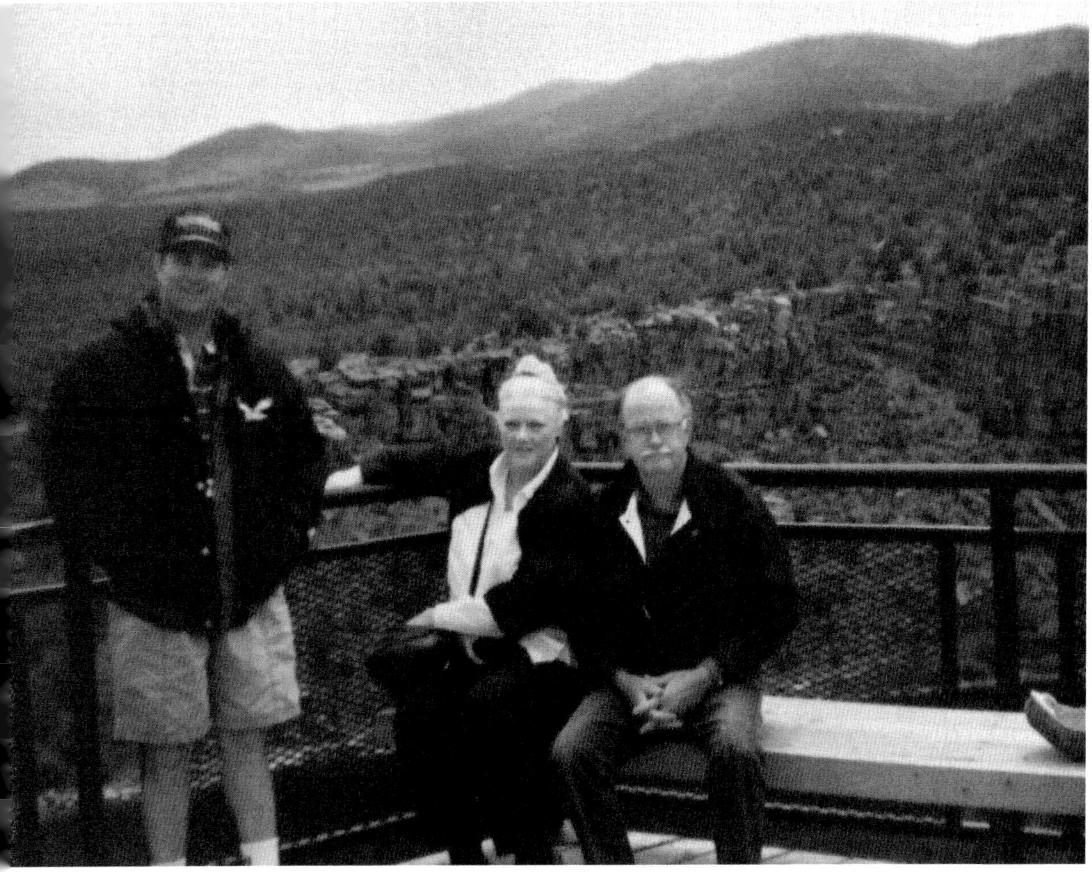

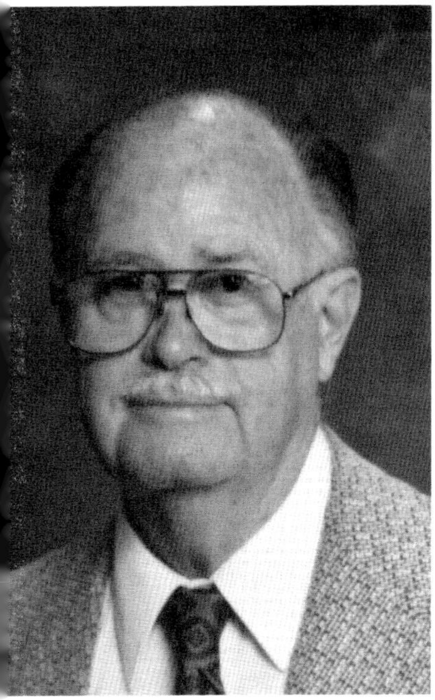

Charles "Charlie" Mozley

"My name is Jim Mozley and I am writing in regards to the nomination for Charles A. Mozley for the Ventura County Hall of Fame. I am the youngest son of a wonderful father, not a perfect one, but that adds to his stature in my book. You see he loved unconditionally and believed in who you were, your potential, not the person who might be struggling or 'messing' up at the time. My father was patient, kind, and sincere in his convictions. There was great peace, joy and warmth in our home due to my dad and I believe much of that exuded from his spirit. Of course, if my father were alive today, he would downplay any role he had and say, 'It was mainly because of your mom,' and that would be true too. The public persona of integrity . . . gentleness, conviction and love he showed for his students during his years in education was no game because he did the same at home. I am the beneficiary of this and I believe some of the skills I have as a minister chaplain in my trade came from him . . . 'Go get 'em Tiger,' my dad might say while you wondered if you could do anything." Charles Mozley is survived by his spouse, Barbara, and their children, Melissa Mozley Coleman, Matt, Joe, and Jim Mozley. Pictured above are Matt, Barbara, and Charles Mozley. (Courtesy of the Mozley family collection.)

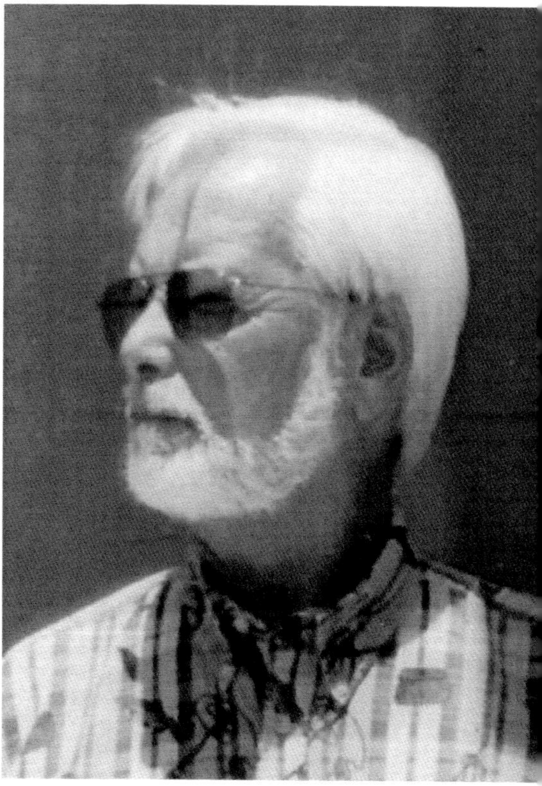

William "Bill" Garfield, A.J. Littman, and Ralph Rees

Bill Garfield taught history at Fillmore High School for many years. He also received a one-year fellowship to study in Singapore. He not only motivated his students, but he also encouraged them to excel and push their limits.

A.J. Littman (not pictured) was a gifted linguist, and he taught Spanish and French and knew German and Latin.

Besides the class work, he had students reading and writing in the language they were attempting to acquire. During the Christmas holidays, he led groups of students as they sang holiday songs in various languages. The students would share their songs at school and within the community. (Courtesy of Kathy Corley Recicar collection.)

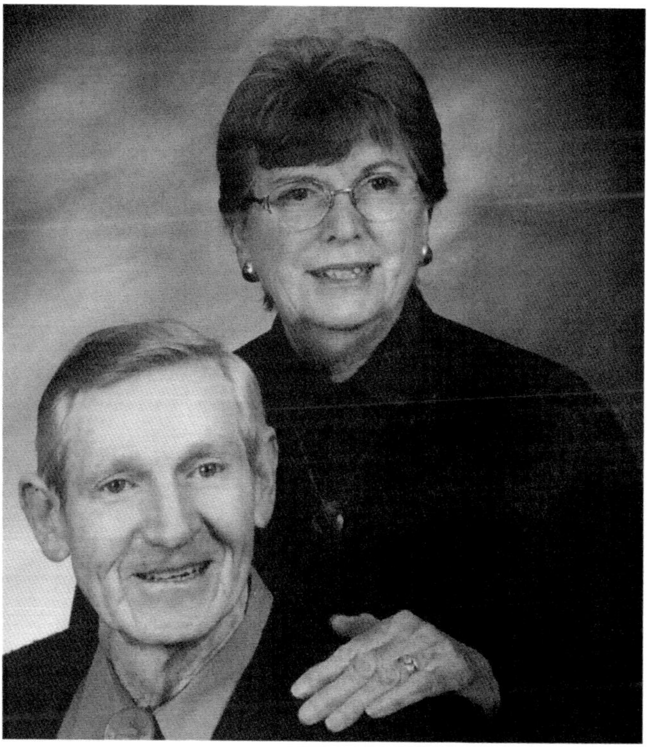

Ralph and Patricia Rees

Ralph and Patricia Rees both taught in the Fillmore schools. Patricia taught elementary grades at San Cayetano School. Ralph taught many industrial arts classes, and he had his students learn how to set up and print newspapers, newsletters, posters, and more. He often had a smile on his face, and he was patient. (Courtesy of Rees family collection.)

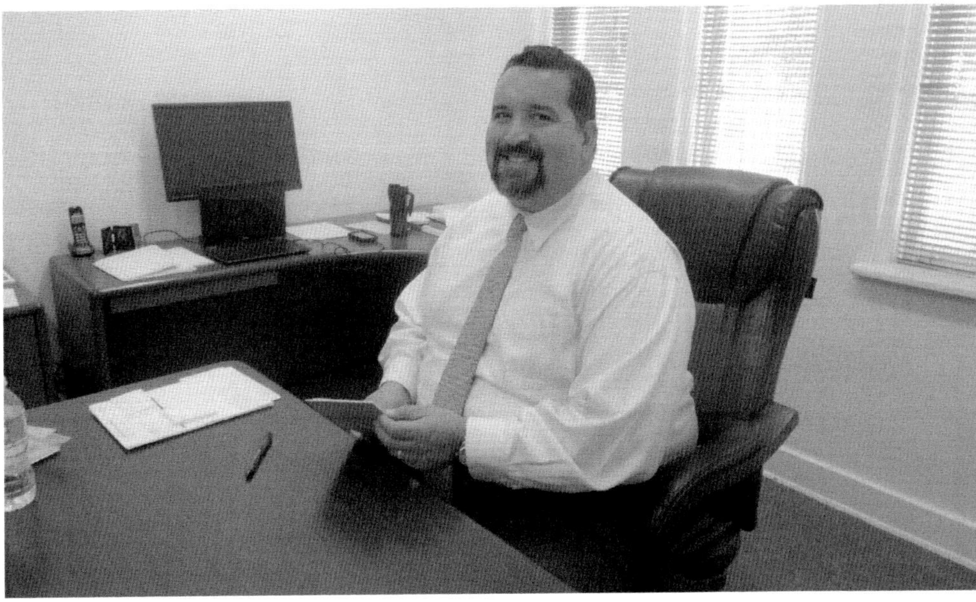

Dr. Adrian Palazuelos

Dr. Palazuelos is the current leader in the Fillmore Unified School District. He also served as a principal in Oxnard, and he understands the challenges facing students in education today—the demands for better technology and the demands of the economy. He and board of trustees strive to lead the students of the Fillmore Unified School District through these with the assistance of all parents and the dedicated teaching staff. Dr. Palazuelos obtained his doctorate from the University of California, Los Angeles, and he lives in Fillmore with his family. His children attend Fillmore schools. (Author's collection.)

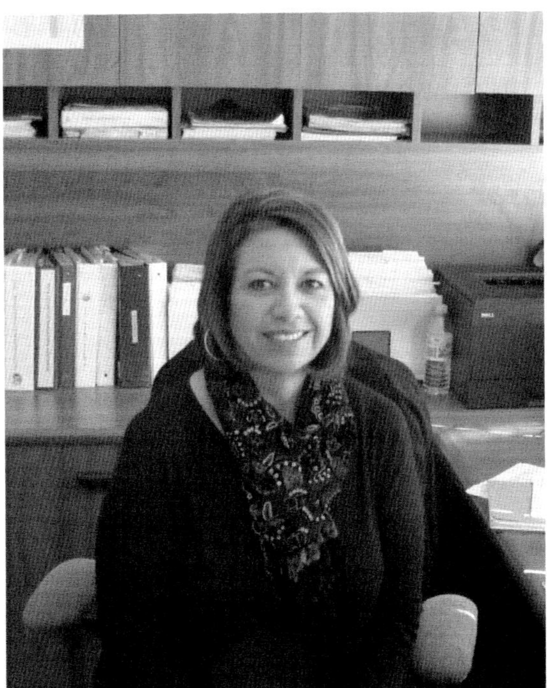

Patricia Gradias

Patricia "Tricia" Gradias grew up in Fillmore and attended Fillmore schools. She aspired to become a principal, and this she accomplished. She is currently the principal of San Cayetano School. (Photograph by Mary Whiteford.)

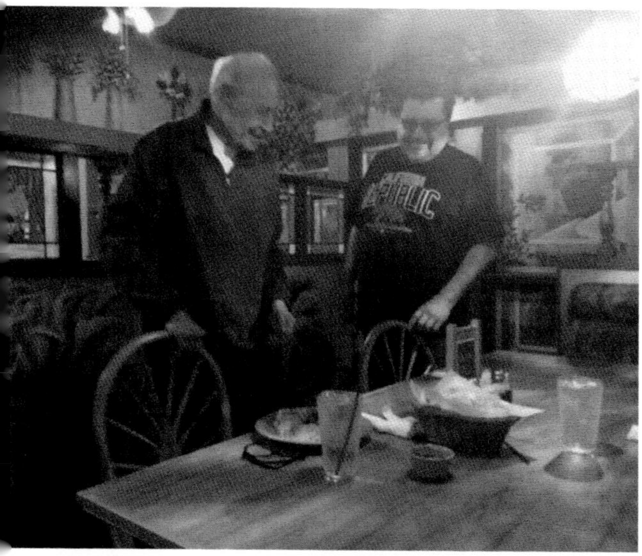

Tony Ybarra and Robert Ybarra

Tony Ybarra (left) was a maintenance worker for Fillmore Unified School District for many years. He is pictured with his nephew Robert Ybarra, reminiscing about the good times in Fillmore. Tony remembers when he and his brothers, "Woody" and Lupe, would help sell tortillas and tamales for their grandma, "Concha," and they would make the deliveries to all the neighbors. (Author's collection.)

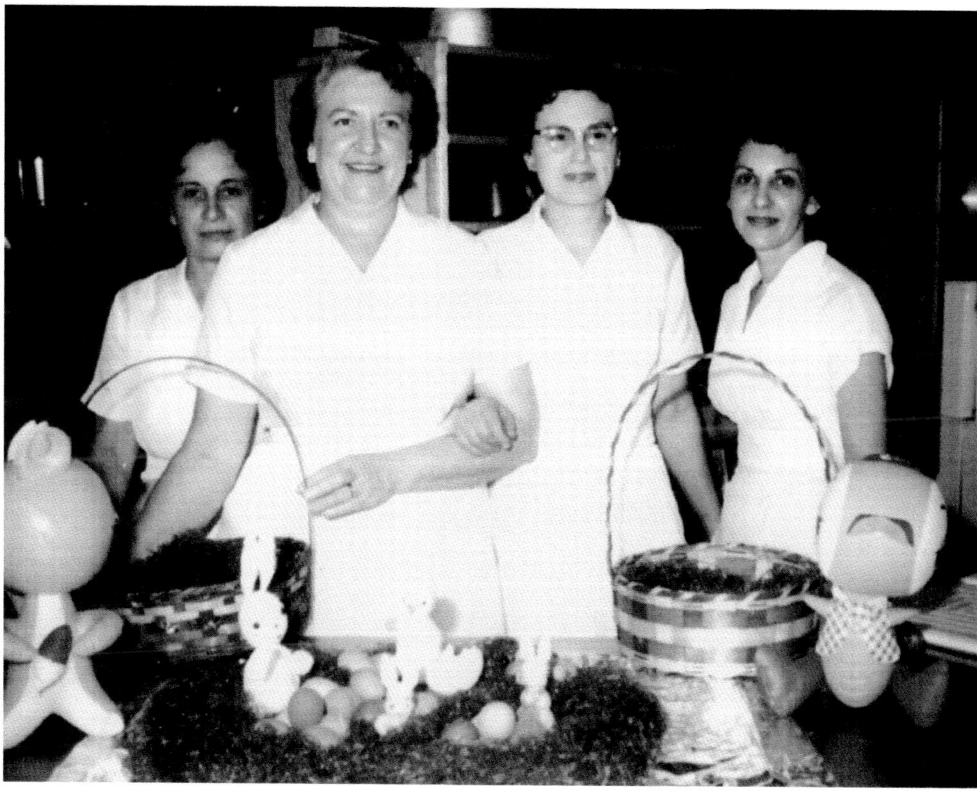

Cooks in the Cafeteria

This photograph shows the ladies who used to cook in the cafeteria. All cafeteria personnel support teachers in the classroom, and they assist the student population as needed. These ladies were no different. Pictured from left to right are Bea Kaufman, Alethea Thomason, Evelyn Paragien, and Kay Curnett Wilson. These ladies cooked nutritious lunches for the students at San Cayetano School. They always made special things for the children for the holidays. (Courtesy M. Ybarra family collection.)

Todd Schieferle

Schieferle stands between Martha Hernandez (left) and trustee Lucy Rangel (right). He is now the director of human resources for Fillmore Unified School District, of which he is also a product. He grew up in a very proactive, educational environment. His sister Darby Schieferle teaches in the high school. When Todd was a very young child of three, he went to Darby's classroom with his mother to help the class make pumpkin pies. His mother was a parent volunteer, and before Thanksgiving, she assisted the teacher and students in placing crusts on pie tins, mixing the pumpkin filling, and pouring it in. Woody Ybarra helped her take the pies to the cafeteria oven for baking, and everyone enjoyed a piece of pie after lunch. The exercise helped students learn about fractions and teamwork. (Author's collection.)

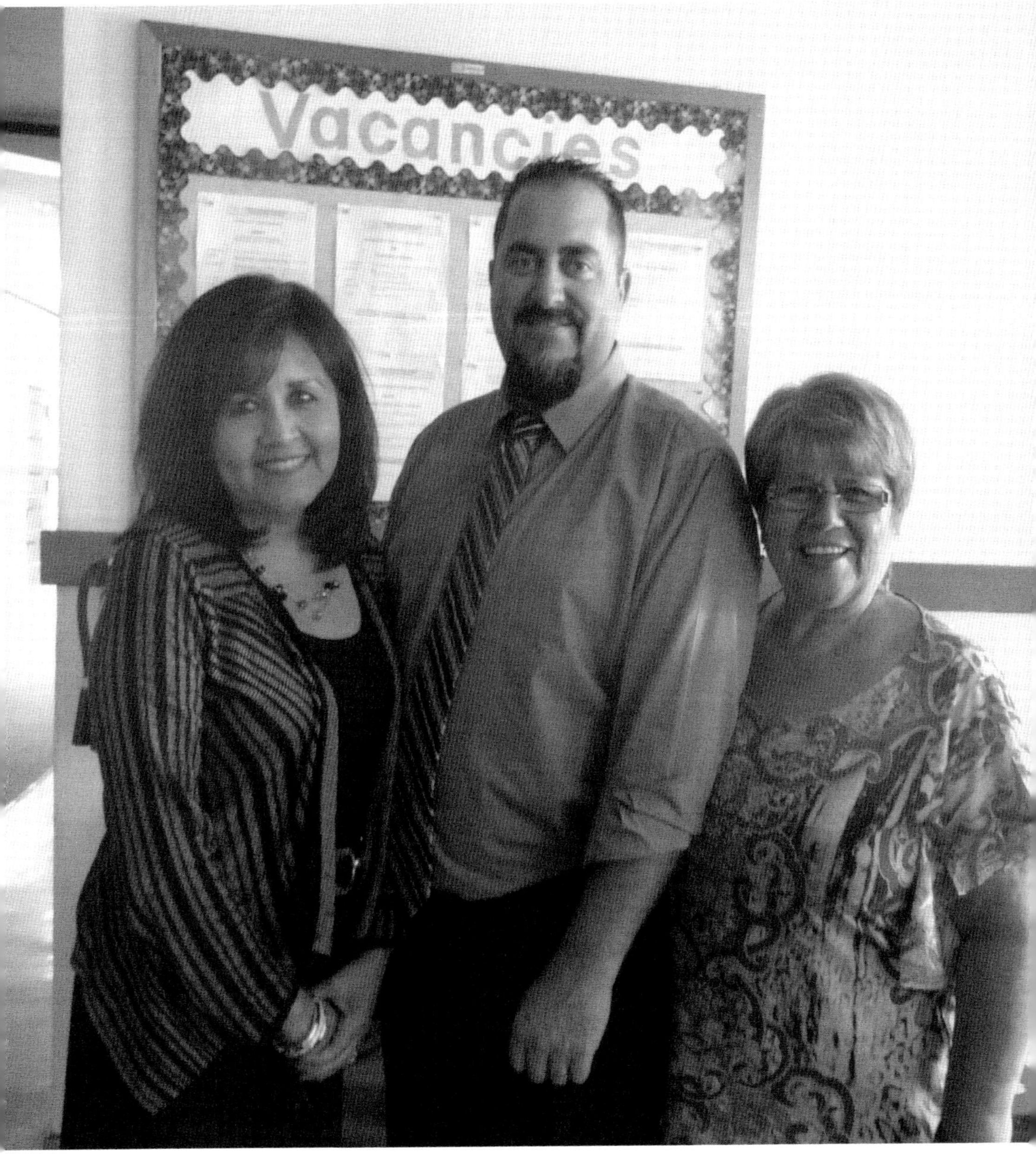

CHAPTER SEVEN

Heroes in Uniform

Men and women from Fillmore, Bardsdale, and Piru have served their country in the armed forces. Numerous sons and daughters have sacrificed their lives or put them on hold in order to participate as a member of the Army, Navy, Air Force, Merchant Marine, or Marines. Others are part of the National Guard.

Charles Michel and Albert Wiklund served in World War I, and Woody Ybarra, Fidencio Ybarra, Jack Warring, Harold Michel, Pete Carrillo, and countless others served during World War II. There are those who served during the Korean War, such as Lupe Ybarra. Walt Taylor served in the Merchant Marine. Others served in Vietnam, including Bob Cox, a photographer who chronicled the events and depicted the Vietnamese population and American soldiers during this conflict in the early 1970s. Then there are those who were lost—Toby Gritz, Walter Sánchez, Ignacio Sánchez, and many others. The Veterans Memorial Building in Fillmore has a listing of all Fillmore veterans. If mothers ruled the world, one can imagine that there might be an end to all wars.

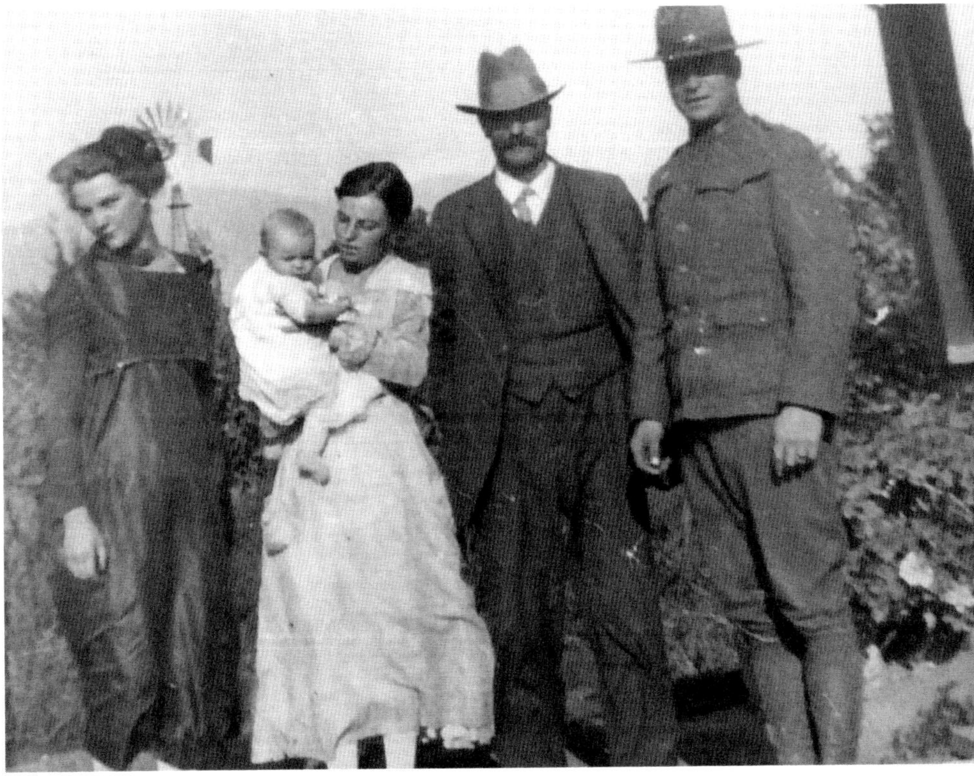

Albert Wiklund and Family
From left to right in the above photograph are Gladys Wiklund, Elvira Wiklund (holding Dorothy), Charles Wiklund, and Albert Wiklund, dressed in uniform prior to his departure for World War I. (Courtesy of Tom Hardison family collection.)

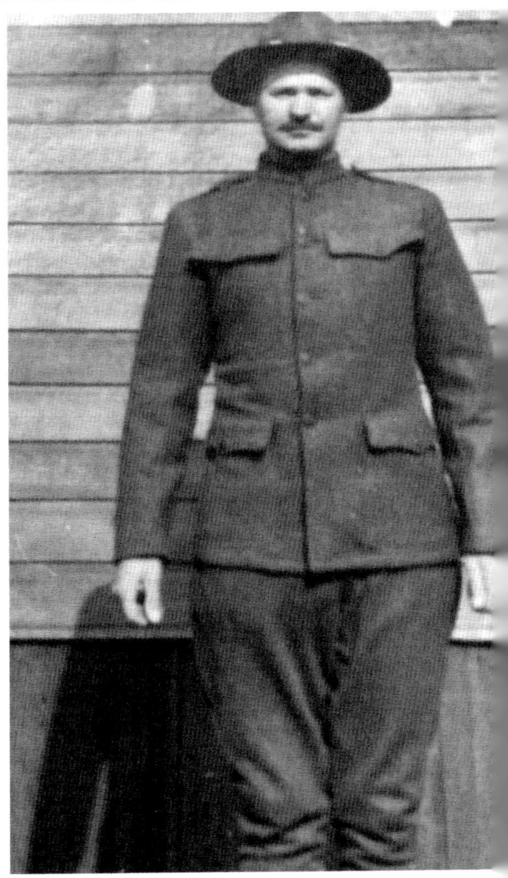

Charles Jacob Michel
Charles Michel is shown here in his World War I uniform prior to his deployment. (Courtesy of Harold Michel family collection.)

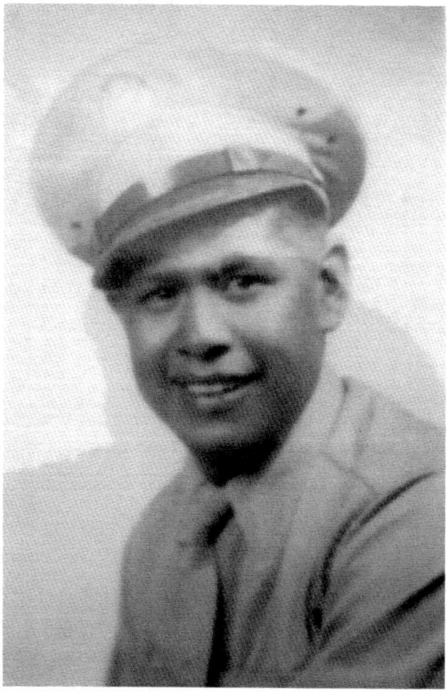

Marcelino "Woody" Ybarra

Woody served as a sergeant in the Army during World War II. He would share the story of serving as a lookout, listening for enemy airplanes. He had especially acute hearing and could distinguish which planes were which as they flew overhead. He was on his way to Okinawa when his ship was caught in a monsoon. He explained that it was extremely dangerous and that the entire crew expected the ship to sink. All of the officers and crew huddled together below deck and prayed through the storm. Suddenly, the storm ended, and they arrived in Okinawa within a few days. Woody played baseball during wartime, and he continued playing as a pitcher for the Fillmore Merchants upon his return. (Courtesy of Ybarra family collection.)

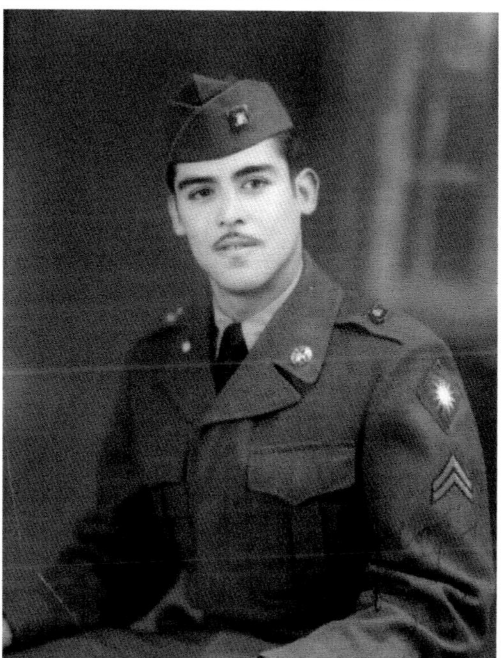

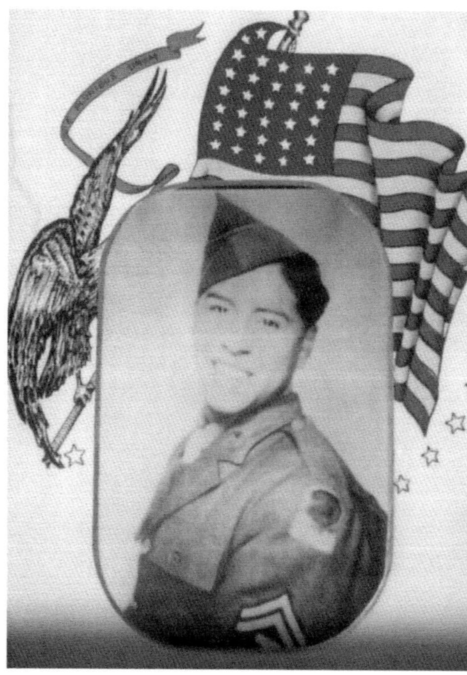

Pete Carrillo and Fidencio Ybarra

Pete Carrillo (left) played baseball upon his return from World War II. Fidencio Ybarra (right) was stationed in France. He hid in a tree for three days during the German occupation of France and survived to return home. The Veterans Memorial Building lists the names of all who served in the armed forces and those who lost their lives making the ultimate sacrifice. Included among the many who lost their lives are Toby Gritz, Ignacio Sánchez, and Walter Sánchez. (Left, courtesy of Michele McKinley family collection; right, courtesy of Odette and James Boblett family collection.)

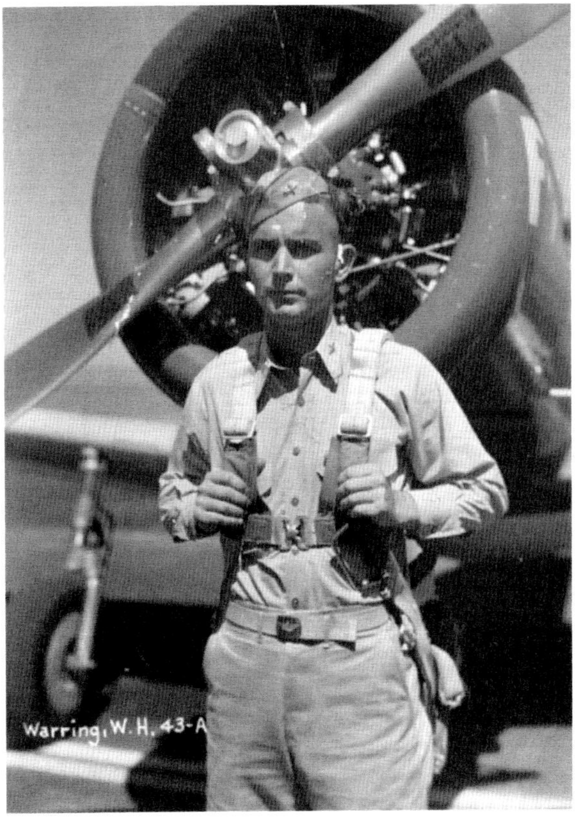

Bill Warring, Fighter Pilot
As a fighter pilot, Jack loved flying and he continued flying planes when the war was over. Bill was captured and was a prisoner of war in Germany for part of the war. The Warring family claims that Jack used to buzz Buckhorn Ranch to let the family know he was nearby. (Courtesy of Missy Pennington Cervantez family collection.)

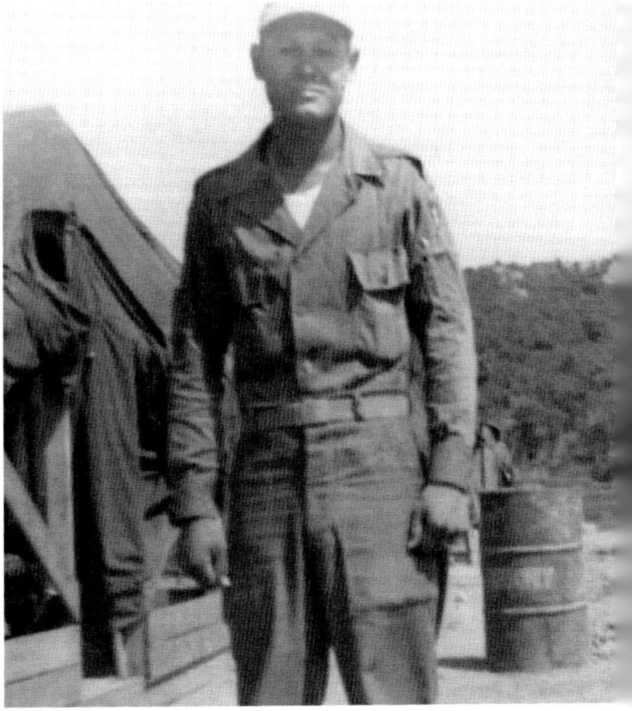

Lupe Ybarra
War is never pretty, and everyone who has served understands that. Lupe Ybarra was in Korea. Numerous individuals in the communities sacrifice their lives to serve and protect the United States of America. (Courtesy of Michele McKinley family collection.)

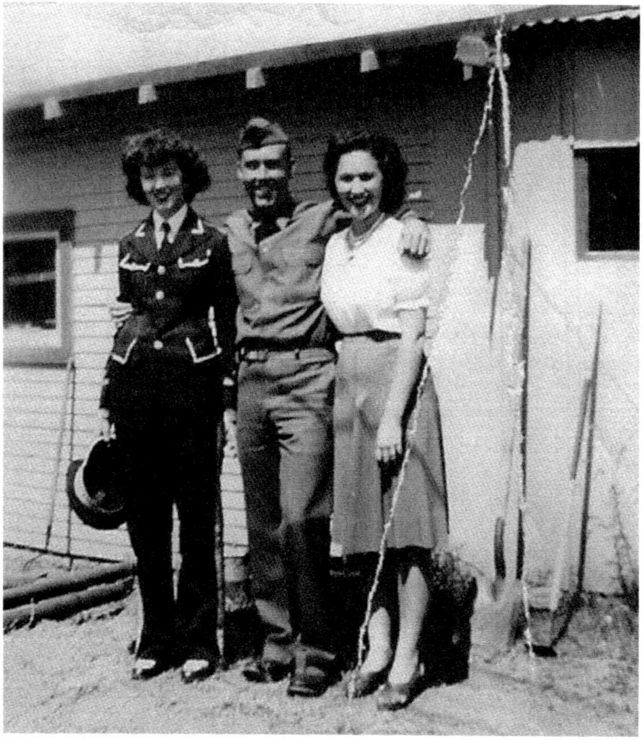

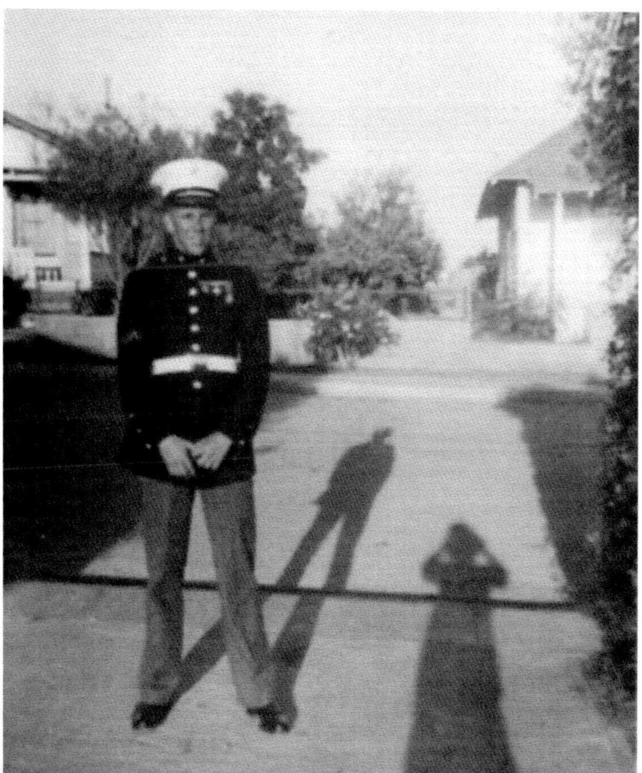

Otis, Buster, and Lee Corley
Otis Corley (pictured above with two friends) joined the Army and was stationed in Bora Bora as part of the 58th Battalion Division. He was also in Manila in the Philippine Islands and in Saipan. Lee Corley (pictured below) served in the US Marine Corps, and Buster Corley was in the Medical Corps. All served their country during World War II. (Both, courtesy of Kathy Corley Recicar family collection.)

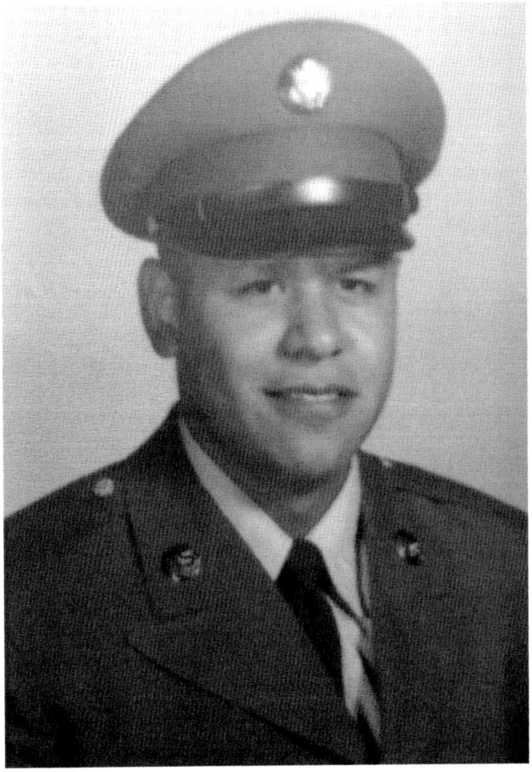

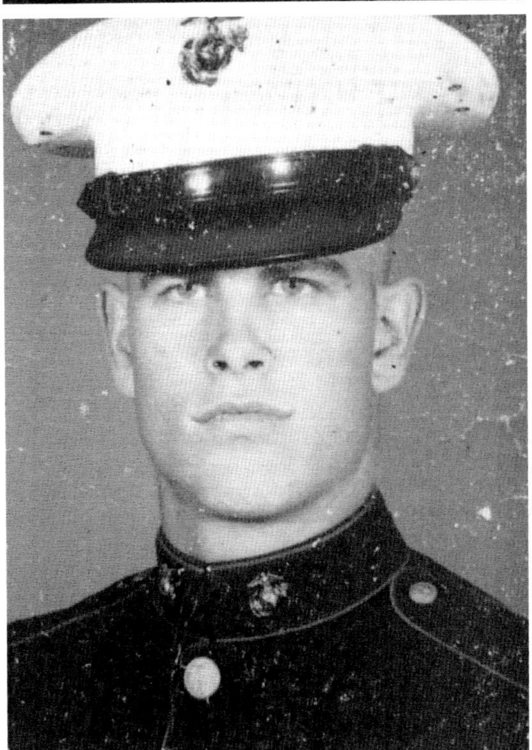

Ed Ybarra and Jim Arundell
Ed Ybarra (above) was stationed in Germany in the 1960s, and Jim Arundell (below) served in the US Marines. War is a sacrifice, and anyone who has served understands this, as do their families, especially spouses and mothers. (Both, courtesy of Ed Ybarra family collection.)

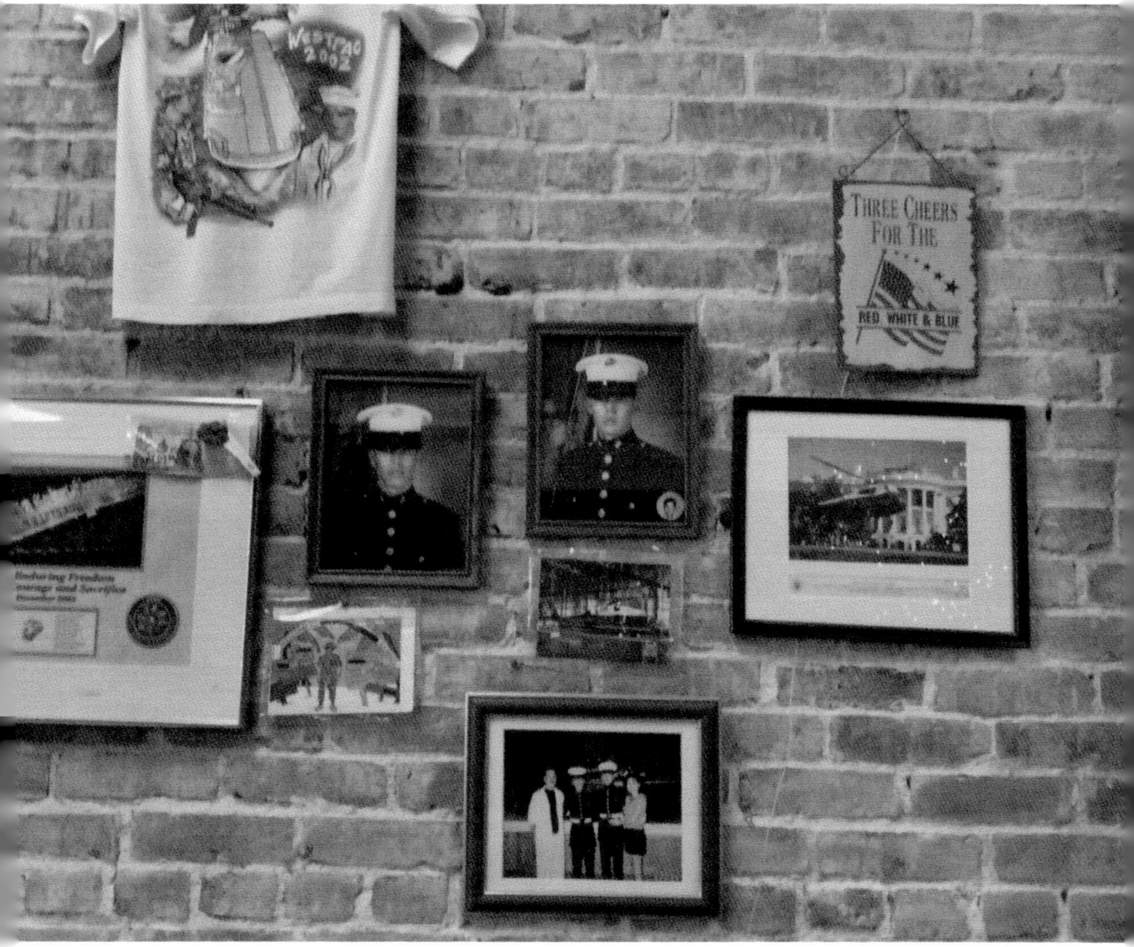

Eric Amaro and Marcos Amaro

Jess and Norma Castro Amaro's sons both served as Marines. Eric Amaro served in the Presidential Squadron and in the Helicopter Squadron. Marcos Amaro served two tours of duty in Iraq. They both served their country with dedication and much sacrifice. Their brother Jess Amaro owns a landscape business, and all three Amaros grew up in Fillmore, California. Jess Sr. and Norma Castro Amaro own and manage Vintage Pleasures in Filllmore. (Courtesy of Norma Castro Amaro family collection.)

INDEX

INDEX